Decolonizing Education

To the youth today for a more just tomorrow.

Decolonizing Education

Nourishing the Learning Spirit

◇

Marie Battiste

PURICH
PUBLISHING
LIMITED
SASKATOON, SK. CANADA

Purich Publishing, an imprint of UBC Press
2029 West Mall; Vancouver, BC; Canada; V6T 1Z2
www.ubcpress.ca

25 24 23 22 21 20 19 18 17   6 5 4 3 2

Library and Archives Canada Cataloguing in Publication

Battiste, Marie, 1949-, author
    Decolonizing education : nourishing the learning spirit
/ Marie Battiste.

Includes bibliographical references and index.
ISBN 978-1-895830-77-4 (pbk.)

    1. Native peoples — Education — Canada. 2. Native
peoples — Education — Government policy —Canada. 3. Native
peoples — Canada — Intellectual life. I. Title.

E96.2.B355 2013   371.829'97071   C2013-905316-6

Edited, designed, and typeset by Donald Ward.
Cover photograph: J. Youngblood Henderson.
Cover design by Jamie Olson.
Index by Ursula Acton.

Canadä

UBC Press gratefully acknowledges the financial support for
our publishing program of the Government of Canada
(through the Canada Book Fund), the Canada Council for the
Arts, and the British Columbia Arts Council.

Printed and bound in Canada by Houghton Boston Printers &
Lithographers, Saskatoon. Printed on 100 per cent post-consumer, recycled,
ancient-forest-friendly paper.

Contents

Foreword

Tawow! Tawow! Tawow! I can hear the echo of this greeting as visitors arrive at my grandparents' home. The literal translation of this greeting being: *there is room here* [for everyone] (often repeated three times). It is an appropriate start to the foreword for this book.

It has been a privilege to be part of an ongoing conversation on education with Marie Battiste over the past 30 years plus, each of us having made a lifetime commitment to be part of the change in our respective cultural communities and in the larger spheres of public educational institutions and society — and the world, in general. I first met Marie in the early 80s through our affiliation with the Mokakit Indian Education Research Association, founded in 1983 to challenge the Eurocentric research paradigms and to support and foster educational excellence in our communities.[1] The dominant research paradigm of the day, based on deficit theory, often resulted in an essentialization of Indigenous peoples, followed by a litany of pathologies. Marie was completing her doctoral work and later serving as Director of Education in her home reserve of Potlotek at the Mi'kmawey School, in the first bilingual education school in Mi'kmaw territory on Chapel Island, Cape Breton, Nova Scotia. I had left the classroom to join the staff of the newly formed Gabriel Dumont Institute of Native Studies and Applied Research, as Coordinator and later Director of the Saskatchewan Urban Native Teacher Education Program. It was an exciting time professionally and politically, as the advocacy work of so many First Nations, Métis, and Inuit had finally paid off across the country and new institutions were being created to advance our stories, languages, and being of this place. I think Marie would agree that we were privileged to be a part of these undertakings. These actions, along with the support we receive from our families and communities of spirit around the globe (interrogating the basic

---

1 Mokakit is the Blackfoot concept for excellence. It is also significant to note that many of the original members of Mokakit had and/or continue to play leadership roles in education in Canada.

tenet of western knowledge — critical theorists, feminists, anti-colonial theorists) anchors our continuing advocacy and commitment to education.

It was also about this time that the world's Indigenous peoples began gathering on many fronts. One such front was the World Indigenous Peoples Conference on Education (WIPCE), held every three years and continuing, bringing together Indigenous peoples, educators, and their allies from all over the world with themes that underscore that *the answers are within us*, in our languages and cultures, and in the stories of our relationships to place. In the context of these supportive relationships with individuals and communities of like mind and heart, we were able to give wing to our dreaming and consciousness as Indigenous people — no less creative or imaginative than any other people inhabiting this earth — as we resist, remember, re-right, recover, reconcile our place in our respective nation states. One of the more comprehensive and exciting projects, for which we formalized our relationship, was the work of the Aboriginal Learning Knowledge Centre of the Canadian Council on Learning, awarded to the Aboriginal Education Research Centre, College of Education, University of Saskatchewan and the First Nations Higher Education Consortium of Calgary, Alberta. Dr. Marie Battiste and Dr. Vivian Ayoungman served as directors for this project, while I served one of the 2.5 positions in a co-ordinating role. Marie also assumed an additional role as an Animation Theme Bundle Holder (out of six themes) for *Nourishing the Learning Spirit*.[2]

Inspired by an exchange with Willie Ermine, Cree ethicist, Marie's re-collection and re-thinking of Aboriginal education in *Decolonizing Education: Nourishing the Learning Spirit* represents a fundamental shift in thinking of decolonization as a process that belongs to everyone. As such, it has huge implications and possibilities for re-imaging our relationships as envisioned in treaty and/or embedded within Canada's Constitution, as Canadians and as world citizens in the context of the natural world, which sustains all of our existence. The work is unfinished. Having just completed the work of the *Joint Task Force to Improve Outcomes in Education and Employment for First Nations and Métis* in Saskatchewan, I am cognizant that there will need to be much more to our conversations than "gaps" in educational outcomes. If we are to realize our full potential as a nation state and as conscious Earth citizens, we will need to "remake our world in more holistic and far sighted ways."[3] Perhaps, as Marie suggests, to transform our educational systems that reflect shared aspirations and goals *with* First Nations, Métis, and Inuit, it begins with consideration of what a truly inclusive culture is for Canada, one which moves

---

2   For more information, visit http://www.ccl-cca.ca/.

3   Turok, Neil. (2012). *The Universe Within – From Quantum to Cosmos*. CBC Massey Lectures. Canada: Harper Collins Canada Ltd.

beyond the maintenance of an identity, language, and culture of a colonial society derived from a historically biased position. Without a shared culture, nationally and locally, is it possible to know how we might measure the success of our educational endeavours in our educational systems?

In this book, Dr. Marie Battiste shares her personal journey and story of inspiration, resistance, and transformation — with influences personal, theoretical, philosophical, and global, which have shaped her thinking and being — as a Mi'kmaw educator making a difference in the Canadian education systems that she has been a part of. To unpack the evolution of Aboriginal education policy and developments in Canada, the perspective she has chosen is from the standpoint and experience of the Mi'kmaw. Despite the horror and trauma of the racist ideology that has shaped educational policy and developments through state and church, she provides extensive references, for the record, to show that the Mi'kmaw have never lost sight of the importance of culture and language in their continuance as a people. Nor have they lost sight of their distinct rights embedded in treaties and/or in the Canadian Constitution, now recognized as part of the *United Nations Declaration on the Rights of Indigenous Peoples*.

It will be quickly apparent that the broad strokes of the picture she paints, resulting from her work in her home community and province of Poletuk, Nova Scotia, her work locally with colleagues at the University of Saskatchewan, and others nationally and internationally, is a familiar one shared collectively by Indigenous people and their allies in Canada and the world. She claims that, despite the dislocation of Indigenous people from their lands, they have continued their struggle to maintain culture and language as core components of education, based on distinct rights recognized in treaty and in the Constitution, and they have continued to resist policies that seek to erase their sense of being as Indigenous People. In this "tortured space" she shares how her own family and community has been making their own way; and, while there have been losses, they have survived. Even now, as her community is faced with many challenges, they are not looking for governments to provide the solutions. Rather, they are seeking *reconciliation* of their rights as Indigenous people and they want to be participants in creating a better future for themselves and for all Canadian citizens. This sentiment is echoed in the final report of *Voice, Vision and Leadership: A Place for All — The Joint Task Force on Improving Education and Employment Outcomes for First Nations and Métis People* (2013), work I have just completed in Saskatchewan with Gary Merasty (chair) and Don Hoium. The report states, "First Nations and Métis people in Saskatchewan and Canada have a strong history as nation builders. Even in tough times, they have worked to retain and regain the strengths and gifts to help build their communities, the province of Saskatchewan, and Canada. Nor do they think that governments will solve all of their challenges, as they recognize the importance of strengthening their own capacity as individuals and communities. However, there are times they need government and institutions to respond in meaningful ways to their needs."[4] I would add to this, "and aspirations." The latter point, of the importance of responsive governments and institutions, is not lost to Marie, either. Her "discursive arrow" is pointed "not at teachers or their methods but largely at the federal and provincial systems and the policy choices made and the inequities coming from them" (p. 14). Further, she notes "the Canadian government has a vital constitutional role to play in protecting the country's remaining Aboriginal knowledge, languages, and heritage" (p. 66). I agree. Those who are aware of Dr. Battiste's work will know she is no stranger to the discussion and critique of Aboriginal education in Canada. Once again, with an undaunted learning spirit, she brings to bear her own unique gifts through listening, sharing, taking heart, and acting to bring about change with others on the damage wrought by racism and its economic effects on children, an eroding land base, and natural environment.

The book represents a formal shift of thinking and writing from a modernistic, expository prose of grand western narratives to a more storytelling manner as a way of uncovering — revealing — a nuanced and balanced perspective of a colonized history and, through it, unmasking the faulty logics of knowing grounded in objectivity and eurocentric theorizing that have undermined Indigenous peoples' knowledge systems. As she writes, "maybe this is wisdom taking its rightful place" (p. 17).

Throughout, she offers a critical gaze, bringing together activism, research, and scholarship to advocate for systemic change and trans-systemic reconciliation of diverse knowledge systems (in the humanities and sciences). However, she cautions that structures and guidelines must accommodate the fundamental concept of *diversity*, because "no single Indigenous experience dominates other perspectives, no one heritage informs it, and no two heritages produce the same knowledge" (p. 66). In creating institutional and systemic change, she offers a way out guided by the *United Nations Declaration on the Rights of Indigenous Peoples* and *an ethical space* (inspired by the work of Cree ethicist Willie Ermine). An ethical space is a theoretical space created among human communities for retreat, reflection, and dialogue to share understandings and to work together to create *a shared future*. It beckons a co-operative and an ethical order of good relations.[5] More fundamentally, though, Marie observes,

---

4   Voice, Vision and Leadership: A Place for All — The Joint Task Force on Improving Education and Employment Outcomes for First Nations and Métis People (2013)

5   Willie Ermine, in *Significant Leadership and Ethical Space Transforming Educational Opportunities for First Nations and Métis Learners in Saskatchewan* (2009) by Michael Cottrell, Jane P Preston, Joseph V. Pearce, and Terrence R. Pelletier. Saskatoon: University of

"Indigenous peoples must be the ones renewing and reconstructing the principles underlying their worldviews and languages, and how these inform their own humanity" (p. 68).

This book is also an invitation for all of us to work together — as Indigenists, to offer our unique gifts to the important work of decolonization, moving beyond cultural awareness and inclusion — challenging racist ideology as we rethink and re-imagine ourselves in relationship with one another sharing place — one earth. The work requires us to care deeply about learning, to love it, she writes. How will we enter into those ethical conversations? What will it mean for the curriculum we offer to our children and youth? How will we measure our progress to meet our aspirations and goals? There are no excuses for doing nothing, either. She reminds us there are covenants, such as the rights of Indigenous people and our own Canadian Constitution to guide us; but the important work must come from the heart, as relationships are matters of the spirit that cannot be legislated.

Neil Turok in *The Universe Within — From Quantum to Cosmos* (2012), observes that we have gained immensely from powerful scientific, technological advances created by the human mind in the past three centuries as we sought to understand a universe that is eternal. However, we will need to dig deeper into a diverse human consciousness, with the entry of new cultures into the scientific community as vital sources of energy and creativity in the future and consider how science can ultimately serve "society's goals and creating the kind of world we would like to inhabit."[6] What humanity has achieved, Turok observes, comes from "our capacity to understand, invent and create: from *The Universe Within*."[7] If we heed Marie's invitation to rethink the premise of Aboriginal education in *Decolonizing Education: Nourishing the Learning Spirit*, perhaps it will take us a few steps toward the journey envisioned by Turok. "As we link the intelligence to our hearts,"[8] the common ground might be an understanding that we are all part of something greater than our differences.

Grateful that you have taken time to read this passage and grateful for today — thunder sounding in the distance and a promise of rain — I offer my thanks and gratefulness. *Marsi, Ninanâskomon!*

Rita Bouvier

Saskatchewan, Dept of Ed. Admin., SELU.

6   Turok, Neil. (2012) *The Universe Within - From Quantum to Cosmos*. CBC Massey Lectures. Canada: Harper Collins Canada, Ltd. p. 249.

7   *Ibid.*, p. 212.

8   *Ibid.*, p. 257.

CHAPTER 1

Introduction

Listen, there are words almost everywhere. I realized that in a chance
moment. Words are in the air, in our blood, words were always there. . . .
Words are in the snow, trees, leaves, wind, birds, beaver, the sound of ice
cracking; words are in fish and mongrels, where they have been since we
came to this place with the animals. . . . Words and thoughts retain their
capacity to create, to cause and to change.

> Kimberly M. Blaeser. 1996. *Gerald Vizenor: Writing in the Oral
> Tradition*. Norman: University of Oklahoma Press.
> (Quoting Vizenor from "Landfill Meditation 8," pp. 18-19)

AS A NEW MEMBER OF THE TEACHING FACULTY at the University of Saskatchewan in 1993, I was given an opportunity to create a special topics course in
my areas of interest for a cohort of graduate students from Prince Albert (PA).
I chose to develop a new course, "Decolonizing Aboriginal Education." Every
other weekend, I traveled north to PA, where I offered the course to a talented
group of men and women as our department's first distance-delivery masters
degree program. My students were largely Cree from neighbouring First Nations communities, mostly teachers within the First Nations schools seeking
to get a graduate degree. I recall one, Willie Ermine, remarking one day, "This
course should be called Decolonizing Education, not Decolonizing Aboriginal
Education. The whole system needs to be changed!" I have often thought about
that comment, and I have called this book *Decolonizing Education: Nourishing
the Learning Spirit*, as I have long accepted that decolonizing education is not
a process generated only for Indigenous[9] students in the schools they attend or

---

9 Many terms such as Indigenous, Aboriginal and First Nations, Métis, and Inuit
   are used in this book. I acknowledge that these, like the term Indian are not
   terms that the People call themselves for most have their own terms, like Lnu
   among my people for their civilization although they have been called Micmac
   or Mi'kmaq in literature. I try to use Indigenous when considering the people
   beyond Canadian borders and use Aboriginal or First Nations, Métis, or Inuit

for students in First Nations programs in universities. Throughout my career since my coming to the University of Saskatchewan, I have aimed my research and discursive arrow not at teachers or their methods, but largely at the federal and provincial systems and the policy choices and the inequities coming from them. Empowered by years of administration and teaching in First Nations schools, serving on boards and committees, and writing and speaking across Canada and beyond to faculty, students, teachers, administrators, and federal and provincial agencies, I am more than ready to address what I see as issues within the whole system. Through this book, I share my critical perspective, activism, research, and scholarship that have put me solidly in the camp of advocating for systemic change and trans-systemic reconciliations. I am Mi'kmaq, and as a professor at the University of Saskatchewan for the past two decades and some before in other schools and universities, I have been forging a path of critique of current Eurocentric education and its practices while also researching and writing about a newer agenda of Indigenous science and humanities, both of which must be part of a global reclamation for education scholarship.

While much of my writing is found in fields of educational policy, curriculum theory, and educational practice as it relates to Indigenous students and Indigenous knowledges, this book shares the foundations for how those issues and insights emerged over my career as an Indigenous educator. Over the past 25 years, I have offered analysis and inspiration from the experiences of the many Indigenous people, particularly as my dissertation unfolded as the history of my ancestors' literacy experiences and history of education. That professional story was not so different from my own family story, but narrative writing has not featured as a large part of my work, regardless of venue. Storytelling is very much part of the tradition I was raised in, but such narratives were not welcomed and encouraged as good methodology in the academy.

My mother was a gifted storyteller, and I a respectful listener. I lived in a home where my mother shared stories of all her relations and her memories of each, their character, and the life events that affected them. My dad was not so much a talker as a listener, until he got with his "old timer" friends, then the stories flew out of him, too. He was a handsome man who lit the room with a big smile and gentle eyes. My aunties and uncles shared those characteristics of storytelling, and I came to enjoy all the benefits of a wide range of

---

when referencing the nations in Canada of Indigenous peoples. I acknowledge the tensions around the terms that my colleagues have long addressed, and offer that these terms, and the merits of the arguments for and against Aboriginal are not meant to offend. I also acknowledge that it is a common protocol today to capitalize Aboriginal as it is a nationality much in the same way as other groups are respected with capitalizing. I do so for Indigenous as well.

knowledge, just by being present and listening and able to stimulate conversation with my questions. As the youngest in my family, I was particularly bold in asking questions, which were largely encouraged. My mother often shared with me how often one frequent male visitor would come and talk incessantly. Everyone would just let him go on and on from one topic to another, listening but not doing much than the perfunctory nod or in Mi'kmaq the discursive holder "eh-heh." One day I climbed up to the table, and after listening for a while, I asked, "What are you talking about?" The adults all howled with laughter, as this was on their minds as well.

There were many silences to my questions, which, as the years went by, I realized were related to the layers of oppression that Mi'kmaq people had lived under. It was about the politics of knowledge production, their intersections with power, race, poverty, and gender, and the processes of colonization, including a patriarchal government and Indian agents. There were stories of people who suffered at the hands of these people, and I could see how our own experiences, though better in many ways because of where we lived, were similar. But there was a notable difference in our experiences. Few, if any, of those of my parents' generation had gone to school beyond a few years, and few cousins my age had finished high school, or even elementary school. During the potato harvest in Maine, many families would come for weeks with their children to work in the industry. In Maine where I grew up, potato harvest went with closed schools, but not in Canada. So my cousins would leave their school for several weeks; some caught up later, but others did not. Residential schools were still ongoing, and while I did not have to go, my cousins and older sister were among the survivors. My own history was held in stories and in the people who experienced multiple layers of both good and bad, all shared widely. My early education did not answer those questions; rather, it ignored them or marginalized the people to singular ideas embedded in grand narratives about country and history. It was not until I got to graduate school that I found classmates and a few professors who understood the plight of the poor, the classed society, the nature of difference, and educational underachievement.

As my learning spirit connected, I yielded in time to being a writer and a teacher, not of stories of my own, but sorting out inequities left unresolved, seeking theory to name what Indigenous students experienced in schools, or visioning of transformations to make the circumstances of one's birth less significant to success or quality of life. It was then that I went back to my family, my mother in particular, to sort out what her life was like and how things came to be from her perspective.

The opportunity came after my father died, and my mother came to live with my family for short periods before returning to her home in Potlotek. Trying to share with my mother her mourning, and to break the silence, I sat with her often, sometimes quietly doing some cooking or watching television, or at other times urging her to talk. She was obliging when I asked about family and friends, and I was amazed at how sharp her memory was, so crystal clear that she could remember certain days or times, who was there, what people wore, and what they said. As the weeks went on, I asked if I might take notes, thinking this may be important for my kids one day. My own memory was bad, maybe because I did not do like my mom did and tell the same story over and over. So I got inspired and asked her if I might be allowed not just to write her story but also to tell her life story in writing. She agreed and we set out with a new purpose, spending hours talking about her childhood and youth, the major diseases that nearly killed her mother, and how she got the dreaded diseases too, her early romances, and finding my dad and our family life. Each day we worked a little bit on the story and after she tired, I went to my computer to type my notes. For a time this went on, but we did not finish the storying then as there were many changes going on with both of us. I had to go back to work after the summer off, her health was changing, and my sister decided to leave Boston and move in with my mother so that she could continue to live with her in her own home. What a blessing this was for us all. When I did finally give the story back to my mother, many months later, my older sister first learned of her own fated path going to residential school in Shubenacadie, Nova Scotia. She learned about the struggles the family endured, and how life unfolds in many difficult ways. After the years of her own struggle, my sister began her own healing journey, starting with coming home to be with our mother and beginning to learn about her own history. This was the only publication that detailed my family life, which was my mother's story, not my own (Battiste, 1993).

Outside this experience of family life writing, I rarely shared my family stories in subsequent writings, even when the postmodern theorists called for it as a way of distinguishing one's location or position as an insider versus outsider, or positioning a counter dialogue, or confirming notions of authenticity. But at the time of my explorations in writing as a Mi'kmaq, I was not following anyone's lead, *per se*, for few writing models inspired me. Rather, in my work and my writing I was driven to get the knowledge to make a difference as a teacher, an administrator, a curriculum developer, or a professor. My search was ongoing, and I read profusely to find where current research and knowledge approached understanding the conditions and scenarios that were related to diverse groups such as Indigenous peoples.

Theorizing oppression and the deconstruction of educational histories of my people and the patterns of Eurocentrism and the decolonizing strategies in education have been my most productive writing moments, as I drew on a growing number of Civil Rights and Human Rights authors who were inspiring me. As the balance of disciplines began to shift in education from modernistic expository prose of grand narratives to more storytelling, to personal narratives and postcolonial analysis of colonization, to research in one's own perspectives, I took greater delight in reading and writing and found that the shift had brought my own analysis into a different light. It also helped me find a greater balance with my own history and offer those as partial analyses of the choices and paths that I took. Maybe this is wisdom taking its rightful place.

bell hooks has noted that women from oppressed groups have stories to tell, and to tell those stories is an act of resistance. Speaking in and through stories then becomes a way to engage self-transformation, a kind of rite of passage. So as I write this book, I am aware of the value of story and its ability to transform my research, and resist the Eurocentric frameworks that privileged other peoples' stories and analyses of Indigenous peoples' lives. It is also transforming me and bringing back life to living.

Within my stories are not my personal struggles with schools or teachers or curricula, for I remember little about my Eurocentric education or the conventional approaches that I had been part of. I tried to stay under the radar of the teacher, not to be noticed or labeled dumb. Little is there I care to remember. Many memories I have long ago let go. But what I think is important is my own path toward understanding the collective struggles of Indigenous peoples framed within a patriarchal, bureaucratic enterprise of government, with education used as the manipulative agent of various intended outcomes, some well-intentioned, some not, but all strategic. These collective struggles are the transforming points of my learning and vectors from which I grew into new responsibilities. In this introduction, I focus on a few memories of growing up that affected my choices. These are forms of guidance that have shaped the course of my scholarship and life. I choose these as a way to take out my story and connect to the lives and wisdom of others who have been my teachers.

Several friends and elders have helped me through my journey. My husband, Sa'ke'j Henderson, of course, my hero and love of my life, whom I met at Harvard and who was my tutor in a public school law class at Harvard. But there are others. I acknowledge Saulteaux Elder Danny Musqua for his generous stories that have been an inspiration for me throughout my years in Saskatoon. His sharing of the foundation for Anishinabe teachings on learning has given me a depth of understanding of the learning spirit. His stories also complement my own Mi'kmaw teachings drawn from my Mi'kmaw heroes such as Elder Murdena Marshall and the late Kji Keptin (Grand Captain) Alex Denny, who both have been closest in guiding my learning spirit with their humour, activism, and wisdom that helped me to understand more fully my

Mi'kmaw consciousness. They have shared their lives in typical Mi'kmaw[10] fashion, guiding, teaching, humouring, supporting, and sharing generously with humility and grace.

I have come to understand more fully my own life journey. Saulteaux Elder Danny Musqua constantly reminds those willing to listen that each of us has a journey on earth that is solely about learning. Learning, he often says, is the purpose of our life journey. We carry both a physical and spiritual energy that is both constant and changing. The constants come from our spiritual energy that is connected to spirit guides that have traveled with us before our birth, and the changing is the physical form that transforms constantly through life to death. At conception, our spirit enters the physical form of our body (after it has traveled through six other stages of development before arriving in a human body), together with other guiding spirits that travel with us throughout our life journey, providing inspiration, guidance, and nourishment to fulfill the purpose of the life journey ahead. Elder Musqua notes that our life spirit knows what the life journey of each person is and travels with each person to offer guidance to keep us on course. This does not happen deterministically, however, as each person's free will and desire will take them in diverse paths, and in each there is learning. Learning is both difficult and enjoyable, but ultimately it helps us shape the person we are.

It is like the deep struggle I had with coming up with my dissertation topic, and when it came, it was a bright moment; there was clarity in life, and a purpose that kept me motivated and focused. My spirit guides were guiding me to that moment. This cosmology or theory of being is one that is repeated in ancient stories of tricksters like Kluskap, Badger, Nanabush, Wasakechuk, Raven, Napi, and others in many diverse situations who inspire us in life with their experiences, always learning and transforming from their learning, and being the inspiration for others in understanding the various bumps and bruises of life as well as the great leaps of faith and change that come from making our choices. These stories offer great benefits from their learning.

We are all on a journey to find our unique gifts given to us by the Creator, Elder Danny Musqua tells us. *Knowledge is held by the spirits, shared by the spirits and comes from the spirits . . . our body then can be seen as carrier of the learning spirit* (Elder Danny Musqua, in D. Knight, 2001). The "learning spirit," then, is the entity within each of us that guides our search for purpose and vision. Our gifts unfold in a learning environment that sustain and challenge us as learners. Pueblo educator Gregory Cajete believes such a setting enables learners to "find their heart, face and foundation" (2000). The face is our iden-

---

10 Mi'kmaq is a noun used to reference the collective of Lnu people and Mi'kmaw is the adjective always preceding a noun.

tity, our heart is the passion that engages our life purpose, and the foundation is the talents and skills needed to put the passion to work. But that source is ultimately connected to a spiritual source, and these are vital foundations of Aboriginal learning.

My spiritual story began on the other side when I chose my parents — or maybe they chose me, or maybe together we chose each other. I was born in Houlton, Maine, during potato-picking harvest, in 1949, while my parents were on a seemingly brief seasonal work stop in Maine. When I was born, my mother and father and their two other small children were living behind the potato farm in a one-room tarpaper shack, as most Mi'kmaw farm hands tended to do at that time. Seeing this seeming poverty and perceived hardship with a new baby, the barren wife of the potato farmer thought she could help. I heard this story many times as I grew up. She had developed an instant connection to this tiny fair-skinned infant, an emotive bond that women feel upon cuddling newborns, and relayed to my mother what she thought she could give to me. She wanted my mother to allow her to adopt this baby. It was not even tempting, my mother said. Despite the seeming context of scarcity, my mother saw no burden in her children, and despite her seemingly impoverished situation, it was all she, like all Mi'kmaq, knew. My mother took pity on her, though, and as consolation, she did let Harriet Bither name me. She chose a name that was near and dear to her: Marie Ann. After having taken pity on her and given her this privilege, my mother did not have the heart to tell her that she already had another daughter named Marie Eleanor who was in residential school in Nova Scotia. So like one of the old comedy television shows featuring the two Daryls in a family, we have two Maries in the family.

My parents, John and Annie Battiste, ended up staying twenty-three years in Maine before returning home to their reserve. Chapel Island Reserve was renamed later to its name that Mi'kmaq always called it — Potlotek in Unama'ki (Cape Breton, Nova Scotia). Twenty-three years is a long time to remain away from their "home," and often I wondered why they did not go back earlier. I recall my mother talking about the many times she had to leave "home" to sell baskets with her mother or aunts, and the many experiences with white people. While she often was away, home was Potlotek, and it was the only one she talked about with fond memories. She often spoke of when she would go "home," what she wanted in the house they would build, and the life with the relatives that such a life would afford. They did not stay in Maine for the great job opportunities or the prosperity showered on us from being there, for we started out living in a tarpaper shack behind a potato house in Linneus, Maine, and gradually moved into low-cost rented houses and apartments, living always on the edge. My dad was a hard worker, but unskilled and untrained in the modern sense of employment. He was big and muscular, and was often hired to do the hard grunt labour of carrying the heavy stuff. My mother was a pretty, petite but stout woman who had a love of cooking and a knack for cleaning. Like many Mi'kmaw women in her early youth, she was hired as a domestic, cleaning homes, often two or more a day. Once it was learned that she was also a great cook, she was enlisted to be the cook for many years for the nuns in Houlton and later for the priests. Often I went with her to help her get through her work more quickly, and I developed these needed family skills. In particular, I developed a love for cooking and keeping a tidy house.

Scarcity was always a challenge, one that required my mother and father to draw on their creativity and cultural resources to make ends meet. Although they survived marginally by being labourers and domestics, in times of great need they made baskets from ash and maple trees, beautiful colourful baskets that they sold after working several days on them. When the baskets were all done and piled high in the shed, my mother would gather them in a sheet and start her trek, going house to house in many locations to sell the baskets for a dollar or two. She often told me stories of these transactions when she used to sell baskets with her mother. At the end of a day they would ask for lodging where they were and get sometimes a bed or a floor, for which they traded a basket. This basket-making was a long-time family enterprise and one that has deep significance to Mi'kmaq.

All of us (two sisters and a brother) were enjoined to learn how to make those baskets. It was a cultural economic enterprise that all Mi'kmaq knew. Getting the wood for the baskets meant for me and my sisters Geraldine and Eleanor, sitting in the woods with our mother or in the car for hours, while she told us stories. Eventually my dad would emerge from the woods with a sweaty face, carrying a long thick log with the axe on his shoulder. After putting it in the trunk, he then would then return to the forest for the second or third log. His muscular build warranted his being called by the local families, affectionately, "Big John" after a song that was popular at the time.

Once home, my father prepared the raw materials, pounding an axe into the wood, splitting and shaving the logs until they stood in straight splints. Each one would be shaved and then pounded evenly with the back of the axe until each splint would split and could be pulled apart. My mother finished off the splints, shaving them with a sharp knife into fine thin strips that she would then soak and dye in many bright colours. When dried, the splints were woven into the floor of the basket, intertwined with the coloured, thinner strips for the sides and top. My brother, sisters and I eventually were taught how to weave the sides. When we were done, my mom would finish the top and add any needed embellishments, and my brother and dad would make the handles and pound in nails on the potato baskets. Creativity was a requirement of the poor, so when potato season was gone, my dad also made axe handles or strapping for seats of old chairs, or he took work as a labourer wherever they would take him. Racism was probably the most frequent issue, but that was what life was like for Native people living in Aroostook County in Maine.

Then why did they stay so long in Maine? Why would they leave the reserve, where they could be assured of some government-supported housing, to live without supportive family around them and having to make do with the minimal? As my dad often reminded us, life on the reserve was hard, too, and there was little available in the way of jobs or education. So they stayed in Maine, and later in Boston, largely for the education that our residency promised. At the time they left the reserve, no Mi'kmaq had made it beyond early elementary school, and no one went to college.

Centralization was a federal policy that removed the Mi'kmaq from their traditional homelands to centralized reserves. Residential schools were still looming. My dad had a notion that my birth in the States and my brother and sisters' going to school there would assure us an education that would make life better for us. I heard that so often that I came to believe it, and it became an inspiration for my continued perseverance throughout my education.

After my parents settled into a home in Houlton, Maine, they went to get my sister from the Shubenacadie Indian Residential School in Nova Scotia. After three years her inner spirit was broken, her identity shattered, and her voice taken. She came home to find me, a new sister in the family. Attending the residential school was the worst thing that could have happened to her, yet attending racist public schools in Houlton was the next challenge. My mother told her often to look after her younger brother, and look after him she did. I often wondered when she came home with a bloody nose if that was what school was going to like for me, too, and if I would have to fight my way through school. But I was the youngest child, raised with my loving parents, and I did not have to take responsibility for anyone outside myself. I could take advantage of the situation of being youngest, of being light skinned, and having older siblings who looked after me. My dad said life required that I do my best in everything I do, and as my mother was always helping my sister, I benefitted from her tutelage, and her teaching my sister Geraldine to read and do math. Life got a little better when my mother transferred us all to the Catholic school system, easing us through some of the elementary school years, although my mother had no idea the trauma bringing my sister to the nuns would be for my sister Eleanor. Residential school had traumatized her too deeply to benefit much from that school. As a result, my sister left school after grade 8, and I continued my education through high school in Houlton before my family moved on to Boston.

Thankfully, my family remained in the United States until I, the youngest, graduated from university. I was a teenager of the 60s. This was a time in the United States when social programming was ripe, when bilingual education was emerging as a consequence of federal initiatives trying to create improved outcomes among disadvantaged children who had little access to the curriculum due to their language and cultural backgrounds, then called "disadvantaged and culturally deprived." Black activist Martin Luther King, President John F. Kennedy, feminists Betty Friedan and Gloria Steinem, American Indian leaders Russel Means and Dennis Banks, among others, were raising the issues of equality and civil rights, human rights, and Indian rights. All of these shaped my emerging social consciousness, as I gained a better awareness of poverty's effect on children, and the economic effects of racism and discrimination. At the time, I believed that it offered hope for those less fortunate, as immortalized in Martin Luther King's speech, "I Have a Dream." I recall memorizing passages as they lifted my spirit, even as my friends in the college dorm knew little and were never challenged about their complicity in creating and sustaining poverty, racism, and colonization. They enjoyed the performance of my speech, eloquently and passionately memorized. It would take many more years before the discourses of whiteness and white privilege would illustrate their complicity in the social issues of the day.

These are but a few of the passages that would emerge as significant for me, an Indigenous scholar and activist, though the story is far from done. The chapters in this book — some parts from my dissertation, from writings on cognitive imperialism, from my work in Aboriginal languages, from my work at the United Nations, and from my research and writing on decolonization, while others are taken from speeches I have given — bring together parts of a life journey that brings my perspectives and my journey to light. I offer these to my children Jaime, Mariah, and Annie, to my grandson Jacoby, and to the many graduate students who have called on me to ask about my life, my inspirations, and my intended legacy. So many graduate students have graced me with their appreciative words about how I have helped them articulate their own directions in reclaiming their Indigenous selves and their collective heritages. I dedicate the book to educators seeking to make changes in their thinking and in their work, knowing that the decolonization of education is not just about changing a system for Indigenous peoples, but for everyone. We all will benefit by it.

CHAPTER 2

The Legacy of Forced Assimilative Education for Indigenous Peoples

Not exclusive

I ASK YOU TO IMAGINE FOR A MOMENT THE EXPERIENCE of Aboriginal peoples in Canada. Imagine that for hundreds of years your peoples' most formative achievements and traumas, their daily suffering and pain, the abuse they live through, the terror they live with, are ignored and silenced. Their compelling voices and stories, largely cast in romance novels or on television in stereotypes for the public, are occasionally brought forward, used to sanction some programmatic innovation, or to support some theory of opposition or resistance, and then re-positioned in the margins of knowledge and curriculum.

Consider that for more than a century, Indigenous students have been part of a forced assimilation plan — their heritage and knowledge rejected and suppressed, and ignored by the education system. Imagine the consequence of a powerful ideology that positions one group as superior and gives away First Nations peoples' lands and resources and invites churches and other administrative agents to inhabit their homeland, while negating their very existence and finally removing them from the Canadian landscape to lands no one wants. Imagine how uncertain a person is whose success is only achieved by a complete makeover of themselves, by their need to learn English and the polished *French* rules and habits that go with that identity. They are thrust into a society that does not want them to show too much success or too much Indian identity, losing their connections to their land, family, and community when they have to move away as there is no work in their homeland. Assimilation. This context is important to postcolonial education, as I offer ways we can continue to reflect upon this experience in a proactive way. This experience continues to challenge our consciousness and our quest for healing. This chapter shows how the horror inherent in this educational process came to be for Mi'kmaw peoples in Canada a familiar path to all First Nations, as evidenced by their having the same patriarchal system of Indian agents, government, Indian residential schools, and contemporary education systems. It is a subject that every citizen of Canada should know, because every citizen in Canada is connected to it.

Forced assimilative education among Aboriginal peoples in Canada is distinct from the choices that immigrants have to make when they arrive from other lands. Immigrants, including refugees, make their way to Canada knowing that they will have to learn a particular culture. For some, the choice of living in a culturally similar community or having a school that guides them along the way helps them make this transition. Aboriginal people in Canada have entered into a relationship with the Crown through treaties and subsequently with the Canadian government to provide teachers and schools to assist them in making a livelihood after the original forms of livelihood were reduced or taken away. The central concepts of the Aboriginal and treaty right to education were an enriched education of First Nations that supplemented the learning system that is integral to the transmitting of knowledge, identity, and life skills to First Nations children.

Aboriginal and treaty rights are unique to First Nations, made distinctive by signed treaties or specific agreements between Inuit, First Nations, or Métis with the federal government of Canada, and affirmed in the Constitution of Canada. These arrangements are not recognized for other Canadians. First Nations education is both an Aboriginal and a treaty right, and affirmed and recognized in the new constitutional order of Canada. Three models of an independent Aboriginal right to education exist: (1) the retaining of First Nations choice in the treaties as an Aboriginal right; (2) the right of Treaty First Nations to choose an appropriate educational system for their children as a prerogative and an obligation; and (3) implementing "appropriate education" for Treaty First Nations, as other treaties allow, within federal discretion. In exercising federal discretion against First Nations choice in the treaty education clauses, however, the courts have imposed a fiduciary duty and the honour of the Crown doctrine (Henderson, 2007, chap. 33).

Treaty First Nations recognize that the treaty rights to education have not been implemented, but have been subverted by governmental interests and policies. Aboriginal and Indigenous elders are also aware of the eroding environment and land base that will require new ways of thinking and interacting with the earth and with each other. Aboriginal peoples are not the only ones experiencing a growing awareness of the limitations of technological knowledge and its capacity to provide solutions to our health, environment, and biodiversity, as we witness the undiscovered potential capacity of knowledge systems rapidly eroding and in need of urgent reform and action.

Aboriginal peoples in Canada and Indigenous peoples throughout the world are feeling the tensions created by a Eurocentric education system that has taught them to distrust their Indigenous knowledge systems, their elders' wisdom, and their own inner learning spirit. Neither the assimilative path of residential schools and day schools in the first half of the last century, nor the integrative approaches of the second half of that century in Canada, have succeeded in nurturing many Aboriginal students beyond high school. Most consider education an ongoing failure. In 2006, only 30 per cent of First Nations, Métis, and Inuit had received a certificate, diploma, or degree, compared to 50 per cent of non-Aboriginal Canadians (Statistics Canada, 2008). *What are the stats 2017*

Educational institutions and systems in Canada are also feeling the tensions and the pressures to make education accessible and relevant to Aboriginal people. With the rise in Aboriginal populations, especially in the northern territories and prairie provinces, and with the expected future economy depending on a smaller number of employed people, the pressure on conventional educational institutions to make Aboriginal populations more economically self-sufficient through education increases (Avison, 2004). In addition, educators are aware of the need to generate a more diverse population of trained workers, as they seek to address the diversity that exists in the population at large. As diversity is recognized, so also are questions about the processes for engendering inclusiveness, tolerance, and respect. In 2010, a report of the Canadian Councils of Ministers of Education, affirmed by much of the literature on Aboriginal education, directed its criticism at the increasing achievement gap within elementary, secondary schools, and universities among Aboriginal and non-Aboriginal students. The gap shrinks somewhat with students attending trade schools and colleges located close to their communities, as well as with an increasing number of Aboriginal women attending school. Interestingly, even Aboriginal single women with children are more likely to go to school than Aboriginal men. Reports of labour market relationships with schooling are strong, which may account for why Aboriginal people are sitting at the bottom of the labour market because of low education. Eurocentric education policies and attempts at assimilation have contributed to major global losses in Indigenous languages and knowledge, and to persistent poverty among Indigenous peoples. In Canada, the Royal Commission on Aboriginal Peoples (RCAP) conducted a six-year study and wrote a five-volume report on the massive damage to all aspects of Aboriginal peoples' lives. The 1996 report was the result of a huge mobilization of Canadian scholars and public servants in an effort to unravel the effects of generations of exploitation, violence, marginalization, powerlessness, and enforced cultural imperialism on Aboriginal knowledge and peoples. The Royal Commission's conclusions and recommendations reflect the broad consensus of 150 distinguished Canadian and Aboriginal scholars, and the deliberations of fourteen policy teams comprising senior officials and diverse specialists in government and politics (RCAP, 1996, pp. 5, 296–305).

The Royal Commission's report creates a postcolonial agenda for transforming the relationship between Aboriginal peoples and Canadians. It affirms how the false assumption of settler superiority positioned Aboriginal students as inherently inferior. This false assumption contaminated the objectives of residential schools and led to the systematic suppression of Aboriginal knowledge, languages, and cultures (1, pp. 251, 331-409). The report argues that this demeaning and ethnocentric attitude lingers in current policies that purport to work on behalf of Aboriginal peoples. Although the assumption is no longer formally acknowledged, this does not lessen its influence on contemporary policies or mitigate its capacity to generate modern variants (1, pp. 249, 252-53). The report proposes that Canada must dispense with all notions of superiority, assimilation, and subordination and develop a new relationship with Aboriginal peoples based on sharing, mutual recognition, respect, and responsibility. Unfortunately, the report, entitled *Gathering Strength,* has gathered more dust than strength, as the government of Canada has done little to acknowledge its contents or its value.

Many Aboriginal and Indigenous scholars and postcolonial writers have been imagining new restorative education programs. Like those who took part in the Royal Commission, they see that education is the key matrix of all disciplinary and professional knowledge and more. They also recognize that education and literacy have not been benign processes, for cognitive imperialism, licensed by dominant English languages and Eurocentric discourse, has tragically diminished Indigenous languages and knowledges and contributed to the discontinuity and trauma Aboriginal peoples continue to experience.

After taking a course in cultural imperialism at Stanford with Martin Carnoy, I had fashioned a name for that experience I had lived in and felt confined to and for which most Aboriginal students resisted with their feet. When Indigenous knowledge is omitted or ignored in the schools, and a Eurocentric foundation is advanced to the exclusion of other knowledges and languages, these are conditions that define an experience of cognitive imperialism. Cognitive imperialism is about white-washing the mind as a result of forced assimilation, English education, Eurocentric humanities and sciences, and living in a Eurocentric context complete with media, books, laws, and values. Indigenous people understand the crisis they live in and feel the urgency for reform. For many, their hopes were put into their own schools in their communities, yet for most they have had to have at least some of their education in public schools where changes are more about measuring success along the lines of their own content. The crisis is best described in a discourse of a decolonized education that seeks to reconcile contemporary education with the past and with the peoples' present, ensuring that the ideological and self-interests within Eurocentric education are not imposed on Indigenous peoples and they build their own present with their own agency and power intact. Kanu (2005) further explains decolonization:

The recent calls . . . to decolonize Indigenous education is part of a larger effort to reflect critically on the impact of colonization on Indigenous people, in particular internal colonization whereby carefully selected mechanisms, such as the subjugation of Indigenous knowledge and the use of colonial ideology to cultivate psychological subordination in the colonized, are employed by dominant groups to subordinate or regulate Indigenous populations. (p. 1)

Some provinces have begun to work through understanding the importance of diversity and cultural inclusion and in some instances making it a priority, yet they have not understood entirely what is at the core of the issues for inclusion for Indigenous peoples, and what ways to make this happen without repeating past problems. The core of understanding relationships built with First Nations, Métis, and Inuit peoples is first and foremost a distinction that is embedded in relationships built from treaties and later agreements that framed the relationships of people in place to the immigrating settler populations. This is least understood in Canada. Most Canadians today still view Aboriginal peoples as first settlers, not First Nations. What they notice first is what is on the surface, racialization and government spending, and both fill them with anxieties that come to the surface when treaties and Aboriginal rights are asserted. Yet, the rising population of First Nations, Métis, and Inuit has caused concern for the future of the Canadian economy.

In 2004, the Council of Ministers of Education, Canada (CMEC), the national body of all the provinces' heads of education, agreed to make Aboriginal education a priority, and the work of finding an appropriate pedagogy, content, and inclusive processes in all the provinces and territories began (Avison, 2004). The 2004 CMEC Report found:

- First Nations graduation rate is at 42 per cent compared to 78 per cent for the general population.
- 31.3 per cent take and pass provincial examinations in Grade 12 English.
- 5.5 per cent take and pass Mathematics 12.
- Grades four, seven and ten use Foundation Skills Assessment (like Canadian Tests of Basic Skills), showing significant gaps in performance between Aboriginal and non-Aboriginal students.
- Reading scores in grade 4 are well below non-Aboriginal students, suggesting a need for early childhood education and literacy programs (Avison, 2004).

The CMEC established the tenets of the priorities for Aboriginal education:

- Recognize early childhood education as a key to improved literacy.
- Provide clear objectives and a commitment to report results, including working closer with Government of Canada and Aboriginal communities.
- Institute strong teacher development and recruitment.
- Improve accountability arrangements with Aboriginal parents and communities.
- Share learning resources.
- Support the elimination of inequitable funding levels for First Nations schools.
- Create a National Forum on Aboriginal education. (Avison, 2004)

Since 2010, the CMEC has established priorities for Aboriginal education in each area of early childhood learning and development, elementary and secondary education, post-secondary education, and adult learning. Each of the recommendations are suitable and necessary for the provincial institutions to contribute to affecting the educational gaps, yet there is more underlying the surface of cultural inclusion. The challenge is not so much finding receptivity to inclusion, but the challenge of ensuring that receptivity to inclusive diverse education is appropriately and ethically achieved with First Nations, Métis, and Inuit support, and that the educators become aware of the systemic challenges for overcoming Eurocentrism, racism, and intolerance. The "add and stir" model of bringing Aboriginal education into the curricula, environment, and teaching practices has not achieved the needed change (RCAP, 1996), but rather continues to sustain the superiority of Eurocentric knowledge and processes.

Subsequent reports and task forces — such as Canada's Senate Subcommittee on Aboriginal Education (2011) and the Report of the National Panel on First Nation Elementary and Secondary Education for Students on Reserve (2011) — seem to reveal similarities of issues across Canada. Again, while each of these reports offer analyses and recommendations for Canadians and politicians to understand the needed structural changes, each refer to inequities, racial discrimination, and student resilience, the differential treatment of schools across federal and provincial fiduciary responsibilities, and the differential knowledges across the cultural divides that prevent communities and parents from feeling welcomed or appreciated in the schools. There continues to be a lack of materials and resources, and lots of tension and sometimes apathy, in making inclusive, culturally responsive, anti-oppressive education. The challenge also continues for educators to be able to reflect critically on the current educational system in terms of whose knowledge is offered, who decides what is offered, what outcomes are rewarded, and who benefits, and, more importantly, how those are achieved in an ethically appropriate process.

The key in designing meaningful education in Canada must begin with confronting the hidden standards of racism, colonialism, and cultural and linguistic imperialism in the modern curriculum and see the theoretical incoherence with a modern theory of society. No theory of Canadian society exists that reflects its order as an eternal pattern of human nature or social harmony. In this predicament, education theory has to confront the line between truth and propaganda.

Often, the purposes of the educational institutions betray this current explanatory theory. Their purpose is to create and transmit an imagined culture of Canada or the provinces in a market-driven society. But the imagined culture remains elusive. It is a culture of nationalism imposed by the state. It is not reflective of the heritage, knowledge, or culture that the students bring to education, or their skills and shared traditions. It is not reflective of the normal everyday one that they live with their families. It is only reflective of an imagined and aspirational "other."

Since there is no agreement about transmitting knowledge, heritage, and culture, the resulting curriculum is made normative by a cloak of standards and expectations on all educators and students. The current structure helps preserve class structures and a ruling elite rather than sort out everyone according to their inherent capacities. The status quo also argues for family or parental responsibility to be passed to the state in the form of compulsory education. These educational purposes imply a disintegration of the family and culture for the abstraction of the society as defined by a standard curricula, and its defined outcomes and successes as identified as graduation from high school and now some post-secondary school, college, or university.

Aboriginal peoples' invisibility continues to be ignored under modern educational curricula and theory, and psychic disequilibrium continues (Canada, House of Commons 1990, pp. 29–35). As the twenty-first century turned, we need to take a look at where we have been and where we are going. For many of us, we have become painfully aware of what has happened to the children and Aboriginal youth across Canada, and we have statistical reminders of how that education has affected them. We must find resources to enable all children to have the fundamental human rights outlined in the *United Nations (UN) Charter of Human Rights* (1948), the *UN Convention on the Rights of the Child* (1989), and now the *UN Declaration on the Rights of Indigenous Peoples* (2007). Like the provisions in the Victorian treaties and the National Indian Brotherhood (NIB, 1972) policy paper on Indian Control of Education, the *Convention on the Rights of the Child*, to which Canada is a signatory nation, provides that "education of the child shall be directed to . . . the development of respect for the child's parents, his or her own cultural identity, languages and values." Article 29 (2) affirms the right to establish and direct educational institutions that conform to the minimum standards of the state. In 2009, the Committee on the Rights of the Child issued general comment No. 11 on Indigenous children and their rights under the Convention, which calls for basic measures to be taken in support of the implementation of the rights of Indigenous children and provides guidance on how these obligations are to be implemented by States parties with respect to Indigenous children. In 2012, the UN issued a thematic report on the rights of Indigenous Children in the Secretary-General's report on the Status of the Convention on the Rights of the Child (A/67/225). The report noted that Indigenous children suffer extreme forms of exclusion and discrimination, but they are rights holders and are therefore entitled, without discrimination, to all the safeguards that are necessary for their survival, development, and protection (s. 9). The situation of Indigenous children is inextricably linked to the histories and experiences of the wider Indigenous communities in which they live. Issues of a cross-cutting nature impacting upon all rights of Indigenous children include respect for cultural identity, protection from discrimination, and the implementation of the rights of Indigenous children (s. 15–23). They are protected in international law by both individual and collective rights and freedoms. Indigenous peoples' collective freedoms are specifically guaranteed under article 27 of the *International Covenant on Civil and Political Rights*, in the *Convention on the Rights of the Child*, in the *International Labour Organization (ILO) Indigenous and Tribal Peoples' Convention, 1989 (No. 169)*, and in the *United Nations Declaration on the Rights of Indigenous Peoples* (sections 11, 12). The report considers the measures needed to address the rights of Indigenous children in education (sections 26-39).

These principles present the challenge to the Canadian education system and Aboriginal parents to design meaningful and honourable education for Aboriginal people that recognizes, respects, and integrates Aboriginal knowledges, heritages, and ways of life as an integral part of education, instead of biased fragmented concepts of culture buried in Eurocentric discourses.

Education theory teaches a social science that presents humans as the product of culture and motivation and interest stemming from those structures the society creates. Once modern society became convinced of the absolute right and virtue of its values and institutions, either real or imaginary, it set out to convert all other societies with which they came into contact. What it saw was largely defined by what it was — by the assumptive knowledge it was heir to, and the particular rhythms of contemporary thought in its own culture. The modern educational system was created to maintain the identity, language, and culture of a colonial society, while ignoring the need to decolonize. Culture in this educative context is a mask for evolutionary or racial logic. Its theory is derived from a biased position.

Culture was an educational concept that allowed Euro-Canadians to focus on empowering the deprived and the powerless, yet not having to confront any explanation or evaluation of the effects of racism or colonialism on these cultures or people. In this sense, civilization is taken as a possession of Euro-Canadians, and the contents of other cultural realms are understood as merely comparative. These cultural borderlands are understood as exceptions in modern thought rather than central areas for inquiry and empowerment. But modern educational thought finds actual human consciousness too messy to be studied, which may account for why youth get the facts but not the discussion of what their own purpose is within the life in which they are submersed.

Most often, Indigenous people, including Aboriginal peoples of Canada, have been depicted as members of a "timeless traditional culture": a harmonious, internally homogeneous, unchanging culture. From such a perspective, the Indigenous cultures appear to "need" progress, an economic and moral uplifting to enable their capacities. This developmental perspective serves as a self-congratulatory reference point against which modern society can measure its own progressive historical evolution. The civilizing journey is conceived of more as a rise than a fall, a process more of perfection than degradation — a long and arduous journey upward, culminating in being "them."

The decolonization and human rights movements among Indigenous peoples, teachers, and students have had to face this culture problem. Because the classic works in the curricula do not present clear or fair interpretations of their world views or languages, they have had to suggest a total revision of anthropological and social analyses. Around the globe, Indigenous thinkers have had to prove that the received Eurocentric notion of culture as unchanging and homogeneous was not only mistaken but irrelevant. They have had to prove that their world view is distinct from the cultural ethnographies constructed about them through the historical and political processes of modern thought. They have had to prove that they are not brute, timeless events in nature, that the so-called classic works confuse local cultures with universal human nature. They have had to demonstrate how ideology often makes cultural facts appear natural. They have had to use social analysis to attempt to reverse the process: to dismantle the ideological in order to reveal the cultural (a peculiar blend of objective arbitrariness and subjective taken-for-grantedness). The interplay between making the familiar strange and the strange familiar is part of the ongoing transformation of knowledge.

Although efforts have been made to sensitize teachers to part of the cultural and psychological context of Indigenous pupils through in-service programs, little has yet been done to include a realistic portrayal of their knowledge, languages, heritages, histories, or governments into the standard curricula. Rather, what schools have had to contend with in terms of materials are false and pernicious representations of Indigenous peoples as vanishing Canadians, Indians of childhood, savage warriors, and images of redskins, performing Indians, celebrity Indians and plastic Shamans, exotic and spiritual Indians, and problem protestors (Peters, 2012). There is no right for Indigenous peoples to offer their own self-representation in curricula, or their own visions for education, because all of that was decided by elite groups who decide what goes into the curricula, how much, and from what perspective.

The problem, thus far, has been assumed to be about enhancing the integration of Indigenous children into school cultures so that they can learn Canadian curricula. The education system has not yet ensured that non-Indigenous children develop an accurate understanding of the Indigenous peoples in Canada and their knowledge systems, much less who is their neighbour. Instead, education systems perpetuate a biased construction of the strength of colonialism posing as globalism, Eurocentric institutions, economic survival of the nation, cultural institutions, and reasoned democracy alongside the idea that Indigenous peoples are primitive, uneducated, justly conquered people who would have been assimilated long ago but for their cultural backwardness. This is the discursive legacy of museums of anthropology and regional and local history.

The educational discourses for analyzing the problems and the experimental strategies for change have created several eras and narratives around culturalism. Culturalism is a strong and influential tradition in Indigenous education. Culturalism is a complex mix of ideologies, discourses, and practices that serve to legitimate Eurocentrism in its many forms of scholarship, law, and social practices so as to make them invisible to those who benefit from them. Culturalism, like other similar terms such as cultural racism, has developed strategies that mask its Eurocentric foundations and purposes of education and its privileged consciousness and perspectives. Informed by the assumption of superiority, culturalism is a strategy of "othering" that effectively dismisses and de-legitimates diverse thought and values, knowledge and heritage, treaties and rights, and culture (McConaghy, 2000).

Cultural transmission and socialization, societal restructuring through assimilation and integration, empowering communities through self-determination, counter-hegemonic, anti-racist, anti-oppressive, post-structural, post-modern, and postcolonial discourses have offered diverse theoretical lenses of analysis of situations involving Indigenous children and youth. Depending on the agents of the lens and perspectives, Indigenous education has been analyzed extensively and criticized widely over the past fifty years by both Indigenous and non-Indigenous scholars, educators, policy analysts, and administrators. Yet the core issues of how student successes are identified and measured, or by what methodology or approaches successes will be achieved, remain elusive.

In designing meaningful and honourable education for Indigenous people in the 21st century, the need for an adequate and relevant educational program that recognizes, first and foremost, cognitive imperialism and its multiple strategies and replaces it with reconciliation through affirmation of the diverse heritages, consciousnesses, and languages of Aboriginal peoples. The next measure is for a trans-systemic evaluation of both Indigenous knowledges and Euro-Canadian knowledges and how they can be framed so that neither is entirely lost but sustained by a new cognitive framework for curriculum, systems, and training.

Where Indigenous knowledge or epistemology survives, it is transmitted through the Indigenous languages. Aboriginal languages in Canada provide a direct and powerful means of understanding the legacy of Aboriginal knowledges and provide deep and lasting cognitive bonds, which affect all aspects of Aboriginal life. Through sharing a language, Aboriginal people create a shared belief of how the world works and what constitutes proper action. The sharing of these common ideals creates a collective cognitive experience for tribal societies that is understood as Aboriginal or Indigenous knowledge systems. Indigenous knowledges are diverse learning processes that come from living intimately with the land, working with the resources surrounding that land base, and the relationships that it has fostered over time and place. These are physical, social, and spiritual relationships that continue to be the foundations of its world views and ways of knowing that define their relationships with each other and others. Indigenous elders have transmitted the functions and knowledge inherent to their living on the land and made clear that what the land reveals is that all things are interconnected, it is sacred, and our people must be stewards of its continued protection.

The next chapters will begin to expose, elaborate, question, and critique these Eurocentric assumptions as the foundation that failed First Nations education. By reviewing the current systems of education and how they have defined diversity, educational discourses within systems of racism and cognitive imperialism, I assert that discourses of achievement, diversity, and inclusion have not been successful because educators have assumed that the problem resides in Aboriginal students, in what is projected onto them as discourses of lack of capacity rather than on the operating assumptions and structures of the Eurocentric system that hides its power and privilege in whiteness, and ignores complicities with dominance, difference, and disadvantage. The next chapter will start with an overview of the historical foundations of First Nations education, highlighting some events and processes leading to the treaties, especially as experienced by Mi'kmaq. It will then focus on the treaty process, and the British sovereign arrangements with First Nations, as well as address the colonial apparatus underlying assimilative Eurocentric education.

CHAPTER 3

Mi'kmaw Education: Roots and Routes

IN THESE PAST TWENTY-FIVE YEARS OF MY PATH, my scholarship and my voice about the trajectory of colonial education in Canada and a path for change has been threaded through a discourse of decolonization. I have been inspired by Indigenous elders, early visionaries, activists like Ida Wassacase, who was a leader in the creation of the First Nations University; Dorothy Lazore, whose tireless persistence in creating materials for a Mohawk language immersion program gave success to one of the first Aboriginal language immersion programs in Canada; and Maori educators Linda and Graham Smith whose voices and activism in their homeland of Aotearoa (New Zealand) helped build Kaupapa Maori language nests that would initiate the restoration and revitalization of their language. These examples of revolutions were led by people with Indigenous core values, vision, determination, and deep relation to their place. But revolutions are not just about people; they are ideological, too.

I recall Linda Smith telling us (Smith, Battiste, Bell, & Findlay, 2003) that the revolution in Aotearoa was not one that came from the changing of the country's legislation that officially recognized their Maori language, although this helped immensely in the building of the educational programs. The revolution was not the Ko Hunga Reo itself as a space for building the languages. Rather, the revolution was built on the strength of young parents' convictions to be the initiating change for their children, providing them with the opportunities to learn the Maori language within the Ko Hunga Reo language nests. This one act by every parent led to the extraordinary revolution of grounding their activation in many different venues, grounding their responsibilities to their children in a commitment to be present every day and give back to the nation. What a change it did make! Linda Smith's book is important reading to anyone seeking to understand Indigenous peoples and decolonization. Her framework has emerged from her historical study of Maori people, but it is very important in its applications to other Indigenous peoples who have experienced colonialism and its various forms of diminishment and deprivations. She writes:

> Decolonization . . . is about centring our concerns and world views and then coming to know and understand theory and research from our own perspectives and for our own purposes. (Smith, 1999/2012, p. 41)

This has been empowering work for her, and for me as well as I developed my own research. At the beginning of my doctoral work, I too wondered what the future would hold and recall for a good long part of my doctoral studies at Stanford, I was looking desperately for that ultimate research problem and question that would finally frame my dissertation. This is the first question every new graduate student comes to dread. What is your research question? I knew it started with a problem, but when I looked at education from an Indigenous perspective, I saw *everything* was a problem. The literature review that was intended to help locate this problem did little to solve my dilemma, as from every disciplinary angle, Indigenous peoples' situations were problematic, and I could not escape the discursive Eurocentric lens that measured everything against itself, and therefore, Indigenous peoples were always found lacking and ultimately to be acted upon by some government initiative. Early on I realized that part of my own problem in the search for the research I would ultimately do was that I was looking *out* and not *in*. I thought there was a magical answer outside myself.

Then one rainy night, on the way from Stanford to San Francisco, I was to find a life-changing moment. I had invited a Stanford faculty friend professor, Beatrice Arias, to attend with me a Chicano art exhibit where another friend was showing his artwork. She approached the idea with adventure, especially to meet new Chicanos who were part of my inner circle of friends from my husband's law school days. We had talked often about the "dissertation problem" I was having, and that night, I just wanted to relieve myself of that tension and asked her not to ask me anything about my dissertation question, problem, or method. That discussion, too, I was to discover, is stressful to any graduate student. So we settled in, her driving in the rain, and me, a good companion, babbling about home and family and then about my community in Nova Scotia. Her own interests were in bilingual education and desegregation, and she asked me if my community had schools with bilingual education. "If only we could get over which writing system is best, we may get there," I responded. "We have three writing systems, all with their advocates and all competing for which one will be the writing system of choice." So then I shared with her what I knew about the missionaries who brought their writing systems and their variant literature, the current advocates and motivations, and the new system being developed in Cape Breton by collaborations with Mi'kmaw language elders and knowledge holders. After listening to what I knew from being immersed in the literacy issues in my community, and when we were almost in San Francisco, she said, "Why don't you do your dissertation on that?" Wow, what a moment! It was like I was hit by cognitive thunder and lightning. What an idea . . . do a dissertation on something I already knew something about! That felt so right. So it began, my journey . . . *in* and then *out*. And it has not stopped.

Living on the far eastern coast, the Mi'kmaq are distinctive for having been among the first tribal nations to meet the European explorers, missionaries, and sailors. Mi'kmaw oral tradition holds many stories of these encounters; especially humorous are the stories of missionaries whose limited but growing Mi'kmaw language got them into lots of funny situations, especially at the confessionals when they would misinterpret and then offer their own conflated advice. Other stories are found in written journals kept by European explorers and missionaries who codified their memories of those early first encounters. For the most part in these journals, they offer biased accounts of the people they met on the shores of what became America. In these accounts they also offer clarity to their own ethnocentric motivations, values, beliefs, and practices while living among the First Nations.

I first discovered one of these journals when I was teaching summer school at the University of New Brunswick in 1979. One Saturday afternoon, at a time long before the Internet became the vogue, I was browsing the book racks looking for something nonspecific when I came across one of the journals of a Catholic missionary by the name of Christian Le Clerq (1691; Ganong, 1910). The book cover was made of delicately bounded leather with gold calligraphy, with thin paper that relayed a missionary's accounts of a people called the Gaspésians, or people of the Gaspé region of Quebec. Reading through the first chapters of the book, I was immediately interested in the introduction to a people that this missionary met, appalled and intrigued simultaneously by the negative caricatures of an ancient time when people lived in their wigwams, survived by the sea and the animals in the forest, and lived simply but lavishly. I was also amused by the accounts of men and women and their attitudes and experiences, as I could easily imagine my own family mirrored in some of those descriptions of their love of family, spirituality, and adventure. The afternoon fled swiftly, and soon the librarian reminded me that it was closing time. This book turned out to be a reference book, not allowed to circulate outside the library. It took some doing, but I was able to convince the librarian that, as a sessional lecturer at the university, I could be trusted to bring back this book first thing Monday morning. So I got the book out and tucked it under my arm and headed home. That evening and through the night, I curled up with it until I was finished. I was mesmerized by the times, the events, the stories, and an inner view to Mi'kmaw life in the 1600s.

Europeans' entrance into our land called Mi'kma'ki stretched over what is now known as the five Atlantic provinces: Quebec, Newfoundland, New

Brunswick, Prince Edward Island, and Nova Scotia. The Mi'kmaq were called many terms in the literature of the ancient explorers. Sometimes they were Etchimins, Gaspesians, savages, depending on how the writer located them in their own space and time. In each of the accounts, they were notably big, well built, lean and athletic, perceptive, acutely aware of their surroundings in both the day and night. They could travel through the darkest of night with great speed, knowing the dangers and the familiar paths. The explorers like John Cabot often relayed that the Mi'kmaq were open, sharing, hospitable people with large families, but fierce and highly regarded for their courage, and feared among many neighbouring nations, whom Mi'kmaq called Kwedej or Mohawk. So when the journals spoke of the meeting of nations with European explorers, it was with interest I read that the relations were cordial and not hostile. Father Christian Le Clerq (1697; Ganong, 1910) relayed stories of how they came to know of the coming of the white man. One dream was of a floating island with trees with empty branches and animals in white skins that were travelling on the sea. These had already been discussed fully in council with the elders, but without much consensus on its meaning. Then one day the sea brought forth what seemed to be a small floating island, with empty branches on which travelled men in white skins. They watched from the forest's edge as the newcomers came to shore and planted a cross in the ground. The cross was like the one that had framed another dream, and which they had already put in their wigwams and wore around their necks. Le Clerq assumed they had been visited by other Christian explorers and tried to find out how it could be that they had been introduced to the cross. Finally the eldest was brought forward to share how the cross came to them through a dream during a great famine. They were instructed to bring the cross to their wigwams, to their village, and to wear it and the famine would lift. The elder then explained how this had changed the circumstances, and they were once again prosperous in their hunting. These events laid a foundation for the newcomers, who came with their own cross, and despite other protocols, this one seemed to assist in the new relations in Gaspesia.

Because travelling across others' homeland was a common occurrence among first peoples, they had well established protocols that were known and practiced among the nations, including one protocol with wampum to help one get safely through one region to another. White wampum and purple wampum told of different intentions and purposes, and these would be addressed in council when the wampum was delivered to the right people. The lands were meant for hunting and other living arrangements within established relationships and alliances, and the people traveled through with their protocols of wampum, but did not stay beyond their known welcomed boundaries. These protocols of place shaped relationships, responsibilities, and ceremonies that eventually were well established among travelers, although not yet known or understood by the European travelers.

In this chapter I examine two aspects of Mi'kmaw education, looking at the historical events that have affected how Mi'kmaq have experienced education through their own learning in home and family and through formal systems. It begins with the historical record that led to the Mi'kmaq developing relations with the French that engaged them in ceremonies that led to their adopting Catholicism. Then there were the relations with the English, different from the French in that it was not about trade and commerce but was about their being diminished, despised, and disposed of through scalp bounties and later trained to be their domestics and slaves. Once the English had a foothold on the land, and no longer needed help in surviving in this environment, they looked to how they could make their own settlement more like their own homeland. Unlike the French, who often adopted a more native lifestyle to survive, the English came with their own lifestyle and thought it could be transposed onto these lands, including remaking the Indians into settled farmers by the use of their own language, literacy, and schooling.

Blending Mi'kmaw Knowledge with Catholic Knowledge

Mi'kmaw systems of education were characterized by communal participation, observation, pragmatic and experiential learning, both formal and informal, and were highly dependent on intrapersonal, interpersonal, kinaesthetic, and spatial learning, as expressed in oral language and active engagement in the daily life of the people. Cyclical and patterned knowledge from living with nature reinforced in ceremony, tradition, and teachings are important referent points for the knowledge holders. The languages and oral traditions have necessarily been socialized within these priorities and ways of knowing, and thus embed many teachings, stories, traditions, and foundations that reflect these understandings and are vital to the continued connectivity of knowledges from the past to the future.

The explorers and missionaries who ventured into what was to them the New World immediately wrestled with the problems of language and their own survival. Though the search for gold, spices, furs, and other marketable items was uppermost in their minds, the early colonists' survival necessitated certain practices with the people they initially called "Indians," as the early explorers had assumed they were en route to India. Travel literature of the fifteenth, sixteenth, and seventeenth centuries relays two approaches with regard to their relationships with the local peoples they encountered, leading to their learning languages. Thinking that all the peoples they met spoke the same language, and envisioning them as interpreters and messengers, some explorers kidnapped local people and, in other instances, invited them on their journeys. For those who agreed to go on these voyages with European travelers, and even the prisoners, Mi'kmaw curiosity and sense of adventure may have appeared at first encouraging. Since the Mi'kmaq were so well acquainted with their homeland and waterways, they could easily find their way back home by land or water. However, the explorers soon became aware of the wide language diversity among tribes and the difficulty in learning any of them, much less all of them.

The second practice of the missionaries and travelers was to keep journals and attempt to codify the languages they heard in order to learn them, and to aid others in their journeys among the natives. During the early colonial period, when several countries were investigating the resources of the New World, the laws and language of each of the individual countries determined the conduct and intercourse with the Indian nations. Since the Church formed the basis of their law, missionaries were the first international diplomats, who established trade and loyalty to their country's interest. Dictionaries which emerged from these encounters were sent to the Church and Crown, providing what appeared to be evidence that these pagan souls could be saved through religious instruction in the local languages. Most of all, the expansion of empire and the securing of resources for the explorers' homeland depended on the religious conversion of Native peoples as required by the Church in order to claim the land. Conversion of the Natives was not a humanistic attempt to bring the light of reason and the true faith to Indians, but rather missionaries were given the responsibility to establish consenting paradigms of trade alliance and allegiance with the Crown that sponsored their expeditions.

The European countries investigating the resources of the New World raised an important question in international politics: how were the land and riches of the New World to be allocated among the various European powers? In all instances, the pope, God's authority on earth, was to justify any occupancy of Indigenous territory. Two papal bulls were enacted to give legitimacy to a process. The first, enacted by Pope Nicholas V in 1452, allowed war to be waged against all non-Christians throughout the world and promoted the conquest, colonization, and exploitation of non-Christians peoples, territories, and nations. The second, in 1493, recognized the Christian domination of the New World. These two papal bulls provided the strongest influence and power over the other European countries, and ultimately the agreed-upon method of allocating the resources was intimately tied to the conversion of the Natives. Thus, learning the Native languages was intrinsic to the missionaries' goal.

While Mi'kmaq were cross bearers and had some entrance to the symbolism of the new religion, Christianity challenged traditional tribal beliefs and practices, which could only be effectively addressed, so the pope reasoned, in the everyday language of the people. Missionaries, then, were sent with the explorers with their rudimentary linguistic skills to discover the languages of the New World. However, learning the languages of the many tribes and the conversion of even a few Native interpreters were insufficient. This, then, would be a long-standing mission and goal that might take years to accomplish, but missionaries and explorers were persistent, and this led to the long and arduous task of codification of these languages for themselves and others who would follow them. This also assured their continued financial support from the benefactors.

While many French missionaries and priests ventured into Mi'kmaw territory in the eastern seaboard of what is now Atlantic Canada and the United States, several missionaries stand out as having had a significant effect both on the development of written languages of the local tribes for converting them to Christianity and for politicizing the intentions of the European leadership. In 1610, Mi'kmaw Grand Chief Membertou and about 140 of his followers were baptized, after which Chief Membertou gave his promise to bring all Mi'kmaq into alliance with the Holy Roman Empire, a feat that was completed in the mid-eighteenth century. The political alliance was celebrated with wampum that was given to the pope's representative Father Jesse Fleche (Battiste, 1986; Henderson, 1997). The alliance, and the wampum belt that is believed to be part of this ceremony, has been well advanced in Henderson's account of the Concordat of 1610 (Henderson, 1997), and shared in oral traditions with one of the current members and hereditary descendants of the Grand Council Stephen Augustine in his Mi'kmaw Creation Story (Augustine, 2008). The baptism of Chief Membertou and his family and friends did not radically or marginally alter the existing beliefs and spiritual practices of the Mi'kmaq at the time, as writers would later relay that the event was seen more as a political alliance than a spiritual one. But how much could one know of the core of religious beliefs with scant knowledge of the Mi'kmaw language? Father Biard, a well-known writer of the Jesuit journals who followed Father Fleche, who baptized Chief Membertou, found him later to be totally unprepared for Christianity, having little or no understanding of the precepts of the religion. Subsequent historians agree that Chief Membertou could not have had knowledge of his baptism and the foundation of the Church's doctrines, which he had supposedly fully accepted (Sargent, 1936). Yet, despite this acclamation of knowledge and acceptance of its truths, this historical event has been described as "superficial" (Conkling, 1974, p. 11) and no more than "a symbol of alliance" (Thwaites, 1856–1896: I, p. 89; Kennedy, 1950, p. 3).

With Membertou's baptism completed and friendship developed with the Mi'kmaq, a large French expedition was sent to Mi'kma'ki under the leadership of Isaac de Razilly, who set up Fort Sainte-Marie-de Grâce and established a new settlement at La Héve in the summer of 1632. Fifteen families and three Capuchin missionaries were housed in the fort. The Capuchins were an order of Catholic monks whose founder, St. Francis of Assisi, was known to have lived among the poor, preaching and living a lifestyle in solitude. The New World offered them just the kind of natural living that gave rise to their order, and soon after their arrival among the Mi'kmaq, they opened the first boarding school in Mi'kma'ki, one that would be for the use of both the colonists and the Mi'kmaq who lived in the surrounding area. It was the beginning of a blended educational system.

The conversion of Mi'kmaq to the precepts of Christianity was an ongoing, gradual process that would consume the attention of the missionaries in Mi'kma'ki. Yet their daily life required their moving from place to place, hunting, fishing, and gathering foods for various seasons and seasonal gatherings in different areas. However, from the time of Membertou's baptism and beyond, missionaries tried to remain on the periphery of Mi'kmaw life. Unaccustomed to the wandering habits and relatively harsh life of Mi'kmaw daily life, the missionaries were largely found where Mi'kmaq gathered in large groups. Most regular were their annual spring and summer nation gatherings in Malagawatch and later at Chapel Island. From a very early date, the rituals of Christianity were absorbed, but without much change to conventional spiritual practices (Thwaites, 1896: III, p. 145).   *Lac-Ste-Anne*

During the off-times from being among Mi'kmaq, the missionaries continued to write what language they heard, practicing from their scribbled notes and sharing their emerging skills with their counterparts in their journals. The object of all of this was that they should be able to engage Mi'kmaq as fully as possible so as to convert them. Language translation, word usage, and varietal functions continued to be the crux of the problems among many of the missionaries, who did not remain long enough with the Natives to become thoroughly acquainted with the Native languages and to have much of an effect on their beliefs and habits (Conkling, 1974, p. 11). Words or preaching alone did not do the job of convincing Mi'kmaq of the merits of being Catholic. The more successful were those missionaries who brought with them medicines from their home country. Mi'kmaq's exposure to European diseases were beginning to be deadly for many, and missionaries who were able to have an effect with medicines from their homeland could help convince some Mi'kmaq of the merits of Christian spirituality (Johnston, 1960).

One of the first missionaries to step beyond the spiritual and healing boundaries and aid the political cause of Mi'kmaq with encroaching settlers was Father Antoine Gaulin. His mission in Cape Breton began in 1713 and continued until 1732. He is best known for establishing a mission at Malagawatch, Cape Breton, which was the headquarters of the Santé Mawio'mi (Grand

Council of Mi'kmaq) meetings. These meetings brought an annual assemblage of Mi'kmaq to hear the discussions and annual reports of the Council and continue the shared teachings and protocols of families and communities. Approximately 120 families were counted as attending one of these meetings in Malagawaj, coming from all directions of Mi'kma'ki in their canoes with their families. The protocols of the gathering were elaborate, and local hosts met the canoes in the water and sang and danced upon their arrival. The families set up their wigwams in villages. The meetings of the Grand Council, like today, were often with the missionaries. Father Gaulin reportedly met with the Council in a letter to the Chancellor of France, noting that the Indians "wished to be united in a single village" and suggested that the River of "Arthigonisesche" be that site and that a church be built there that should house a resident priest (Johnston, 1960, pp. 63–64). In 1724, the chapel was completed in the area of what is known as Antigonish, Nova Scotia.

In 1732, Father Gaulin was recalled to Quebec, leaving his assistant, Father Michel Courtin, to continue the ministry among the Mi'kmaq (Johnston, 1960). However, Father Courtin's mission was abruptly terminated when he was lost at sea that same year, leaving the Mi'kmaq without a missionary priest. Father Gaulin, who had learned the Mi'kmaw language during his nearly twenty-year mission among Mi'kmaq, had subsequently instructed Father Courtin, and together they had been able to put together the first Mi'kmaw catechism and "other basic texts" which were intended for those missionaries who would come after them (unsigned letter, 1739, in Upton, 1979, p. 33). These would begin a legacy of religious literacy that would continue through the twentieth century.

Father Antoine Pierre Maillard was the next most influential missionary among the Mi'kmaq, for many reasons. Father Maillard's mission originated in 1735 and lasted through his death in 1762. He is best known among the Mi'kmaq for his quick study of Mi'kmaw language and further supporting literacy in two forms, hieroglyphics and roman scripts, although the latter he attempted to keep from them for some time. He was also known for being instrumental in negotiating political alliances and treaties between the Mi'kmaq and the English. Within a year of his arrival at Cape Breton, Maillard had learned enough Mi'kmaq with the help of an interpreter, Louis Benjamin Petitpas, who had both Mi'kmaq and French ancestry, to deliver his first sermon in fluent Mi'kmaq (Rand, 1850, p. 30). The Mi'kmaq were so surprised by this man's almost miraculous fluency and speed in learning their language that they attended much more seriously to his instruction and to his teachings of the religion (Rand, 1850, p. 31). Maillard was known to have met frequently with the old men and shared with the people through an interpreter of the old times, of God, and also of the French (Maillard, 1863, 310).

While to the Mi'kmaq, it appeared miraculous that he had learned the language so quickly, Maillard reported in his journal that he found this language learning an arduous task to which he had to put most of his time. "I do not dare to guess the number of years I have spent in this work — eight years, almost exclusively occupied in doing nothing but [learning the idioms], [that] proved insufficient," he wrote (Maillard, 1863, p. 361). His abundant and meticulous notes on his knowledge of the language, evidently in part his own learning tool, became an asset for those who would try to use these notes for other purposes than Christian advancement. In his manuscripts, he advanced a theory of Mi'kmaw grammar and explained many of its idioms (Maillard, 1759). Using French explanations, he prepared elaborate transcriptions of songs, prayers, and instructions. These manuscripts became the basis for Father J. M. Belanger's thirty-nine page *Alphabet Mikmaque,* published in 1817 in Quebec. Later, in 1939, Father Buisson Pacifique used these same notes as the basis for his *Lécons Grammaticales Theoriques and Practique de la Langue Micmaque,* developing favourably the language inflections, so much so that this priest became known to Mi'kmaq as the "Lnu"-speaking priest. Lnu is the term the Mi'kmaw people use to describe their civilization, and is still the term used for all identification with the people.

With his almost-magical talents immortalized, Maillard soon held considerable influence over the populous Mi'kmaw territory, and often used his influence among them to champion his own and the political interests of the French. Being equally influential among Lnu and newly settled "Acadians," Maillard was appointed the Bishop of Quebec's Vicar General for Île Royal in 1740, a position of significant political influence in the Catholic Church. His political influence among Acadians, French leaders, and the English was richly endowed by his connections and communication with the populous Mi'kmaq who also had relations with surrounding local native populations that could affect relationships among the French and English in Acadia and Île Royale.

An astute politician, Maillard was cautious about how much he shared with the Mi'kmaq about the politics of his own country, particularly as it affected them. One element of their culture was its literacy, which could be a dangerous knowledge that could be controlled if they were to learn how to read and write using the French scripts. Maillard realized early that the delicate relations between the French and English could be upset with Mi'kmaw intervention, and he did not want them to have any entrance into the political debates of the day. Maillard observed and commented to his superiors that Mi'kmaq were very clever people who had proved to be good students in learning what he wanted them to learn, in particular the prayers and catechism in hieroglyphic, a system he picked up from the children as they wrote on birch bark. So deflecting their curiosity about reading, he quickly figured out that the system they were already using could be modified for the purposes of teaching prayers and other religious concepts. In his journals, he shared how he learned of this from watching the children as they learned their prayers and made memory marks with charcoal. He adopted this system and elaborated on it to make many more characters than the children already knew, thus crediting himself to his superiors with this discovery of hieroglyphics. Maillard also realized that the Mi'kmaq were already fluent speakers of French, and it would not be long before they had all the skills needed to advance their curiosity and learning. Many of them had already complained to him about the growing losses and encroachments on their land and their livelihood by the English settlements, and this was becoming worrisome to him. He was also aware that to teach them the manner of reading with the Roman alphabet would give Mi'kmaq access to religion and politics and to information that Maillard (Maillard, 1863, p. 368) felt would cause them to use their "inquiring minds" to his church's disadvantage. In his letters to his superiors, Maillard cited his concern about the possibility of their exchanging agitating letters if they could read and write like the French using the French script. He worried that this might excite their anger against the French as well. In the end, he wrote to his superiors that "If they could read or write our language, they would be able to induce a lot of troubles among the nation both at the religious and political levels . . . that would be a mistake for them and us" (p. 362).

In an effort to discourage Mi'kmaq from developing widespread literacy, Maillard reinforced a mythical conception of written material as being sacred in nature. As part of this ruse, he prepared only texts of religious significance in the hieroglyphics, which he insisted they use. However, despite Mallard's warnings and fears, Mi'kmaq had many opportunities to become acquainted with the written language and the culture of the French. They had begun trading their resources for material goods, and in this respect, observed the Frenchmen's use of writing in accounting manuals and developed an interest in a small but growing library of books they brought with them. The literature of the Frenchmen at Louisburg at the far end of the island included several types of books, including the myths of the gods. When some Mi'kmaq questioned Maillard on his narrow analysis of the use of Roman script writing, he responded by insisting that the Frenchmen were trying to trick the Mi'kmaq into believing that the writings they heard were not spiritual but secular (p. 362).

As time went on, Maillard adapted to the lifestyle of the Mi'kmaq and moved with them from camp to camp, and in these places experienced what to him were the hardships of life experienced by Mi'kmaq making a living from nature. He wrote extensively to his superiors within the Church and with political leaders of their ways of life. While analyses of their grammar interested him, he began writing letters to his superiors and to French officials for financial support for the Mi'kmaq. A fervent advocate for the Mi'kmaq, given their lifestyles, he became a liaison of merit between the European leadership and the Mi'kmaq. Aware of the loss of hunting lands that supported the tribes, Maillard frequently corresponded with French leaders for aid and support of the Mi'kmaq who, he assured his superiors, were loyal allies of the French. As the French needed to meet with the Mi'kmaq to discuss matters of land and their future permanent settlements, Maillard was called upon to translate documents for the Mi'kmaq using the roman script. When treaty making came as a next step for relation building, he was also singularly responsible for translating the treaties and other political arrangements into Mi'kmaq using the Roman script. These transcriptions were presented in original text in the official proceedings of the events, such as the Treaty of 1752. Thus, despite Maillard's deliberate attempts not to teach Mi'kmaq the uses of the roman script as secular writing, they witnessed many uses of it by the French and later the English, and perceived its potential for themselves.

Among his responsibilities, Maillard visited Mi'kmaw camps throughout the province and eventually succeeded in persuading them, by way of addressing their leadership to sign the peace treaty with the English at the conclusion of the French and English war. A Treaty of Peace and Friendship was signed by their chief's marks in 1752 and renewed in 1761. These treaties were translated into Mi'kmaq with Maillard's help; he was also instrumental in getting them to agree to it. His translations, however, were found to be inadequate to the Mi'kmaq who complained to him that what they said in Mi'kmaq was not translated adequately. Maillard responded by telling them that he was first loyal to the King and did not wish to disobey him, and second, it was impossible to say word for word in translation what they said in Mi'kmaq (p. 359). These variances would later be the source of many misunderstandings and interpretations about strategic positioning with the French and the Mi'kmaq.

Religion was at the heart of the strategic plan of the new English government of Nova Scotia. In 1758, it decided to terminate the French Catholic priests, sending them either to Quebec or back to France. The Mi'kmaq, however, had now had the experience of learning more deeply about the Catholic ceremonies and teachings of the Church and had been Catholics for more than a century. Seeing the effect that faith and loyalty had on the Mi'kmaq with the French, the English launched a policy and a campaign to convert the Mi'kmaq to Protestantism and to assimilate them into more English ways of living. This would require a very different approach than the French, who lived beside the Mi'kmaq, befriending them and seeking only their loyalty to the King of France. The French approach was one that did not require their change in habits such as the English were inclined to do. The French population was small and their presence was limited to a few fishing villages erected with Mi'kmaw consent (Barsh, 1982, p. 4). Furthermore, the lingua franca of the area was a Mi'kmaw Basque dialect used largely in trading and little else (Upton, 1979, p. 23). The missionaries largely conducted internal affairs with the Mi'kmaq in the Mi'kmaw language.

English policy, on the other hand, did not separate acculturation from conversion, for they were seen as one. The English governors frequently complained that the Catholic missionaries had done "an inadequate job of converting Mi'kmaq," meaning that conversion and civilization were the same (Upton, 1979, p. 154). The task for the English therefore seemed doubly difficult. Their goal was not only to root out Catholic beliefs and practices that the French missionaries had instilled in the Mi'kmaq, but also to acculturate them to English manners and ways of being, thus ending their wandering habits and settling them onto lands that they would farm in the manner of the English. The Mi'kmaq had little interest in either.

In the last days of the French and English war, Maillard pleaded with the English to put aside their bigotry and make peace with the Indians. Making peace was achieved through treaties, and the English governor began in earnest to find ways to achieve this using Maillard as translator and peace negotiator. They assumed that after the peace was established they would work more effectively on implementing the transition plan for their policies that would enable them to convert Indians finally to their Protestant faith and to their culture. The plan was to employ the aging and ailing priest Father Maillard in the final pacification and peace making with the Mi'kmaq, while also preparing a successor for Maillard who they hoped would lead the Indians more effectively to conversion to the Protestant Church. From that time on, Dr. Thomas Wood, a doctor and Anglican minister, accompanied Father Maillard in his ministries and meetings with the Mi'kmaq. Yet the time for learning Mi'kmaq from Father Maillard was cut short by the ailing priest's demise.

Dr. Wood was among those first called to be at Maillard's side before he died (Johnston, 1960, p. 73). Wood later capitalized on these last moments with Maillard, telling the Mi'kmaq that their revered priest had appointed him at his deathbed to be his successor. At Maillard's funeral, Wood gave the final prayers, reading the prayers that Father Maillard himself had composed, but that he himself did not understand, and even used the sign of the cross in the hope that he might deceive the people into believing that his religion and that of the deceased priest were one and the same (Johnston, 1960, p. 73). Yet, despite the many attempts at ministering to the Mi'kmaq and the support of several other ministers among the Mi'kmaq, there was only one known conversion of a Catholic Mi'kmaq to the Protestant religion, and he, on his deathbed, reverted to Catholicism.

Nova Scotia Intervention in Mi'kmaw Education

The population of English settlers continued to grow from 1800 to the date of Confederation in 1867. An estimated 22,000 Scots; 13,000 Irish; 2,000 Englishmen; 1,700 Blacks from the United States, Quebec, and New Brunswick; 1,700 from Newfoundland; and 600–700 disbanded soldiers came to the colony between 1815 and 1838 (Henderson & Marshall, 1980, p. 362). Most of the population settled on the shores, leaving the interior lands and harder-to-reach coastal areas to the local tribes who would continue their daily pursuits that guaranteed their survival on the water and in the forests in all seasons. They hunted various game, fished in the waters, trapped animals, gathered berries, fruits, vegetables, moss, and other foods and resources, and made new tools and objects from the traded goods given to them. Many of these objects, such as baskets, chairs, coats, books, and ornamental goods were creatively embellished with designs particular to their nation. These items, now in museums around the world, have demonstrated the exquisite manner of the Mi'kmaq assimilating new levels of skills with new tools into their imaginative creativity. They easily adopted cloth, knives, pots, and hunting implements. Yet, with the growing mass of Europeans descending upon their lands, the Mi'kmaq took particular issue with the new settlers trespassing on their hunting grounds, clearing trees and grounds, chasing game away, and making it nearly impossible for the Mi'kmaq and other First Nations to survive in their traditional patterns in some areas.

The pressure also continued into the nineteenth century to make Mi'kmaq settled farmers. As a preliminary step, the government established a committee with the aim to "consider the condition of the Indians" and to consider how they could encourage, by various means, to remake the Indians in a style more compatible to their own. Upon consideration of the lifestyles of the Indians, the committee felt that the primary means to achieve any change would be by way of their children. Among the first school options made by the Nova Scotia Assembly was to attach a free school tuition clause to an act that prohibited the sale of spirituous liquors to Indians (Nova Scotia, S.N.S, 1829). By way of this appended clause, the government determined that education in the white man's school was the only means of dealing with the problem of "wandering" natives, if only they could get them to accept this option. Thereafter, any Indians who wished to go to school could attend any publicly supported school free of charge, although few did and those few not for long.

Encroachment of European settlers on Mi'kmaw land continued to be a problem for the government as the settlers did not abide by any rules, as established by the Royal Proclamation of 1763, which provided only the Crown could consensually purchase their lands. The Nova Scotia Committee reports of the Department of Indian Affairs repeatedly called for some additional action to be taken to protect the Indians from encroachment of white settlers. In 1820, prompted by dire warnings, the Legislative Assembly of Nova Scotia established reserved land for the sole use of Indians, stipulating further that the land was to be held in trust by the Crown. In 1842, the Government of Nova Scotia passed the first *Indian Act*, establishing a Commissioner of Indian Affairs responsible to and "under and in subordination to" the Governor and Her Majesty's Executive Council. While the intent of the Act was to establish permanent settlement grounds so that the provincial government could better protect and preserve the lands, the Act neither commanded, nor could it command, the tribal hierarchy of the Mi'kmaq Nation to comply. Rather, it merely stated:

> It shall be the duty of such commissioner, under such Instructions (from the Governor, by and with the advice of Her Majesty's Executive Council) to put himself in communication with the Chiefs of the Province, to explain to them the wishes of the Government, and to invite them to cooperate in their permanent settlement and instruction of their people (Nova Scotia, S.N.S., 1842, p. 16).

Believing that the major problem of assimilating Mi'kmaq into English society lay in the prior French influence and in the lack of an English education, the English colonial government of Nova Scotia developed policies that would root out the French influence and further restrict what they negatively perceived as the Mi'kmaw nomadic lifestyle. The Nova Scotia Assembly believed that through various restrictive and manipulative strategies, they would eventually be able to transform Mi'kmaw ways of living and values to be more amenable to those of the encroaching white community.

In 1842, an *Act to provide for the Instruction and Permanent Settlement of the Indians* (Nova Scotia, S.N.S., 1842) had the effect of enlarging governmental control and management of Indian lands and lives as well as forging a new national treasury built from the sale of Indian lands. In an effort to encourage settlement and curb Indians from moving freely on their land, the government provided funds for "purchasing implements and stock, erect[ing] a School House and place of worship" (Nova Scotia, S.N.S., 1842). In addition, the Commissioner of Indian Affairs was authorized by the Act to arrange for Indian children to go to school, although no restrictions were placed on them as to which school they were to attend. The act further mandated documentation of the progress of "Indian civilization" in yearly reports that would be the responsibility of the Commissioner.

Throughout the years 1842 to 1930 these annual reports provide the best evidence of the persistence of the government to make Indians into willing pawns to their goals, as well as the resistance Indians exerted in forgoing their traditional habits in favour of this more settled English existence. The few Mi'kmaq who took advantage of the schools did so without much commitment. Additionally, there were not any known examples of Mi'kmaq who actually succeeded with this education, especially in assuming any position of authority in English-speaking society. Mi'kmaq were not giving up their way of life, including anything they had learned by way of their introduction to literacies, including their hieroglyphics and the roman scripts they had now absorbed into their daily lives, corresponding with one another throughout their territories. From the outset of Nova Scotia's establishing funds for the support of education among Mi'kmaq, the Committee reports indicate that Mi'kmaq were not interested in European literacy and the domestic habits leaning toward farming that they fostered. Commissioner of Indian Affairs Joseph Howe wrote in the first report of the Department of Indian Affairs:

> The Education of the Indians was one of the most important topics to which my attention was called, by the enactments of the Legislature, and by your Excellency's instructions. With few exceptions, I at first found nearly the whole tribe strongly prejudiced against learning to read or write any other language than their own. Their books, which contain prayers and portions of their religious services, are more numerous than I at first supposed, and if not found in every wigwam, are carefully preserved and constantly referred to in every encampment. By visiting the camps, conversing cheerfully with the Indians — giving them familiar illustrations of the value of our rudimental branches, to themselves, and showing how much they had lost from not knowing how to secure lands as the whites had done, or to protect those which they had, an impression was gradually made upon some — while, by explaining the character and utility of different Books in my Library, and reading passages to them, others were interested. By writing letters about their own business, and receiving answer, I endeavoured to convince them of the superiority of the Post Offices over the Courier de Bois. (Nova Scotia, N.S., D.I.A, 1843, p. 7 of Appendix No. 1)

During this first year, Howe could report only one major success in all their education efforts. A Sunday school had been established at a chapel in Dartmouth, Nova Scotia, which for several weeks was well attended by Indians, but when winter drew near, they all left for the woods to prepare for the winter (N.S., D.I.A, 1843, p. 7). For those who did attend, Howe remarked on their progress, citing an example of a man who "with scarcely any instruction, wrote in a few weeks, a copy book very much better than persons often do who have been twelve months at school" (p. 8).

Parents' choice whether to send their children to school was tempered by their priority to maintain the seasonal migrations that sustained them throughout the year. These were noted in the Commissioner's report in 1843; a school at Bear River had twelve enrolled Indian students (p. 121). Howe reported, however, that the Indians seemed "desirous of obtaining a knowledge of reading and writing, but they cannot afford to spend their whole time at it" (N.S., D.I.A, 1843, p. 122).

Noting the strong religious nature of the Mi'kmaq in the reports of 1844, the Committee recommended that religious groups "to which Micmacs were attached" be given control of the money and education so that they might continue to "improve their moral and religious character" (N.S., D.I.A, 1843, p. 164).

While the Jesuits were credited with converting the Mi'kmaq to Catholicism, the government criticized them for having done a poor job of "acquaint[ing] Mi'kmaq] with the arts and industry of civilized life" (N.S., D.I.A, 1843, p. 118). Despite over a hundred years of contact and cooperation with the French and English, Mi'kmaq had solidly retained their traditional way of life and livelihood, following the seasons, the migrations of animals, the customary ways of living and transmitting their knowledges to succeeding generations. Their own forms of communicating and recording of their knowledges were held in forms of oral traditions and the mnemonic ideographic forms of literacy that had survived from Father Maillard's ministry. These books were so treasured as to have been ornately beaded and kept as sacred objects. But oral traditions did not go without some symbolic elements, as were found in pictographs, petroglyphs, notched sticks, wampum, and iconic symbols that covered all parts of their territory. Through their orators, their beadwork, and storytelling they held onto their past and present and shared this important knowledge throughout their country and among all their members. Birch bark scrolls were known to have been held by certain knowledge holders as evidence of their library of knowledge. Mi'kmaq were curious people and held multiple literacies, as was reported in 1847. Then Commissioner of Indian Affairs, Abraham Gesner, reported,

The Micmacs have a written language, which consists of hieroglyphics, resembling Chinese characters. Manuscript books of prayers, and portions of Scripture, introduced by the Jesuit Priests, are common among them. Their sacred music is also written. A few individuals can read English, and several children have been taught in the common schools of the country. (N.S. Administration of Indian Affairs [N.S. A.I.A.], 1843, p. 118)

From as early as the Act of 1842, the Nova Scotia Assembly had committed monetary support for Mi'kmaw assimilation through formal schooling and farming; however, the Commissioner's priorities with regard to Indian health and provisions for settling them in farm labour took precedence, delaying school construction and teacher recruitment. Committee reports indicate that very little effort was made to establish schools or encourage attendance. The bulk of the monies were used to pay doctor's fees for attending to the Indians who had contracted foreign diseases and whose diet had been changed by the loss of traditional hunting and fishing activities. What remained of the government monies was used for purchasing settlement provisions.

Until Confederation in 1867, when the federal government took over control of the education agenda, Indian schools were supported for the most part by missionary societies, religious orders, and Indian bands. The missionaries were primarily interested in maintaining Catholic liturgy and rituals, and did little at this time to affect Mi'kmaw habits and customs. Since both missionaries and Mi'kmaq had few funds to support education, teachers' wages were low and attendance was poor. As a consequence, the schools were thought to be ineffective (N.S. A.I.A., 1843, p. 127).

In 1847, the Commissioner recommended integrated schooling with white children in English, but where schools were established for Indian children only, he recommended that they be instructed in their own language (N.S., A.I.A, 1843, p. 122), a policy which would remain in effect until 1920. He also affirmed the policy of having Catholic clergy instruct them, as they were knowledgeable of the Mi'kmaw language and more inclined toward teaching in that language. As a final note on education, the Commissioner recommended that, when possible, day schools should be phased out and boarding schools established which were to be erected at some distance from the Indian communities (N.S., A.I.A, 1843, pp. xxi–xxii).

Canada's Intervention

Canada's commitment to federal education came with a treasury and fiduciary obligations created by treaties with the various nations across Canada. The sale of Indian lands initiated in these treaties brought a settlement base for new settlers and Canada's first treasury base. In all cases, Indians and Canada signed treaties in good faith to assist Indians in the changing landscape of settlement and provided lands for the new settlers. In return for these exchanges, First Nations committed themselves to peace and friendship. In some treaties, like those in the eastern seaboard, there were no exchanges of lands like the numbered treaties in the west. First Nations received in the peace and friendship treaties the government's truckhouse, trading relations, a court process to deal with any disagreements, yearly provisions at Treaty Day, and in later treaties, schools and teachers, medicine chests representing health, treaty monies, gun powder, and other trade goods. The First Nations saw these obligations as sacred promises for their friendship, moving and allowing settlement on their lands, while subsequent governments saw these treaties as ways t o get more land and as part of their assimilation plan, to be conveniently forgotten until they needed them.

Confederation of the new identified territories was achieved with the *British North America Act* (BNA) in 1867, an act that formally created the federal government as defined as the current structure of the House of Commons, the Senate, the justice system and the taxation system. In the enumerated sections of the BNA Act, the foundation of the federal government's authority, roles, responsibilities, and obligations were defined, as well as for the four included provinces — Ontario, Quebec, Nova Scotia, and New Brunswick. In another section, called Miscellaneous Provisions, are several important general and specific responsibilities, including section 132 covering treaty obligations that has been the largest responsibility of the government yet.

Two sections of the BNA Act are significant to education, one for First Nations and one for the settlers. Under Section 91(24) of the BNA Act of 1867, the federal government is charged with responsibility for "Indians and lands reserved for the Indians," implementing the obligations of these treaties within Canada for the Crown, with whom the Indians entered into the treaties. This is a broad constitutional obligation. The BNA Act thus transfers from the confederating provinces to the newly created Canada the obligations for Indians. Section 93 relays, among other things, the constitutional authority of each of the provinces to make laws in relation to education for its citizens. Section 93 thus also provides the constitutional basis for the establishment of both Catholic and public education systems, as well as the administration of schools and universities. Basically, the *British North America Act,* as the first constitution of Canada, created dual systems of education and health, one for provincial citizens and one for First Nations.

After Confederation in 1867, Canada's treasury was created by a legislative act that would implement the treaty obligations. The *Indian Act* thus took over administration of the treaty obligations and was held by the Secretary of State. Until then, most schools had been supported by missionary societies, religious orders, and treaty bands. Each of these had different missions and goals for education and used different approaches. The missionaries were primarily interested in maintaining Catholic liturgy and rituals, and did little to affect Mi'kmaw habits and customs. Prayers and religious traditions were taught, and where reading occurred it did so with religious literature, such as catechisms. Since both missionaries and Mi'kmaq had few funds to support education, teachers' wages were low, student attendance was poor, and the schools were reported to be ineffective (N.S., D.I.A, 1843, p. 127). The reports of Indian schools, thereafter, were sent to the Department of the Secretary of State, a branch of which was made the administrative office for Indian Affairs. While these reports continued to show some increases in school population within schools erected for Indians, they reported no significant change in Mi'kmaq livelihood. In many instances, Mi'kmaw children were being placed in English homes for training.

Taking children from their homes was a common practice that was criticized at least by one Englishman, Walter Bromley, representing the North American Indian Institution. He wrote a letter criticizing the manner of taking children from their homes, asserting that "If Indians were to be civilized, it could only be done by general consent of the tribe" (Bromley, 1814, p. 46). In particular, with regard to Indian policy, he urged the government to provide education and the comforts of "civilized society" as well as encourage religion. "Increase their knowledge, increase their wants," he asserted, "and honest industry will follow" (Bromley, 1814, pp. 50-55).

From 1867 to 1945, the Government of Canada continued to root its policies in forced assimilation and relied on missionaries such as the Roman Catholic Oblates and the Anglican Church to "raise Indians to the level of whites." Much of the work involved both day schools and residential schools, largely using religious personnel belonging to various Christian orders and organizations across Canada. How these policies continued to work against the people were the topic of many subsequent reports from Indian Affairs. One report pointed out that the Indians did not learn much from the schools because the teachers of Indians were ignorant of their language, were considered outsiders, and were not trusted (Vetromile, 1866); second , the report criticized the manner of the government selecting American Protestant teachers for the Indian schools because, as he pointed out, the Indians did not trust either Americans or Protestants. Vetromile ended on an encouraging note, however, saying that many Indians now "know how to read well, and some capable of writing" (Vetromile, 1866, p. 102).

Local day schools were populated only part of the year. Parents still continued in their seasonal pursuits across their lands, taking the families and children with them. In the 1895 report, the Commissioner wrote that Indians were indifferent to the day schools. Of the eight schools that were intended solely for Indians, the attendance of 102 pupils was reported to be irregular. Sickness and disease, especially tuberculosis, were rampant. Some Indians had left their wigwams, abandoned their farms, and moved nearer to towns to obtain jobs (Bock, 1966).

The double hardship of isolation and protection were forced on the communities. First Nations children were removed from their families and forced into confinement, with harsh punishment and isolation by gender and age. He noted the pathways to becoming "white" were treacherous, punitive, and traumatic for children. They were being forced into religious prayers and church attendance, forced daily into child labour as ongoing responsibilities in the schools, and punitive measures were meted out for using their ancestral language, including removing connections among siblings and with their families and communities. The creation of full citizenship in Canada was an assimilation plan that not only included their full adoption of an English-speaking white identity but also the loss of their rights to live with their families and communities on lands that were now "reserved" for them. To finish off the assimilation process were policies that cut them off from their tribal communities. The idea of absorption into the Canadian fabric was integration, although this was not equal participation, just equal to one's status at the bottom of the class system.

1. Planting Out

Schools were only one form of education. A practical education in an English settler home provided what some early commissioners encouraged. As early as 1814, a system of "planting out" was established that had as its purpose to apprentice Indian children in the nearby homes of English settlers. Subsidies were allocated to both parents and settlers for this purpose. In Sussex Vale, Nova Scotia, thirty-five Mi'kmaw parents were given a weekly allowance for staying away from their children. Each English family was given a yearly stipend for having Indian children in their home, a stipend that equalled the salary of a labourer for a year. Child labour and sexual abuse prevailed under the system (Upton, 1979, p. 163). Boys were taught the trade of farming, while girls were taught to clean and sew. The system was kept intact for many years, with encouraging reports coming from the Commissioner. Without any investigation of the outing system's effects on children or on their physical, mental, or sexual health, the Commissioner in 1917 reported that the outing system was still going well (Canada D.I.A., 1917).

In 1918, the government's goal for educating the Indians was articulated as follows:

> By education, the department endeavours to give the rising generation of Indians such training as will make them loyal citizens of Canada and enable them to compete with their white neighbours (Canada D.I.A. 1918, p. 23).

In 1920, the Parliament of Canada legislated amendments to the *Indian Act* of 1876, which was the regulatory mechanism for administering Indian affairs. While the Department of Indian Affairs assumed the administration of all schools for Indians, the schools on the reserves continued to be staffed largely by religious orders. The amendments to the *Indian Act* created policy that made English language mandatory in the schools, thus ending what some religious orders had been informally using, such as those in Restigouche, Quebec, where the Sisters of Holy Rosary had established a four-grade day school in which they taught "elements of Micmac reading and writing" (Bock, 1966, p. 36) together with catechism and Bible history. Furthermore, the *Indian Act* mandated primary school attendance for children between the ages of six and sixteen years of age, and that rule was to be strictly enforced (Canada, *Indian Act*, 1920). Thereafter, the Indian agents who were legislated to implement the *Indian Act* became more punitive and authoritarian, ending the diplomatic relations that had been earlier established.

2. Indian Residential Schools

The revised *Indian Act* of 1920 laid the foundation for the removal of children from their homes and the massive forced migration of children to a large network of residential schools, leaving families and communities without children and continuing and enlarging the erosion of their core values and knowledge related to their children's learning and to their own sustenance. Boarding or residential schools had already begun before Confederation, starting in the 1840s and continuing through 1996. Over 115 such schools were established across Canada, with over 150,000 students being recorded as having attended these schools (Canada, Truth and Reconciliation Commission, 2011).

In Nova Scotia, after repeated recommendations for a boarding school from the Committee Reports to the Department of Indian Affairs, federal monies were finally released for the construction of a residential school in Shubenacadie, Nova Scotia, which was intended for "orphan and neglected children." In the first year of the school in 1930, the Superintendent General issued a compulsory school clause amending the *Indian Act* of 1920 to keep a pupil in school until the student reached the full age of 18 years instead of 16 years, as was previously authorized. Rather than inviting First Nations to comply, many treaty First Nations children were forcibly taken to schools if there was not a local day school, or if the Indian agent on reserves deemed any children to be neglected or orphaned. In 1930, 286 students were enrolled at Shubenacadie; among them were my father's four sisters and one brother. After giving birth to their seventh sibling, my father's mother died, and my father, John, and his oldest sister, Isabel, were kept at home to help look after the home while the rest of the children were sent to boarding school. His own education took a back seat in the local day school to keeping the fires burning in the school where he was left in charge of cutting wood for the stove. His father eventually removed him from day school, arguing that his daily labour was not doing him any good. With the limited reading ability he got, my father thought he might have got through grade four or five.

The Indian Residential School opened in 1929 under the administration of the Catholic Church and its administrator, Father Jeremiah Mackey. In its first year, Father Mackey attempted unsuccessfully to fashion the school into a manual training and agriculture teaching facility for teenage boys. The following year, the school had a new mandate — to enrol children ages seven to fifteen years old, although younger children were known to have attended. The school eventually adopted provincial curricula in 1932 (Canada D.I.A., 1932), although the boarding school continued to emphasize domestic labour and farming that kept the school cleaned daily and stocked with food. The schools continued to follow the Indian agent style of authoritarian management, using harsh punishment as discipline and age-defined and gender-segregated classes. The strict rules against using the Mi'kmaw language in and out of school was difficult to maintain, as this was the only language the students knew when they came to the school (*Micmac News*, August, 1978). Most children were not allowed to visit their brothers and sisters in the same school. They were also not allowed time with their parents during the year, except for some who lived nearby and could travel home at Christmas. For the rest, they remained in the school for the full year, and some who were orphaned stayed for the entire time until they reached the compulsory age of release. Letters and presents were not given to students, and minor infractions had harsh consequences, even for the youngest of children, such as being sent to isolation in darkened closets (*Micmac News*, September 1978).

Residential schooling was intended to root out and destroy Indigenous knowledge, languages, and relationships with the natural family to replace them with Eurocentric values, identities, and beliefs that ultimately were aimed at destroying children's self esteem, self concept, and healthy relationships with each other and their families. Each decade of the Indian Residential Schools found different staff hired, and different punitive policies and practices used, as students revealed to the Truth and Reconciliation Commission (TRC) in more recent years. However, core themes reverberated in those hearings among former students of the Indian Residential Schools of their stripped Indigenous identities; sexual, mental, emotional, and physical abuse; poor nutrition and some death from starvation and abuse; enforced child labour; and the lack of a public school education that was intended to prepare them for anything but church attendance and domestic labour. The effects of this persistent abuse and trauma continue to affect First Nations, Métis, and Inuit students in many ways that are continuing to have devastating consequences. The

TRC is continuing to investigate and reveal the full truth and consequences of this system and to reconcile these students and their families through their revelations, insights, public knowledge, and mutual healing from these truths.

3. Centralization Policy

By 1929, another governmental policy was taking shape that would affect First Nations lives. The Commissioner of Indian Affairs wrote that Indians were scattered throughout the province of Nova Scotia, living on poor agricultural lands in overcrowded tarpaper shacks (Canada D.I.A., 1929). Many of these homes were found near white settlements. His recommendation was to move the whole scattered Indian population to centralized areas, a policy which was to materialize in 1940. The policy was called centralization.

Underlying the new centralization policy was a method for the government to divest itself of responsibility for Indians who appeared to be able to be assimilated into the settler society. A policy of disenfranchisement was developed that would allow Indian agents living among the Indians to decide which Indians demonstrated any capacity for being able to live successfully in white society, and then would have them removed from the rolls of Indian Affairs. These disenfranchised individuals were thus no longer in need of government protection and intervention. Canada's first "disenfranchised" Indians were those who were holding jobs off the reserve or were in the military. Mi'kmaw men and women were thus involuntarily severed from their tribal status, terminating their legal right to live on reserved land. Hundreds of Mi'kmaq fighting in Nazi Germany received their notices on European battlefields (Barsh, 1982, p. 6). Those with education or women who had married out of their community to white men were also disenfranchised. The remaining Mi'kmaq were supposedly to be sent to one of two reserves: Shubenacadie or Eskasoni, where construction of housing, a school, and a chapel would begin, and medical care, welfare subsidies, and education were promised. While the majority of Mi'kmaq ended up eventually making the move, there were many who remained in their ancestral lands, doubting the benefits of the move or that the promises would be fulfilled. When services were slow in being actualized in the newly formed reserves, many Mi'kmaw families either returned to the reserves they had left or decided to try making a living in other locales, such as in Maine or in the urban areas of Boston, where a growing Indigenous community emerged. Since the 1770s, these lands were known as *Pastimkewa'ki* (Boston and the north-eastern seaboard of the United States) and in the range of Mi'kma'ki, the seven districts of the Mi'kmaq. Eventually some of these lands were made into federal territory as the Micmac in Aroostook County, Maine, were federally recognized as a band of Micmacs within the United States in November 1991 with the passage of the *Aroostook Band of Micmacs Settlement Act.*

4. Fiscal Transfers from Canada to Provinces

In 1946, the federal government established a Special Joint Committee of the House of Commons and the Senate to review the *Indian Act* and to make recommendations to Parliament regarding changes to the policies and practices in Indian education. After extensive discussions, meetings, and submissions to the Committee by First Nations leaders, parents, and educators, as well as submissions from administrators of the schools, the Committee agreed with the goals of the Department of Indian Affairs and recommended an increased budget to the Department, and increasing the opportunities for education beyond the residential and day schools to adults and to post-secondary education (Carr Stewart, 2011). The Committee argued that the goals of the Department of Indian Affairs to provide for the education of children could not be achieved without advancing higher education, and funding for post-secondary education to help prepare First Nations "to face the new conditions of life" (Canada, Joint Committee of the Senate and House of Commons on Indian Affairs, 1959, p. 12). Parents also wanted to improve local schools and keep children at home rather than have them attend residential schools, but it would be another three decades before most of the residential schools were closed down.

Another study would help to push Indian education further into the hands of the provinces. Published in two volumes in 1966–1967, *A Survey of the Contemporary Indians of Canada Economic, Political, Educational Needs and Policies* by H. B. Hawthorn, an anthropologist (Canada, Hawthorn, vol. 2, 1967), would raise awareness of the failures of the educational initiatives at the federal level and make extensive recommendations for its improvement. The *Survey* affirmed First Nations' view of education in the treaties, noting that education was a prerequisite to meaningful choices and to the social well-being and economic prosperity of Indian youth. The *Survey* rejected the previous policy that had focused on assimilating Indian children by removing them from the influence of their parents and communities. As well, it emphasized the importance of greater parental involvement and improved communication between the school and Indian communities (p. 130). The *Survey's* solutions, however, taken from a Eurocentric point of view, offered the key solution for the "integration" of Indian children through their integration into provincial systems "with the retention of some of their cultural characteristics such as pride of origin, knowledge of their history, passing on of their tradition and preservation of their language" (p. 28). Recognizing that provincial systems were not well equipped to take on these initiatives, the study acknowledged that compromises were needed in the provincial school system to accommodate the needs of Indian students in their policies and practices. Finally, it urged "remedial" programs for Indian students.

In 1951, Canada entered into financial agreements with provinces and territories for the education of First Nations children to attend public schools administered by the provinces and territories. The agreements provided funds to the provincial local public schools for the tuition of First Nations students who were living on reserve. This funding initiative, in many regions, built the infrastructure of provincial schools to increase their capacity in return for their taking First Nations children, a per-head tuition fee that has grown considerably over the years, from about $4,000 in 1984 when I was an education director in a band-operated school in Potlotek, to a rate of $9,000 per student in Nova Scotia in 2012, as confirmed by the current education director of *Mi'kmaw Kina'matnewey*, Eleanor Bernard. Accountability for the successes of the students under provincial watch continues to be an issue, however, as the Province of Nova Scotia has yet to issue any accountability for these funds as to how the monies directed to provinces have created successes among First Nations students. This lack of accountability has been noted in the Auditor General's reports of 2000 and 2004. An audit of the federal government's education program for First Nations people in the year 2000 revealed that the Department of Indian and Northern Affairs' education programs are the most costly of all its programs — then at $1.3 billion annually. After more than a century of forced assimilation and the failed residential schools, the Auditor General of Canada concluded that the federal government had failed to educate First Nations children on a par with other Canadians. It found that the record of academic achievement of First Nation children living on reserves was dismal.

Despite the continuing and growing payments of tuition from the 50s through the 90s, when First Nations were paying tuition to the provinces, First Nations students were not graduating from high school or attending universities at comparable rates as non-Aboriginal students. Twenty-seven per cent of First Nations students were reported to have graduated from high school; only nine per cent of those attended post-secondary institutions, and only three per cent of those graduated from them (RCAP 1996). In 2000, the Auditor General of Canada examined those tuition payments in a report to Parliament, noting the lack of accountability from the provinces to INAC and to First Nations peoples for those agreements and payments (Auditor General, 2000). Four years later, in another audit of Indian Affairs programming, with more accurate figures from the 2000 audit, the Auditor General's report noted that the number of years for First Nations education to achieve parity with students in the provinces had actually increased from twenty-three to twenty-seven years.

The report criticized two important elements of the work of the Department of Indian Affairs and Northern Development (DIAND). The first was that DIAND had not clarified its own role in education in closing the gap for students, and because of the diverse functions of the department the Auditor General could not decide if DIAND was the funder or the evaluator for education programming, but in all instances it had not been held accountable for outcomes in education and for how government funds were used. The report also acknowledged that, in not taking an affirmative role, the department had chosen to rely on either First Nations or provinces to provide schooling, and to rely solely on the provinces to provide the curricula for First Nations schools. The Auditor General's report concluded that DIAND had no assurance that it was appropriately meeting its objectives to assist First Nations elementary and secondary students in meeting their educational needs and aspirations. They had also not adhered to the federal government's investment in the future economic well-being of Canadian Aboriginal society (Auditor General, 2000; 2004).

The process of handling the various aspects of education across the country has been on a fee-for-service basis, with local communities establishing school committees or school boards to handle local decision-making. These have not served Aboriginal education, as various reports have noted. Given the massive undertaking, the Auditor General of Canada (2000, 2004, 2010) has criticized DIAND — later Indian and Northern Affairs Canada (INAC), now Aboriginal Affairs and Northern Development Canada (AANDC) — for not being able to determine if it is meeting its stated objectives in closing the educational gap, as well as not having clarity in its goals, roles, and responsibilities in the federal structure of AANDC in education. At the time of this writing, a new federal agenda by Prime Minister Stephen Harper is fuelling a First Nations Education bill that again promises to portray a new education future, but without adequate consultation and support from Aboriginal peoples across Canada. As the Idle No More movement has revealed, it will again thrust an unsettling enterprise of education programming on First Peoples without accountability and adequate funding.

5. White Paper Policy on Equality

In 1969, the Minister of Indian Affairs, Jean Chrétien, announced in Parliament a policy shift that he suggested would enable "Indian people [to] have the right to full and equal participation in the cultural, social, economic and political life of Canada . . . [and] lawful obligations must be recognized" (Chrétien, House of Commons Debates, June 25, 1969, p. 10,582). His policy paper became known as the *White Paper* but was formally called the *Statement of the*

Government of Canada on Indian Policy, 1969. Among its core recommendations were for the government of Canada to remove all legislative and constitutional bases of what he referred to as forms of "discrimination," "that control of Indian lands be transferred to the Indian people" (p. 7), and furthermore to ensure that "services come through the same channels and from the same government agencies for all Canadians" (p. 7) — in other words, through the provinces. The policy further sought "to repeal the Indian Act" and proposed transferring all responsibilities for Indians to the provinces (p. 7).

Transferring the failed federal efforts of Indian education entirely to the provinces through a process of federal transfer of treaty obligations for education was a proposal that was firmly rejected by First Nations leadership across Canada, as well as by the provinces, that were unwilling to take on these extraordinary new responsibilities. The uproar was heard throughout Canada. This left the Liberal government of Canada with few alternatives except to find an alternative solution proposed by the First Nations people themselves. The National Indian Brotherhood (NIB) issued their statement calling for the federal government to

> recognize that the treaties are historic, moral and legal obligations. The redmen signed them in good faith and lived up to the treaties. The treaties were solemn agreements. Indian lands were exchanged for the promises of the Indian Commissioners who represented the Queen. . . . Our education is not a welfare system. We have free education as a treaty right because we paid in advance for our education by surrendering our lands. . . . We expect that the promises made when we signed the treaties will be honoured. (1972, pp. 14–15)

6. Indian Control of Indian Education Policy

The policy document was informally called the Red Paper, and formally submitted to the Federal government in 1972 (NIB, 1972), and implemented as policy in 1973 as Indian Control of Indian Education. This First Nations remedy for educational failure was to use the obligatory treaty resources of the federal government to develop their own schools founded on First Nations culture and languages, specifically "to give our children the knowledge to understand and be proud of themselves and the knowledge to understand the world around them" (NIB, 1972, p. 1). The education of Indians was conceptualized as a way of revitalizing Indian cultures and economies, rather than assuming assimilation and lost identities were the only alternative for First Nations people. The NIB articulated this vision of linking education and cultural preservation and promotion as follows:

> We want education to provide the setting in which our children can develop the fundamental attitudes and values which have an honoured place in Indian tradition and culture. . . . We want the behaviour of our children to be shaped by those values which are most esteemed in our culture . . . [I]t is important that Indian children have a chance to develop a value system which is compatible with Indian culture (NIB, 1972, p. 2).

It also stressed that in the past, Indian students were asked to integrate, "to give up their identity, to adopt new values and a new way of life." It stated, "We believe in education . . . as a preparation for total living . . . as a means of free choice of where to live and work . . . as a means of enabling us to participate fully in our own social, economic, political and education advancement." It argued that this approach must be radically altered if future education programs were to benefit Indian children (NIB, 1972, p. 25).

Canada's acceptance of this policy transformation occurred in 1973, which initiated a period of what was known as the devolution of administrative authority to First Nations communities to administer their own education programs. This transfer of management did not change Canada's fiduciary responsibilities for First Nations education, but rather would enable First Nations communities to develop and enhance their own educational capacity to undo the forced assimilation policies enacted in federal boarding schools and day schools.

Not all Mi'kmaw communities and schools chose this option, however, as most communities began slowly with the devolution of administration of their schools. Most felt unprepared but determined, as they had not any experience with the many and varied responsibilities of the administration of their schools. As a result, those initiatives met with varied successes. Indeed, some schools are still emerging through levels of growing capacity as reserve schools and communities have also had to engage conditions where there were few Aboriginal administrators and teachers, given the generations traumatized under the prior federal systems of assimilation and boarding schools. The Catholic or the federal day schools did little to harness leadership among youth or encourage higher education. Without any support for learning in a second language, Mi'kmaq learned English unevenly and imperfectly, struggling to survive in situations in which they were submersed in English. There were instances of a few Mi'kmaw women becoming nuns and later coming back to teach in the communities, and in these cases, they supported the students using their Mi'kmaw language and helping with understanding the vocabulary of English. In some smaller communities, located closer to white communities, a gradual shifting of the home language of the community to an English-Mi'kmaw dialect occurred over the next two decades. But regardless of community, the diminishment of Mi'kmaw youth and their parents led to some ambivalence about taking on the administration and leadership of education in some communities.

In all, the Mi'kmaw communities throughout the period through the late 1970s showed high levels of recidivism (grade repeating) and dropouts or early school leavers. A study of Mi'kmaw enrolments over an eight-year period from 1970 to 1979 in grades K through 12 compared to non-Indian Nova Scotia schools in two rural locations revealed a significant drop in enrolment of Mi'kmaw students at grade 7. Over the eight-year period covered by the survey, the situation worsened in the mid-70s and improved slightly by 1979, although overall figures showed significant drops in enrolment for all Mi'kmaw communities (UNSI, 1979, p. 2).

The Canadian initiative with Indian control had its counterpart in provincial institutions as well. Given that over sixty-eight per cent of First Nations students were involved with provincial schooling at some point (Canada, RCAP, 1996), mostly at the secondary and post-secondary levels, the provinces have had to consider programming and capacity to achieve success with First Nations youth.

Against this backdrop of changing policy in education, the housing and living conditions in many Indian bands continued to be appalling, undermining educational reform:

- Infant mortality rates in Indigenous communities is nearly double that of other Canadians.
- The youth suicide rate is seven times higher than the Canadian average.
- The unemployment rate on reserves is three times the Canadian average.
- Literacy rates are half the Canadian average.
- Most Indigenous people live below the poverty line.

These conditions have existed for more than fifty years and government policies have failed to correct them. The problems continue to mount, as well as calls for innovative educational reform.

7. Canada's Apology

In 2006, the Canadian government announced a $1.9 billion compensation package to benefit tens of thousands of survivors who were abused at Indian residential schools. It proposed, among other things, some funding for commemoration and for a "Truth and Reconciliation" program for Aboriginal peoples, as well as an individual Common Experience Payment for victims of the Indian residential schools. Canadian Prime Minister Stephen Harper apologized to Aboriginal peoples, First Nations peoples in particular, who were forced to attend residential schools. Most important for First Nations, Métis, and Inuit peoples was that the Prime Minister of Canada acknowledged the excesses of the residential school system and apologized for the creation of the system. In a nationally televised broadcast from Parliament, he read his statement, which in part read :

> In the 1870s, the federal government, partly in order to meet its obligation to educate aboriginal children, began to play a role in the development and administration of these schools. Two primary objectives of the residential schools system were to remove and isolate children from the influence of their homes, families, traditions and cultures, and to assimilate them into the dominant culture. These objectives were based on the assumption aboriginal cultures and spiritual beliefs were inferior and unequal. Indeed, some sought, as it was infamously said, "to kill the Indian in the child." Today, we recognize that this policy of assimilation was wrong, has caused great harm, and has no place in our country. . . . The government now recognizes that the consequences of the Indian residential schools policy were profoundly negative and that this policy has had a lasting and damaging impact on aboriginal culture, heritage and language. . . . The legacy of Indian residential schools has contributed to social problems that continue to exist in many communities today. (Harper, 2008, at AANDC website)

Canada's apology to Aboriginal peoples for the destruction of their lives, their loss of parenting skills, and jeopardizing their continued livelihood based on their rich cultures and heritages comes as a welcome first step in creating a responsive education system for Aboriginal peoples. Yet the translation of this apology into concerted policy, action, and change is wrapped in political wrangling over several issues, including inequitable funding of First Nation schools, accountabilities for measuring student achievements, consultations on new legislation proposed as the First Nation Education Act, and on increasing losses of programs showing potential for success. While this apology cannot erase the damage suffered by thousands of people who attended these schools, or the trauma the families experienced and the consequences to their parents and grandparents attending these damaging schools, the apology represents potentially a new beginning, a new consciousness of what that past has been and what it has created, and a reconciliation leading to some healing and a negotiated, consultative future.

As the process of educational reform continues, it is imperative that educators and researchers and Canadians at large understand the structure of doubt and distrust that various Canadian governmental authorities and the educational system have generated among Aboriginal people. Every First Nations, Métis, and Inuit student has been contaminated by a system built on false colonial and racist assumptions that target them as inferior, child-like, or corrupt. The public image of First Nations governance and peoples has generated self-doubt in students, leading them to discount their inherent capacities and gifts, their elders' wisdom and knowledge, and their tribal values and teachings. No educational system is perfect, yet few have been as destructive to human potential as Canada's, with its obsession with paternalism and assimilation and racialized discourses. In this coercive system, more than three out of every four Aboriginal students fail in public schools. The random achievement of the few who do succeed, however, does not directly relate to success in life, nor in parenting, nor in caring for others. The trauma and racism inherent in the system drain students of their capacity for achievement in all aspects of their lives. It robs them of their learning spirit and potential.

It is well past time for Canada to accept its complicities with the failures in Aboriginal education. It is time for the government to reject paternalism and embrace co-operation and collaboration with First Nations, Métis, and Inuit peoples who know what they want. It is time for resources to be carefully assessed for the educational outcomes of Aboriginal peoples based on fully integrating their own knowledge and heritage into a system that values and respects Indigenous ways of knowing and allows Aboriginal students to embrace and celebrate who they are instead of making them doubt themselves. Indigenous knowledges must be part of that future.

Prime Minister Stephen Harper and Parliament have acknowledged the historic legacy of abuse of, and wrongs to, Aboriginal children that were achieved by education policy that diverged from Aboriginal and treaty rights (Harper 2008). The Royal Commission on Aboriginal Peoples has highlighted the multiple layers of the problems and issues created by Aboriginal Affairs and Northern Development and a federal Parliament that creates a gap between what Aboriginal peoples and the general population have received. The Truth and Reconciliation Commission has issued a process for reconciling and healing the country and the individuals to this once-hidden history of Canada. Canada's dark secret has emerged as one that shows individual and collective complicities with the outcomes of colonization, which continues to disadvantage Aboriginal children, their communities, and their future.

Canada has a responsibility to live up to its reputation as a compassionate and innovative nation on the way to becoming a truly just society. We can only arrive at this by acknowledging Canada's relationships with First Nations through treaties, the legacy of benefits that have accrued to so many, yet have left so many out, and by renewing investments in holistic and sustainable ways of thinking, communicating, and acting together.

Under the aegis of Indigenous science, humanities, social justice, and human rights work, educators have begun the reconciliation and the renaissance with negotiated principles for working with Indigenous peoples, new protocols for engaging respectful ethical relationships (Ermine, Sinclair, & Jeffery, 2004), foundations for curriculum change (Western Protocols, 2000), new models for identifying success and collective well-being (CCL, 2007), and new collaborations at the federal and provincial levels, such as the *Mi'kmaw Kina'matnewey* project. Reconciling these constitutional rights to education is a task that the federal and provincial governments will have to continue to work on. The task, then, is to educate Canadian politicians, policy makers, and educators to be more responsive and proactive, to reconcile the national and provincial curricula to the principles underlying Aboriginal and treaty rights, and to make schools a transforming and capacity-building place for Aboriginal students.

The Canadian government has a vital constitutional role to play in protecting the country's remaining Aboriginal knowledge, languages, and heritage. It has demonstrated some measure of good will, good intention, and commitment to completing the process.

The most important educational reform is to acknowledge that Canadian schools teach a silent curriculum of Eurocentric knowledge that is not accommodating to other ways of knowing and learning. Schools that attempt to impose Eurocentric homogeneity by standardizing domesticated curricula are a problem, for they are often at a loss as to how to integrate local content into their prescribed, standardized curricula. Indigenous knowledge is not a singular concept. Homogeneous methodologies for disseminating knowledge in schools are not helpful in the current educational crisis. Any reforms must take into account the fundamental diversity of Indigenous knowledges, and must create structures and guidelines that are capable of accommodating this fundamental concept, keeping in mind that no single Indigenous experience dominates other perspectives, no one heritage informs it, and no two heritages produce the same knowledge.

To effect reform, educators need to make conscious decisions to nurture Indigenous knowledge, dignity, identity, and integrity by making a direct change in school philosophy, pedagogy, and practice. They need to develop missions and purposes that carve out time and space to connect with the wisdom and traditions of Indigenous knowledge. They need to teach holistic and humanistic connections to local and collective relationships. They need to generate educational space that allows them to be challenging, caring, inspiring, and alert to their students' intellectual travails and attuned to their inner conditions. They need to make educational opportunities for students to come together in community with people who bring out their holistic better selves. Only when these changes in thought and behaviour are made can we create an educational system that is a place of connectedness and caring, a place that honours the heritage, knowledge, and spirit of every First Nations student.

CHAPTER 4

Creating the Indigenous Renaissance

Education is recognized as both a human right in itself and an indispensable means of realizing other human rights and fundamental freedoms, the primary vehicle by which economically and socially marginalized peoples can lift themselves out of poverty and obtain the means to participate fully in their communities. Education is increasingly recognized as one of the best long-term financial investments that States can make. Education of Indigenous children contributes to both individual and community development, as well as to participation in society in its broadest sense. Education enables Indigenous children to exercise and enjoy economic, social and cultural rights, and strengthens their ability to exercise civil rights in order to influence political policy processes for improved protection of human rights. The implementation of Indigenous peoples' right to education is an essential means of achieving individual empowerment and self-determination. Education is also an important means for the enjoyment, maintenance and respect of Indigenous cultures, languages, traditions and traditional knowledge. . . .

UN, Expert Mechanism on the Rights of Indigenous Peoples, 2009, pp. 4–5.

IDEAS DO NOT EXIST WITHOUT PEOPLE TO IMPLEMENT THEM. A postcolonial framework cannot be constructed unless Indigenous people renew and reconstruct the principles underlying their own world views, environments, languages, and forms of communication, and re-examine how all these elements combine to construct their humanity. My own reclamation began with my dissertation and then returning to Mi'kma'ki to help restore the value and place of Mi'kmaw language in our community school in Potlotek. That experience and my subsequent publication, *Reclaiming Indigenous Voice and Vision* (Battiste & Henderson, 2000), have been significant highlights of my career. Since then, there has been an emerging critical mass of Indigenous scholars, newly empowered through education, building their own visions, leadership, knowledge, and professionalization. Furthermore, the philosophical and activist agenda inspired by critical theory and anti-oppressive activism in areas such as women's studies, postcolonial studies, cultural studies, queer theory, and decolonizing, and participatory and anti-oppressive methodologies have led to an ever-growing committed group of non-Indigenous allies who are providing additional critical frameworks for addressing issues of inequality, inequity, gaps in education among diverse groups, colonial conscientization, and hegemony in politics, organizations, and institutions, while acknowledging excellence through the proper valuing and respectful circulation of Indigenous knowledge across and beyond Eurocentric disciplines. Indigenous people are also moving beyond critiques to address the healing and wellness of themselves and their communities, to reshape their contexts and effect their situations, and to create reforms based on a complex arrangement of conscientization, resistance, and transformative action.

Collaborative Conscientization

The initial educational struggle for Indigenous educators, then, has been to sensitize the Eurocentric consciousness in general, and educators in particular, to the colonial and neo-colonial practices that continue to marginalize and racialize Indigenous students. This does not come easily to Eurocentrically educated Canadians, for it requires their unlearning as well — challenging their conscious and subconscious notions of meritocracy and superiority learned in life with sometimes well-intentioned but biased parents, grandparents, media, community, school texts and discussions and how privilege is constructed and maintained in a racist society. The second struggle is to convince them to acknowledge the unique knowledge and relationships that Indigenous people derive from place and from their homeland, which are central to their notions of humanity and science, and passed on in their own languages and ceremony. This is the emerging work of Indigenous scholars who have been part of the Indigenous renaissance. Once so convinced, the next tension is for all learners to learn it respectfully with Aboriginal people and without appropriating their new knowledge and experience for their own ends.

Since Indigenous peoples' search for change is still aspirational and inspirational, the conceptualization of the postcolonial has been in part a collaborative conscientization and in part an act of hope, a light in the darkness of educational failure. Yet, what are the social and cultural requirements for this dreamed about or idealized version of education? Moreover, what role do schools, universities, teachers, and faculties have in helping to effect that change? This now takes me to the epistemological current or theme.

In 1982, the inclusion of Aboriginal and treaty rights in the patriated Constitution was a product of collaborative conscientization in Canada. It established a new constitutional foundation for the right to education for Aboriginal peoples. The concept of education as either an Aboriginal right or a treaty right established in Canada the right for Aboriginal people to decolonize the existing education system. Educators and politicians have ignored this innovative constitutional right, until the decisions of the Supreme Court in Canada have revealed the necessity of constitutional reconciliation of the various powers and rights regarding education. In Canadian law, Indigenous knowledge is constitutionally protected as Aboriginal and treaty rights under Section 35(1) of the *Constitution Act, 1982*. The affirmation of Aboriginal and treaty rights under this section is broad in scope, but what it affirms is that the Aboriginal traditions and customs held prior to contact and the specific treaty provisions as part of the negotiations with specific First Nations are acknowledged as part of the Canadian fabric. Unfortunately, the political climate of Canada still enables them to largely ignore any change on the pretext of the need to study the issues before changes to laws, rules, and regulations are enacted. Instead, Canada has left it to the First Nations themselves to seek action by the use of the Courts, and there to judge the merits of their approaches.

In one case, however, the Supreme Court of Canada has determined that the affirmation of Aboriginal rights provides Aboriginal people with recognized customs and traditions unique to their cultures. The Court acknowledged that Aboriginal peoples' having rights should have ways to enable them to keep them. The court then held that to ensure the continuity of Aboriginal customs and traditions, a substantive Aboriginal right would normally include the incidental right to teach such a practice, custom, and tradition to a younger generation (Côté, 1996: para. 56). Similar reasonable incidental rights are in the Court's interpretation of the treaty educational provisions (Sundown, 1999, para. 26–33). As noted however, the main deficiency of the court approach is that federal and provincial educational laws, regulations, and practices have yet to implement or reconcile with the constitutional rights to have and to teach Indigenous knowledge.

Indigenous diplomacy is another act of collaborative conscientization. Through collaborative work with scholars in Canada and beyond to Australia, New Zealand, and the United States, Indigenous scholars and leaders are illustrating the strength of the postcolonial and anti-colonial movements by constructing multiple critiques of the modern discourses within the multidisciplinary foundations in the current system. They are achieving this transformation in multiple sites, where diverse problems engage multiple strategies, strategic goals, and broad political agendas. We have been inspired by Indigenous activist such as Graham Smith, who has pointed out that Indigenous peoples' struggles cannot be reduced to singular solutions in singular locations, but rather they need to be carried out in multiple sites using multiple strategies (Smith, 2000). This means there is no magic bullet, but multiple ways to solve many issues, some by way of academic analyses and research; some political as related to activism, resistance, and lobbying for the merits of various programs, positions; and some by self-reflection and emerging from the chains of the oppressive situations one has been conditioned to be in. Some of the most important work being done by young people is found in the self-reflective narratives that help them to understand their own situation and what has held them there, and reframing what has been cast as negative into more positive ways. They emerge rejuvenated and passionate as they begin to the find the core of truths embedded in the search for their inner strengths — their own learning spirit.

This activation of the human learning spirit is evident in the work being done by Indigenous peoples at the United Nations, where lobbying bodies have raised awareness of the plight of many oppressed peoples around the world. Their provocations have directly influenced the United Nations, as is evident in the number of declarations and covenants embracing or urging the adoption of standards to protect women, children, and cultural minorities. The Idle No More movement has also struck a national and international chord of drumming and singing and placarding so as to bring every conscientized person into the movement, whether Indigenous or not. Many Indigenous peoples around the world continue to suffer trauma and stress from colonialism, genocide, and the continuing destruction of their lives by poverty and government neglect — and in Canada, government ambivalence. The current agenda of Indigenous peoples' activism is to initiate awareness of the continuing struggles of peoples around the world to live with clean water, air, land, and demands for collaborative dialogue on policy issues affecting them. They are seeking to live fully within their own cultural and linguistic communities, and to benefit from the many advancements in Canadian society, many of which have been built on their resources from the land, and work actively for a transformation of ongoing colonial and neo-colonial thought and practices. Their efforts reveal the inconsistencies between discourse and action. They challenge the assumptions and the taken-for-granted, and expose the ills, while continuing to search from within and from our heritage for the principles that will guide their children's future toward a dignified life. With the *Declaration on the Rights of Indigenous Peoples*, finally ratified in 2007, came minimum principles for their protection, something that had already been achieved for women, children, minorities, and refugees.

While educational institutions have a pivotal responsibility in transforming relations between Aboriginal peoples and Canadian society, the Royal Commission on Aboriginal Peoples (1996) firmly held that all institutions should respect Aboriginal knowledges and heritages as core responsibilities rather than a special project undertaken after other obligations are met (Vol. 3, p. 515).

To date, there has been a growing emergence of collaborative work that has offered new transcultural, interdisciplinary coalitions across education, the humanities, the social sciences, law, and more recently in the physical sciences, as issues of eco and biodiversity and globalization pressure institutions to seek new innovative and holistic solutions to ecological and global problems using Indigenous knowledge. As well positioned as these are for research and making critical changes to policy and practice inside disciplines, respect for Indigenous knowledge must begin with Indigenous peoples providing the standards and protections that accompany the centring of Indigenous knowledge.

More work is needed to unpack and rethink the assumptive values of our educational and the social systems on which contemporary society has built its knowledge and institutions, the mythical portraits that have been assumed from a biased knowledge base, and the neglected rich diversity of our nations as a foundation for all students. The knowledge base of Indigenous peoples, as well as other neglected knowledge bases such as those of at least half the world's population of women (Minnich, 1990), can be sources of inspiration, creativity, and opportunity, and can make contributions to humanity, equality, solidarity, tolerance, and respect. The educational significance and justification for respectful dialogues cannot be over-emphasized as a basis for arriving at a decolonized educational agenda. This should take us beyond the prior processes of cross-cultural awareness and inclusion and bridging programs to a new perspective and processes that support Indigenous knowledges, communities' continued enriched livelihood within place, their languages, and self-determination in a new, decolonized way.

Despite painful experiences Aboriginal peoples have suffered in the past century or more, Aboriginal people still see education as having hope for their future, and they are determined to see education fulfill its promise (RCAP 1996, Vol. 3, pp. 433–34). This has been made clear among many groups — the Indigenous peoples themselves in many voices and forums, especially in the Royal Commission's Final Report, in the dedicated efforts of the UN Working Group on Indigenous Populations, and among Indigenous researchers and postcolonial scholars and leaders. No longer can institutions be inactive based on the notion that "we don't know what they want" (Havemann, 1999, p. 70).

We must examine a process of respect in the dialogues, in the development of postcolonial, anti-colonial, and Indigenist strategies for both Indigenous peoples and non-Indigenous educators, and in any research that must continue to be principled on the benefits returning to Indigenous peoples. We must seek the appropriate protocols and respectful methodologies that will help us to enter into a sustaining dialogue and respectful relations. To achieve this outcome will necessarily require the Canadian people and their institutions to view Aboriginal peoples not as disadvantaged racial minorities but as distinct, historical, and socio-political peoples within Canada, with collective rights (Chartrand, 1999).

While it is gratifying to see the bridges being built by some non-Indigenous scholars to Indigenous knowledge (Aikenhead, 1998; Lunney Borden, 2010; Haig Brown, 2005; Barrett, 2009; I. Findlay 2003; Findlay & Findlay, 2011) and some integrative work among collaborations with Indigenous scholars (Aikenhead & Michell, 2011; Battiste, Bell, Findlay, Findlay, & Henderson, 2005; Orr, Paul, and Paul, 2002), the acknowledgement for Indigenous knowledge must begin with Indigenous people themselves. It is Indigenous people who must provide the standards, principles, and protections that accompany the centring of Indigenous knowledge, and articulate and clarify the visions for how these can support self-determination, healing, and the future. Many of us have taken up this challenge in many forms and forums.

The knowledge bases of Indigenous peoples, as well as other neglected knowledge bases, can be sources of inspiration, creativity, and opportunity. They can also contribute to humanity, equality, solidarity, tolerance, and respect. The United Nations is providing Canadian educational institutions with an exemplary opportunity to confront the ethics, theories, methodologies, and lessons of Indigenous knowledge and heritage. The dialogue needed to engage the suppressed knowledge of Indigenous civilizations has been delayed for far too long. The significance and justification for respectful dialogue as a basis for arriving at a decolonized educational agenda cannot be over-emphasized.

Ethical guidelines for responsible research into Aboriginal peoples must also be developed from within Aboriginal and constitutional law. Any guidelines put in place must respect Aboriginal protocols in the exchange of information, and must ensure that benefits from federally or provincially funded grants accrue to Aboriginal peoples and not exclusively to researchers, their careers, or their institutions. The guidelines must respect the fact that Indigenous knowledge can only be fully known from within Aboriginal languages, pedagogies, and communities. They must also respect the limitations, as defined by Aboriginal peoples, of what knowledge is held for certain holders, who can access the knowledge, and in what contexts it can be shared.

Indigenous Methodologies

The Indigenous renaissance is an action agenda for the present and future. Some Indigenous scholars are now calling it an "Indigenist" agenda that is not confined to those who are Indigenous. Rather, "Indigenist" is a term that operates much in the same way that the feminist movement was facilitated, not only by women but also by men who claimed proudly to be feminists. Indigenist, then, speaks to a movement, much like the thrust of the Idle No

More movement that works collaboratively toward Indigenous peoples' goals for sovereignty, self-determination, and treaty and Aboriginal rights reconciliation with the provinces, territories, and the federal government. These must not be an agenda for Indigenous peoples alone, as so many have been complicit in their subordination, and beneficiaries of the relationships that enabled lands to be used, bought, taken, or misused. Non-Indigenous allies must support these as well, although they may have different trajectories for how they enter into the discussion, such as in diverse disciplines, organizations, and research foci. Len Findlay's essay (2000) "Always Indigenize!" is one "indeterminate provocation" that he suggests non-Indigenous scholars can take to develop a connective critical stand from their location to the Indigenous agenda, noting, promoting, activating, defusing, infusing, complicating, and in general putting the Indigenous agenda firmly in the present and not only in the hands of the politicians and the activists. It is an academic exhortation to include Indigenous issues in one's scholarship, recognizing that the desired outcomes "will depend on who is listening and how they understand and act on what they hear or read" (p. 368).

Take, for example, Maori scholar Linda Smith's twenty-five decolonizing methodologies. Her agenda also includes the place for non-Indigenous to take up "Indigenizing and indigenist processes . . . [activated] through centring the consciousness of the landscapes, images, languages, themes, metaphors and stories of the Indigenous world" (2012, p. 147). It is an Indigenist approach that Lester-Irabinna Rigney at Flinders University in South Australia (1999) and Cree scholar Sean Wilson (2013) use, borrowing from the feminists and other critical approaches to include and privilege Indigenous voices. Indigenist research then "reflects an Indigenous view of reality, knowledge, and the gaining of wisdom to shape the future of our communities" (Wilson, 2013) in the many institutions, agencies, departments, and places where we work. Sean Wilson relays that the Indigenist paradigm is one that is not claimed by anyone but is a way of sharing ontology and a practice that contributes to the empowering of Indigenous peoples. Wilson aims to put the contingent relational element to this research work, noting that while Indigenist research does not require that one be Indigenous, it does require one to support and articulate one's ontology and one's philosophy and research in relation to context-based knowledge that is community-based, not book or literature-based knowledge. In other words, the context is derived not from theory from academics but from peoples and collectives and related to place. When one is connected to community and to place, the relational aspects of communities, people, families, and their context become the important elements of how to proceed with knowledge search and production. It grounds one's protocols and thus research processes as Graveline used in her "In-Relation pedagogy" (Graveline, 1998).

There is always a perceived tension, however, between academics using Indigenous methodology and an Indigenist research paradigm so defined. The issue is that there is a perspective and a paradigm inherent to Indigenous peoples that cannot simply be adopted from a Euro-Canadian or Eurocentric perspective. Understanding what locates one or from what position one comes is then a needed element for addressing fully how Indigenous communities are positioned. Len Findlay (2000) aptly notes that the Eurocentric cannon of universities and their scholarship are embedded in the two related fictions — *terra nullius* (empty land) and scientific objectivity that continue to circulate theory, research, and discourses that do not represent Indigenous experience, frameworks, or knowing. Rather, modernity is expressed in governance, structures, economies, and scholarship that shelter the duality inherent in progress and continue to diminish, marginalize, and oppress Indigenous peoples. Several Indigenous researchers have cautioned against assuming that one knowledge system is like another, and that Indigenous systems can be easily infused in Eurocentric knowledge systems. The dangers are immediately noted, as problems that arise from different perspectives that are in research are named epistemological, ontological, and axiological.

The epistemological approach of any research fundamentally shapes a project, beginning with what is deemed worthy of researching, what questions are asked, how they are asked, and how the "data" are analyzed (Smith, 1999/2012). Indigenous researcher advocates have raised concern primarily with the ethically and culturally appropriate study of Indigenous people, and the fit of different epistemologies between the researcher and the researched. Indigenous epistemology is holistic, acknowledging the "interconnectedness of physical, mental, emotional, and spiritual aspects of individuals with all living things and with the earth, the star world, and the universe" (Lavallée, 2009, p. 23). Each community will have its own stories and understandings of how they have come to live in the world, and what they value as to how to live in the world. This ultimately shapes their humanity, their spirituality, and their heritage. Indigenous methodologies then drawn from within this ontology of being connected physically and spiritually with all things are then not theoretically constructed from imaginative thinking that emerges from a fact-finding mission, but conform to Indigenous knowledge according to local cultural imperatives (Porsanger, 2004). Brant Castellano (2000) identifies three sources of Indigenous knowledge which afford a glimpse of what Indigenous knowledge production entails:

Traditional knowledge which has been handed down more or less intact from previous generations. . . . Empirical knowledge is gained through

careful observations. . . . Revealed knowledge is acquired through dreams,
visions, and intuitions that are understood to be spiritual in origin. (Brant
Castellano, 2000, pp. 23–24 [emphasis in original])

An overwhelming number of authors, international and interdisciplinary, acknowledge and agree on the holistic framework of Indigenous epistemologies
that are foundational to Indigenous peoples. Holistic thinking incorporates
the unity of spiritual and physical worlds which may have had a role in some
parts of Western Eurocentric thinking as well, although, as Atleo notes, it is
"doubtful that holistic thinking could be considered an overriding theme in
patterns of Western thought . . . [when there is a] tendency to compartmental-
ize experience and thus assume that some parts have no relationship to other
parts" (Atleo, 2004, pp. xi–xii).

In Indigenous epistemologies, "the greatest mysteries lie within the self at
the spiritual level and are accessed through ceremony" (Sinclair, 2003). The
spiritual aspect of life is as important to the search for knowledge as is the
physical, and accessing the spiritual realm in each of the nations is shown to
include personal and collective engagements at the level of intuition, meditation, prayer, ceremony, dreams, and vision quests, and other forms of intro-
spection that reach another realm. Knowledge received through these means
is a reflection of the Indigenous perception of "living in a sea of relationships.
In each place they lived, Indigenous peoples learned the subtle, but all-import-
ant, 'language of relationship'" (Cajete, 2000, p. 178).

Indigenous methodologies are then thought of as alternative ways of thinking about research processes and have their own ethical guidelines. Brant-
Castellano (2004) suggests that ethics are the rules of right behaviour and are
intimately related to who you are, the deep values you subscribe to, and your
understanding of your place in the spiritual order of reality. Ethics are ultimately integral to the way of life of a people. The fullest expression of a people's
ethics is represented in the lives of the most knowledgeable and honourable
members of the community, often considered respectfully as the Elders or
knowledge holders. Imposition of ethical rules derived from other epistemologies or ontologies or ways of life in other communities will inevitably cause
problems in how one enters a community, what relationships guide the inter-
actions, what knowledge is appropriate to be sought, how it is to be used, and
other issues related to access and benefit, although common understandings
and shared interests can be negotiated.

Constitutional Reconciliation

The Supreme Court of Canada in its attempt to merge Aboriginal and treaty rights with the rest of the constitutional powers has told Canada, the provinces, and the territories that constitutional reconciliation with the holders of these constitutional rights is a critical educational requirement in patriated Canada. Yet, the question remains: what does constitutional reconciliation mean in relation to the Aboriginal peoples right to education? Despite the courts' decisions addressing proactively what the provinces, territories, and corporations and others should do, the provinces have not yet made reconciliation a priority, nor have they even addressed Aboriginal and treaty rights in any of their current transformations. The courts have stressed that Aboriginal and treaty rights must be read with the other constitutional provisions. In other words, the sections delegating education to the provincial Crown (s. 93) must be read together with the reconciliation of educational rights and privileges protected in the federal Crown (s. 91(24)) and in the affirmation of Aboriginal and treaty rights in s. 35 of the Constitution. These are what a responsive education would entail.

Reconciliation is rooted first in the principle that First Nations parents have a right to have an educational choice for their children that includes the foundations of their own knowledge systems and that enables them to benefit from the education in their lives. The transfer of jurisdiction of land to the Crown thus provides the financial means and fiduciary framework for implementing these educational rights for the benefit of First Nations, Inuit, and Métis peoples. The constitutional framework and court decisions affirming customary Aboriginal knowledges then generate what might be seen as a place where an emerging reconciliation of Indigenous knowledge in learning and pedagogy can have an impact on all public forms of education. It creates the context for systemic educational reform to include Indigenous science, humanities, visual arts, and languages as well as existing education philosophy, pedagogy, teacher education, and practice.

The Supreme Court of Canada has stated that the basic purpose of s. 35 of the *Constitution Act, 1982* is the reconciliation of the pre-existent rights of First Nation societies with the sovereignty of the Crown:

> s. 35 (1) provides the constitutional framework through which First Nation, who lived on the land in distinctive societies with their own practices, traditions and cultures, are acknowledged and reconciled with the sovereignty of the Crown. (*Van der Peet*, 1996, p. 508)

Reconciliation needs to be pursued in different forums through engagement with appropriate holders of Aboriginal and treaty rights; these are the people, the elders, the men and women as guardians of their children. This should not to be confused with the federal *Indian Act* band structure, as the chiefs alone cannot resolve the issues of constitutional reconciliation. Respectful dialogues and consultations on guiding principles of reconciliation could identify common ground for (1) renewing relationships in a manner consistent with the constitutional purpose of the recognition and affirmation of Aboriginal rights to healing and treaty rights to health care in s. 35; (2) articulating clear, constitutionally based principles and objectives for explaining Aboriginal and treaty rights to education; and (3) generating positive environments for an engagement by the educational systems for recommended reconciliations.

The aim of constitutional reconciliation and the creation of a conceptual framework for the delivery of education to beneficiaries of Aboriginal and treaty rights is not to produce different explanations. It is to broaden the collective sense of intellectual possibility in Canada, inviting attention to the unspoken exclusions within a history of Eurocentrism in the education system.

As the Court noted in the *Haida Nation* decision (2004), constitutional reconciliation is not a final legal remedy in the usual sense. Rather, it is a process flowing from guaranteed constitutional rights to education that affects federal, provincial, and territorial legislations. Reconciliation of the rights in this new conceptual framework offers the key to establishing a framework for living together, and an innovative paradigm in education in Canada. The courts may clarify rights, but the courts cannot build relationships; people do — by working together on the basis of mutual respect and trust.

The concept of reconciliation is a key theme for renewing relationships with Aboriginal peoples within the Canadian federation. It articulates the relationship principles of mutual recognition, mutual respect, mutual benefit (sharing), and mutual responsibility as the basis for renewing relationships with Aboriginal peoples. These relationship principles have been endorsed by most Aboriginal peoples and have become central for much of the academic and public-policy dialogue on Aboriginal and treaty rights. The RCAP (1996) initially articulated that reconciliation is an ongoing process of establishing and maintaining a framework for living together. It involves the commitment to recognizing Aboriginal and treaty rights and the preservation of the knowledge and language distinctiveness of Aboriginal people within Canada. These interconnected concepts offer a potential organizing framework for the reconciliation of the right of Aboriginal peoples to education and one that every institution must accept as a basic start to their approach to Aboriginal education.

Given the vastly different circumstances of Aboriginal peoples throughout Canada, it is recognized that reconciliation may take different forms — a "one-size-fits-all" approach is not practical for addressing the different holders of Aboriginal and treaty rights in different parts of the country. Perhaps for this reason, many First Nations do not endorse a First Nations Education Act, as it could not cover all the possible variations of situations existing across Canada, yet the *Mi'kmaq Education Act* has illustrated that when stakeholders dialogue and collaborate for specific populations and conditions, they can achieve a standard from which to work. Overlapping constitutional powers, rights, and claims are also important variances that must be negotiated in creating new jurisdictions for Aboriginal education. Conceptual frameworks, policy renewal, and research ethics will need to be pursued in different forums through engagement with appropriate beneficiaries of Aboriginal and treaty rights and the federal, provincial, and territorial governments.

Establishing Transformative Principles in UN Law

The principles elaborated by the United Nations (UN) sub-commission have been incorporated in the International Labour Organization Convention 169, *Concerning Indigenous and Tribal Peoples in Independent Countries* (1989) and in the *UN Declaration on the Rights of Indigenous Peoples* (2007).

1. International Labour Organization Convention 169, Concerning Indigenous and Tribal Peoples in Independent Countries (1989)
The ILO Convention has not been ratified by Canada, but it is part of international law. The Indigenous peoples at the Indigenous Summit of the Americas (2001) reaffirmed this convention in articles 24–25. Article 7 of the ILO convention provides:

(1) The peoples concerned shall have the right to decide their own priorities for the process of development as it affects their lives, beliefs, institutions and spiritual well-being and the lands they occupy or otherwise use, and to exercise control, to the extent possible, over their own economic, social and cultural development. In addition, they shall participate in the formulation, implementation and evaluation of plans and programmes for national and regional development that may affect them directly.

(2) The improvement of the conditions of life and work and levels of health and education of the peoples concerned, with their participation and co-operation, shall be a matter of priority in plans for the overall economic development of areas they inhabit.

Part VI, Education and Means of Communication, in the ILO convention article 26 provides:

Measures shall be taken to ensure that members of the peoples concerned have the opportunity to acquire education at all levels on at least an equal footing with the rest of the national community.

Article 27 of the ILO convention provides:

(1) Education programmes and services for the peoples concerned shall be developed and implemented in co-operation with them to address their special needs, and shall incorporate their histories, their knowledge and technologies, their value systems and their further social, economic and cultural aspirations. They shall participate in the formulation, implementation and evaluation of plans and programmes for national and regional development, which may affect them directly.

(2) The competent authority shall ensure the training of members of these peoples and their involvement in the formulation and implementation of education programmes, with a view to the progressive transfer of responsibility for the conduct of these programmes to these peoples as appropriate.

(3) In addition, governments shall recognize the right of these peoples to establish their own educational institutions and facilities, if such institutions meet minimum standards established by the competent authority in consultation with these peoples. Appropriate resources shall be provided for this purpose.

Article 28 of the convention asserts:

(1) Children belonging to the peoples concerned shall, wherever practicable, be taught to read and write in their own Indigenous language or in the language most commonly used by the group to which they belong. When this is not practicable, the competent authorities shall undertake consultations with these peoples with a view to the adoption of measures to achieve this objective.

(2) Adequate measures shall be taken to ensure that these peoples have the opportunity to attain fluency in the national language or in one of the official languages of the country.

(3) Measures shall be taken to preserve and promote the development and practice of the Indigenous languages of the peoples concerned.

Article 29 of the ILO Convention provides:

> The imparting of general knowledge and skills that will help children belonging to the peoples concerned to participate fully and on an equal footing in their own community and in the national community shall be an aim of education for these peoples.

Article 30 provides:

> (1) Governments shall adopt measures appropriate to the traditions and cultures of the peoples concerned, to make known to them their rights and duties, especially in regard to labour, economic opportunities, education and health matters, social welfare and their rights deriving from this Convention.
>
> (2) If necessary, this shall be done by means of written translations and through the use of mass communications in the languages of these peoples.

Article 31 provides:

> Educational measures shall be taken among all sections of the national community, and particularly among those that are in most direct contact with the peoples concerned, with the object of eliminating prejudices that they may harbour in respect of these peoples. To this end, efforts shall be made to ensure that history textbooks and other educational materials provide a fair, accurate and informative portrayal of the societies and cultures of these peoples.

2. UN Declaration on the Rights of Indigenous Peoples (2007)

The *UN Declaration on the Rights of Indigenous Peoples* (2007), affirmed by nation states that Indigenous people have the right to establish and control their institutions, and educational systems, and provide education in their own languages, in a manner appropriate to their cultural methods of teaching and learning. The General Assembly declaration affirms fundamental principles of equality:

> that Indigenous peoples are equal to all other peoples, while recognizing the right of all peoples to be different, to consider themselves different, and to be respected as such, . . . that all peoples contribute to the divers-

ity and richness of civilizations and cultures, which constitute the common heritage of humankind, . . . that all doctrines, policies and practices based on or advocating superiority of peoples or individuals on the basis of national origin or racial, religious, ethnic or cultural differences are racist, scientifically false, legally invalid, morally condemnable and socially unjust.

They recognized:

the urgent need to respect and promote the inherent rights of Indigenous peoples which derive from their political, economic and social structures and from their cultures, spiritual traditions, histories and philosophies, especially their rights to their lands, territories and resources, . . . that respect for Indigenous knowledge, cultures and traditional practices contributes to sustainable and equitable development and proper management of the environment, . . . in particular, the right of Indigenous families and communities to retain shared responsibility for the upbringing, training, education and well-being of their children, consistent with the rights of the child. . . .

The Declaration proclaimed as the minimum rights of Indigenous peoples in United Nations law (art. 43):

Indigenous peoples have the right to the full enjoyment, as a collective or as individuals, of all human rights and fundamental freedoms as recognized in the Charter of the United Nations, the Universal Declaration of Human Rights and international human rights law (art.1).

All the rights and freedoms recognized in the Declaration are equally guaranteed to male and female Indigenous individuals (art. 44).

The General Assembly proclaimed the right to self-determination equal to other people (art. 3). As part of their right to self-determination, in article 14, it declared:

1. Indigenous peoples have the right to establish and control their educational systems and institutions providing education in their own languages, in a manner appropriate to their cultural methods of teaching and learning.

2. Indigenous individuals, particularly children, have the right to all levels and forms of education of the State without discrimination.

3. States shall, in conjunction with Indigenous peoples, take effective measures, in order for Indigenous individuals, particularly children, including those living outside their communities, to have access, when possible, to an education in their own culture and provided in their own language.

Article 5 proclaims "that Indigenous peoples have the right to maintain and strengthen their distinct political, legal, economic, social and cultural institutions, while retaining their right to participate fully, if they so choose, in the political, economic, social and cultural life of the State." Indigenous peoples have the right "not to be subjected to forced assimilation or destruction of their culture" (art. 8(1)).

Indigenous peoples, in article 11, have the right

to practice and revitalize their cultural traditions and customs. This includes the right to maintain, protect and develop the past, present and future manifestations of their cultures, such as archaeological and historical sites, artifacts, designs, ceremonies, technologies and visual and performing arts and literature, as well as the right to restitution of cultural, intellectual, religious and spiritual property taken without their free and informed consent or in violation of their laws, traditions and customs.

In article 12, Indigenous peoples have the right

to manifest, practice, develop and teach their spiritual and religious traditions, customs and ceremonies; the right to maintain, protect, and have access in privacy to their religious and cultural sites; the right to the use and control of their ceremonial objects; and the right to the repatriation of their human remains.

In article 13, Indigenous peoples have the right

to revitalize, use, develop and transmit to future generations their histories, languages, oral traditions, philosophies, writing systems and literatures, and to designate and retain their own names for communities, places and persons.

Article 15 affirms that Indigenous peoples "have the right to the dignity and diversity of their cultures, traditions, histories and aspirations which shall be appropriately reflected in education and public information." They also have the right to "establish their own media in their own languages and to have access to all forms of non-Indigenous media without discrimination" (art. 16) They have the "right to participate in decision-making in matters which would affect their rights, through representatives chosen by themselves in accordance with their own procedures, as well as to maintain and develop their own Indigenous decision-making institutions" (art. 18).

Moreover, article 31 proclaims:

> Indigenous peoples have the right to maintain, control, protect and develop their cultural heritage, traditional knowledge and traditional cultural expressions, as well as the manifestations of their sciences, technologies and cultures, including human and genetic resources, seeds, medicines, knowledge of the properties of fauna and flora, oral traditions, literatures, designs, sports and traditional games and visual and performing arts. They also have the right to maintain, control, protect and develop their intellectual property over such cultural heritage, traditional knowledge, and traditional cultural expressions.

Nations and educational systems must respect and draw upon the broad principles for decolonization that have been outlined in the International Labour Organization's Convention 169, the Indigenous peoples' polycultural *UN Declaration on the Rights of Indigenous Peoples*, and the *Guidelines for the Protection of Indigenous Heritages* (Weissner & Battiste, 2000), which outlined to the United Nations Human Rights Commission standards for establishing a fair and minimum definition of fair and just education practices.

In the scientific arena, Indigenous scholars and advocates have stimulated an interest in the contribution of Indigenous knowledge to a better understanding of sustainable development. The UN Conference on Environment and Development, the Canadian International Institute for Sustainable Development (CIISD) and the Canadian International Development Agency (CIDA) have all entered this dialogue (Clarkson, Morrissette, & Regallet, 1992). Knowledge of the environment is being lost in communities around the world, and there is an urgent need to conserve this knowledge to help develop mechanisms to protect the earth's biological diversity, among other benefits. The *UN Convention on Biological Diversity* (1992) recognizes the importance of Indigenous knowledge to the conservation and sustainable use of biological diversity, acknowledges the contributions of Indigenous knowledge as innovative approaches to environmental studies, and recognizes the validity of Indigenous science. It also recognizes the value of Indigenous knowledge, innovations, and practices to scientific knowledge, conservation studies, and sustainable development. In 1999, the World Conference on Science, assembled under the aegis of the United Nations Educational, Scientific and Cultural Organization (UNESCO) and the International Council for Science (ICSU), in the *Declaration on Science and the Use of Scientific Knowledge: Science for the Twenty-First Century*, urged governments to promote understanding of Indigenous knowledge systems. The Declaration urged scientists to respect, sustain, and enhance traditional knowledge systems and recommended that scientific and traditional knowledge should be integrated into interdisciplinary projects dealing with links between culture, environment, and development (paras. 32, 83–87).

The UN *Declaration on the Rights of Indigenous Peoples* (2007) has affirmed these rights to sustainable development. Article 23 proclaims:

> Indigenous peoples have the right to determine and develop priorities and strategies for exercising their right to development. In particular, Indigenous peoples have the right to be actively involved in developing and determining health, housing and other economic and social programmes affecting them and, as far as possible, to administer such programmes through their own institutions.

The Declaration affirms that Indigenous peoples' right to development includes the right to determine and develop priorities and strategies for the development or use of their lands or territories and other resources (art. 32). Indigenous peoples have the right to the conservation and protection of the environment and the productive capacity of their lands or territories and resources (art. 27). They have a right to maintain and strengthen their distinctive spiritual relationship with their traditionally owned or otherwise occupied and used lands, territories, waters and coastal seas, and other resources, and to uphold their responsibilities to future generations in this regard (art. 25). These rights include "their traditional medicines and to maintain their health practices, including the conservation of their vital medicinal plants, animals and minerals" (art. 24).

Moreover, Indigenous peoples have the right to the recognition, observance, and enforcement of treaties, agreements, and other constructive arrangements concluded with states or their successors and to have states honour and respect such treaties, agreements, and other constructive arrangements (art. 37).

Section II of the UN Report of the Expert Mechanism on the Rights of Indigenous Peoples, called *Study on Lesson Learned and Challenges to Achieve the Implementation of the Right of Indigenous Peoples to Education* (2009), affirms the overarching goal of Indigenous education:

Education of Indigenous children contributes to both individual and community development, as well as to participation in society in its broadest sense. Education enables Indigenous children to exercise and enjoy economic, social and cultural rights, and strengthens their ability to exercise civil rights in order to influence political policy and processes for improved protection of human rights. The implementation of Indigenous people's right to education is an essential means of achieving individual empowerment and self-determination. Education is also a means for the enjoyment, maintenance and respect of Indigenous cultures, languages, traditions, and traditional knowledge (para. 6, p. 4).

The Report recognized the necessity of having legal provisions for learning centres to recognize education that is reflective of Indigenous knowledges and traditional ways of teaching and learning. It said in section IV at para. 56, p. 13):

Examples of important existing education legislations include those recognizing the integration of Indigenous perspectives and languages into mainstream education, culturally appropriate curricula, mother tongue based bilingual and multilingual education, intercultural education and the effective participation of Indigenous peoples in designing education programmes. Policies of complementary education for Indigenous peoples permit the implementation of intercultural education in schools and colleges with the aim of moving towards multiculturalism and the recognition of the diversity of peoples.

It also stressed that financial support for infrastructure and programming is necessary to implement these initiatives:

Allocating targeted financial resources for the development of materials, testing proposed culturally appropriate curricula, teaching Indigenous languages, providing support for training and incentives for teachers in rural schools and developing education programmes in cooperation with Indigenous peoples are also effective initiatives. An equally important consideration for communities located in isolated and sparsely populated areas is that the allocation of funding for infrastructure should not be made based on a school to population ratio (para. 60, p. 14).

Many opportunities exist to push this education agenda in international forums. In 2013, the International Experts Group Meeting to examine Indigenous youth under articles 14, 17, 21, and 25 of the *Declaration on the Rights of Indigenous Peoples* and the Twelfth session of the Permanent Forum on Indigenous People will be following up on the recommendation on education of Indigenous youth. In 2014, a world conference on Indigenous Peoples is being planned by a 2012 resolution of the UN General Assembly (A/66'L. 61) in order to share perspectives and best practices on the realization of the rights of Indigenous peoples, including pursuing the objectives of the *Declaration on the Rights of Indigenous Peoples*.

Canada has participated in, ratified, and affirmed most of the international obligations (Henderson, 2007). However, Canada's educational institutions have largely ignored, and continue to ignore, Indigenous knowledge and pedagogy. In the educational crisis that has been articulated over the past thirty years, First Nations peoples have drawn attention to the value and importance of Indigenous knowledge in their Aboriginal and treaty right to education. The failures of the past have exposed the shortcomings of the Eurocentric monologue that has structured modern educational theory and practice. In forcing assimilation and acculturation to Eurocentric knowledge, modern governments and educational systems have displaced Indigenous knowledge. It is clear, however, that the exclusive use of Eurocentric knowledge in education has failed First Nations children (Schissel & Wotherspoon, 2003). Indigenous knowledge is now seen as an educational remedy that will empower Aboriginal students if applications of their Indigenous knowledge, heritage, and languages are integrated into the Canadian educational system.

Mi'kmaw Reform of Education

1. Mi'kmawey School: Bilingual Education

The first bilingual education school in Mi'kmaw territory was the Mi'kmawey School in Chapel Island, now renamed to its original name, Potlotek. Situated along the southwest shore of Bras d'Or Lake, 15 kilometres from the village of St. Peters in Cape Breton, Nova Scotia, Potlotek is the historical and cultural centre of Mi'kma'ki, being the traditional gathering place for Mi'kmaq. Here the spiritual, social, and cultural ties of the larger Mi'kmaw community are renewed each year. Though one of the smallest of Mi'kmaw reserves, the community has long held the responsibility for guarding the homeland and the cultural rituals surrounding Chapel Island where the Grand Council meets twice a year.

While crises are troubling for communities, sometimes they lead to something unique and beneficial. For Potlotek, a crisis over provincial education led to the development of a band-operated school in the community. The crisis that created Mi'kmawey School was a common experience that many communities were facing in the days before the policy of Indian control of Indian education. The federal government had already given over Mi'kmaw children to the nearby non-Mi'kmaw community of Johnstown, helping them to construct their school with monies from Indian Affairs so that they might educate the children in Potlotek as well. However, the provincial school's indifference to what the children brought with them in their language and culture and the nature of educational policies rooted in assimilation and paternalism were troubling. Mi'kmaw children's educational needs and the subsequent failures within the different public schools had simmered for decades despite the objections of family members and band leadership.

The Department of Indian Affairs had subjected the Mi'kmaq in Potlotek to different regimes of education, federal day schools, policies aimed at assimilation, individualization of prosperity, removal of children to residential schools and later to provincial schools, all without consultation with any of the leadership or parents. None of the parents were allowed to serve on the school board, because reserve students lived outside the provincial boundaries, and they had no power to redress the needs of their children. These grievances led to the momentum for a band-controlled school, which came in three portable trailers delivered after parents refused to send their children to the provincial school, and after much wrangling with Indian Affairs.

My entrance to this school came shortly after its beginning, when I was asked to return to my community to initiate an education based on the very foundations of my training and scholarship in bilingual, bicultural education gained at Stanford University. In 1984, after completing my doctorate, I took a position as education director and principal of the school. The first aim was to stop parental resignation and provide a community-based model of education that recognized the students' language and learning, including building upon what the elders and parents desired beyond the provincial curriculum. The students' experiences in the public school had been damaging to their identities, self-concept, and self-esteem. So re-establishing the foundations of Mi'kmaw language, knowledge, and trust in what education could do was important and was reflected in the philosophy of the school. "*Ni'n ankamsi, nanasi, kejitu'telita'si, kesalsi, welite'lsi, kejitu kelusi mimajuinui kwlaman nikma'j kisi ankmak, kisi nena'q, kisi jiksitaq, kisi ksalk, kisi wlite'tmk, kejik kelu'sit mimajuinuit.*" This translates to "I look at myself, I know myself, I know what I am thinking, I love myself, I think well of myself, and I know I am a good person, so that I can look at my friend, I could know my friend, I could listen to my friend, I could love my friend, I could think well of my friend, and I know he is a good person" (Battiste, 1987). This philosophy supported the awareness and appreciation of one's self in the context of one's culture and capacities. Since racism seemed to separate students in the provincial school, our approach aimed to build strongly on repairing the damage that had been done and reconcile relations among youth with other communities outside the reserve and with whom they would have to continue schooling in the near future, as the school went only through grade 6. In addition, we needed to help students to become independent learners, able to operate in biased and unresponsive systems so that they could find information, investigate effectively and efficiently, summarize and find pertinent facts to support their problem solving, and apply results to their own situation. They were expected to develop these important skills before they left their grade six. Eight basic independent learning skills were prioritized: reading, writing, research, planning, problem solving, self-discipline, self-evaluation, and orality. Students' practice in highly structured processes to less structure and freedom were ways to help them develop confidence in the assigned projects. With small classes, each student had enough structure, but security in freedom as well.

The school became the hub of community activity that drew on the rich historical and cultural education embedded in the community, the oral tradition of the elders, and their deeply spiritual connections. The teachers spent many hours after school developing their own materials and resources, and we enthusiastically embraced community members who visited and helped in many cultural projects, making the school a thriving learning experience for children and adults. A monthly newsletter called *Kluswaqn* reported on the activities of the school, the visitors and contributions from the community and language learning for parents to support their children, and helped parents with some of the Mi'kmaw language learning that their own children were learning. Everyone in the school assumed diverse responsibilities, from being teacher, counsellor, friend, curriculum developer, home school liaison, and storyteller, as the lines were blurred as to who was an administrator, public relations officer, teacher, or resource person.

Mi'kmawey School at Potlotek demonstrated that Mi'kmaw cultural and language education could effectively prepare students for basic English skills without sacrificing self-concept, causing cultural disintegration, or diminishing their cultural heritage and language. This school that emerged from one crisis has remained a cornerstone of the community of Potlotek. It has grown and prospered over time, gaining legitimacy through its innovations and public relations to become a catalyst role model for other Mi'kmaw communities in the Maritimes. The school's use of Mi'kmaw literacy to retain the heritage of the people through tribal epistemological foundations has been significant. Its innovative teaching methods and its inclusive holistic approach toward Mi'kmaw heritage and language, and its development of independent learners, have been critical to its success. Mi'kmawey School has since grown in numbers and size as well as moved into a new building in the community. It has also joined the *Mi'kmaw Kina'matnewey* to become one of the nine original communities that partnered in the *First Nations Education Act* in Canada

(Canada, 1998). There are currently eleven partnered Mi'kmaw communities. This was a first in Canada.

2. Mi'kmaw Kina'matnewey

The *Mi'kmaw Kina'matnewey* agreement in Nova Scotia is a notable innovation and historical first in First Nations education. It is an agreement among federal and provincial governments and eleven Mi'kmaw communities that recognizes the Mi'kmaw bands' right to self-governing education among the participating communities from pre-K through post-secondary and adult education. Nine, then later two more, Mi'kmaw communities joined together to assume jurisdiction over their community's education as well as implementation of their vision, drawing upon their own ways of knowing, their language and culture, and the wisdom of their elders. This initiative acknowledges the capacity of First Nations to generate an educational system that is comparable to provincial schooling, although comparability is not the limiting vision of likeness to the provinces' education but rather is being built on Mi'kmaw principles that make Indigenous knowledge accessible, transferable, and generative either by itself or within other knowledge systems or technologies. The agreement facilitates educational reform that meets Mi'kmaw capacities and goals. It enables Mi'kmaq to evaluate the old structures, to adopt sustainable new foundations, and to find alternate structures and time frames for learning that are tailored specifically to their own goals and requirements. Such an education requires communities to agree on how they can contribute their collective resources to a system of multi-tiered services comparable to provincial departments of education to assist with common needs across schools. Although the system is still evolving, its accomplishments have already been felt in Mi'kma'ki.

Education under Canada's Constitution resides with the provinces, except in the case of First Nations, whose treaties with the Crown were placed in the administration of the federal government and the Department of Indian Affairs to manage the fiduciary responsibility for "Indians and lands reserved for the Indians" as designated in the 1867 *British North America Act*. Hence, the agreement for *Mi'kmaw Kina'matnewey* (MK) was a trilateral negotiation with federal, provincial, and Mi'kmaw First Nations bands to enable Mi'kmaw peoples to create their own corporate body to be an instrument of their self-governing jurisdiction, and would enable graduates from the schools to be transferred easily to provincial schools. MK is the organization that implements the agreement with its board of overseers drawn from chiefs of the reserves of the participating communities. Through the work of ongoing collaborative, cooperative, and committed professionals in MK, the schools are demonstrating a positive impact in their communities in terms of their capacity to deliver a superior educational program, progress in growing the needed services for those schools and students and teachers, and successes among students in making transitions and graduating from both First Nations and provincial schools (SIDRU, 2004). MK may still have many issues left to resolve around developing parity of teachers' salaries with the provinces, creating language programming as variable to the communities as their real language situations, increasing funding for the schools according to their needs, and capital construction of schools; however, the commitment and progress made with all the communities, parents, and students has been national in scope and many First Nations are examining MK as a model for their communities.

3. Mi'kmaw Immersion

Among the most effective innovation in First Nations education has been the language immersion model that emerged from several models — the early work of Jim Cummins in Canada with French immersion programming, the successful Maori immersion language nests called Ko Hunga Reo, the Hawaiian immersion programs called the Puna Leo programs, and the Mohawk immersion program in Kahn awake under the direction of Dorothy Lazore. Immersion programming was developed in Canada primarily for English-speaking families seeking to have their children learn French, the other official language of Canada. It was built on a model of immersion language learning theory, a natural language method, second language teaching models, trained second language teachers, materials and resources, and supportive parents and administration, all of which would act as supporting mechanisms for the language learner. These supports then mark the difference between immersion and submersion programming, if the latter can be called a program at all.

Submersion learning of English is a process First Nations, Métis, and Inuit students have endured over the years in residential and public schools where they have been thrust into an English-only environment, without supports to scaffold their learning of English. In English-only situations, they are marginalized and silenced, held captive and not allowed to use the only communicative tool they know. The most significant differences of a submersion language context from an immersion language context is that:

- First Nations, Métis, and Inuit parents generally have little opportunity for input into the curriculum and even less for any decision affecting school policy.

- First Nations, Métis, and Inuit parents do not ask for English-only instruction; it is imposed.
- Few First Nations, Métis, and Inuit or bilingual language instruction classes are available as options to the English program.
- In contrast to immersion, English-only programming was never regarded as an experiment to be monitored, assessed, and evaluated prior to policies being made. Rather, English-only programs were strategies intended for assimilating the First Nations, Métis, and Inuit children.
- Aboriginal languages have been viewed historically as impediments to the school progress of First Nations and Métis children and treated as liabilities rather than assets (Heit & Blair, 1993, p. 109). This has come to be known as subtractive bilingualism, when a child has two languages and educational programming that focuses on only one will have the effect of removing the other. Aboriginal language programming has been sporadic in Canada, with First Nations schools being the primary supports for language retention or restoration, yet they are attempting to correct the past neglect and assimilation with schooling mandated with provincial curricula and minimal resources for language programming.
- Probably most important to Aboriginal learning contexts is the school's capacity to reflect Aboriginal epistemologies, cultural practices, and socio-historical contexts in real learning experiences, drawing on community and elder teachings within the pedagogy of the schools, including spiritual teachings, ceremonies, and physical activities associated with Indigenous knowledges.

Research and studies on immersion programming have grown over the years and are considered to be the most successful for improving second language acquisition, reading in two languages, and first language retention. This is especially true in the first years of schooling as students immersed in Aboriginal immersion schools from K to grade 3 have a higher chance of becoming fluent in both the Aboriginal language and English. Immersion specialists believe that 600 to 700 hours of immersion is needed for students to become fluent and to be able to pass the language on to future generations (Johansen, 2004).

Two Mi'kmaw teachers have documented the effects of students who start their early years in Mi'kmaw immersion class, thus documenting one of the best demonstrations of success in Aboriginal language immersion programming. Sherise Paul-Gould and Starr Sock are Mi'kmaw immersion language teachers at Eskasoni Elementary School who have researched both qualitatively and quantitatively the processes and outcomes of the immersion program in their master's theses at St. Francis Xavier University. Interviews with the administrators, parents, teachers, and students participating in the immersion program, and analyses of the test scores of students reading in English after leaving the program, provide ample research evidence that immersion programming has positive effects on students' identities, their attitudes toward schooling, their achievement in English language programming after leaving Mi'kmaw immersion, and most importantly, their own fluency in the Mi'kmaw language (Paul-Gould, 2012; Sock, 2012).

Eskasoni Elementary and Junior High School has had band control since 1981, and Mi'kmaw language instruction since 1986. However, it was not until 1997, with the support of *Mi'kmaw Kina'matnewey*, that the school adopted full immersion programming for students in kindergarten, subsequently adding another grade each year following these children through grade 3. Learning to read has always been a concern of parents, although it has been a concern of many parents that their children were not learning to read at the same pace as non-immersion students. Many parents even thought that teaching them first in Mi'kmaq might have negative effects on their learning to read in English. Yet the study of students who graduated from the first immersion program reveals what researchers have been consistently saying. You only learn to read once.

Learning to read in Mi'kmaq has demonstrated many benefits to students as they move into the English language program. Many teachers of students from immersion classes revealed that these students were reading better, writing longer, were critical thinkers, and able to support their own statements in writing. Research in immersion programming has shown that benefits last several years after leaving the last grade of the immersion programming, especially in areas of English reading levels and with teachers noting their academic abilities across subject areas (Paul-Gould, 2012; Sock, 2012). Beyond the benefits to students' academically, immersion programming has also shown to have benefits to the community, to parents, strengthening relations with elders and their Indigenous knowledges, as well as building capacity in Indigenous language instruction and curriculum development (Paul-Gould, Sock, Murray-Orr, & Tompkins, 2013). With results such as these, one wonders why English-language programming for students who still have their Indigenous languages used in the community would be used at all as the only language of instruction. Decolonizing the minds and hearts of administrators, teachers, as well as parents is a continuing challenge.

At present, Indigenous peoples from all nations, across Canada and beyond, are attempting in their many innovations, resistance, and commitment to self-determination to correct the colonial education processes from the past, born from a colonial notion of the superiority of English over other languages and knowledges. Domination, assimilation, marginalization, and hegemony are the norms, which are far from being banished in contemporary education and society. The context, for Aboriginal people in Canada, is laden with third world poverty, isolation, unemployment, powerlessness, cultural imperialism, and racism (both individual and systemic) as evidenced by run-down schools, inequities in funding, assimilation to English language and Eurocentrism that is now normalized in all schools. The emerging successful efforts of First Nations, Métis, and Inuit peoples in Canada to reclaim their own schools, languages, and knowledges in diverse learning styles and practices are driving a new agenda for transformative education that still has its challenges in resource inequities. To understand these requires one to understand the role of racism and Eurocentrism in Canadian education, past and present. The recognition and intellectual activation of Indigenous knowledge today is an act of remediation, a recognition of the rights of Indigenous peoples, and a renaissance among Indigenous scholars, social activists, and their allies. Their struggles represent a regeneration of the dignity and cultural integrity of Indigenous peoples, where success has been found in affirming and activating the holistic systems of Indigenous knowledge, engaging Elders, communities, and committed individuals. These practices reveal the utility, wealth, and richness of Indigenous languages, world views, teachings, and experiences to animate educational achievement. Once again in the struggle, Aboriginal languages are the most significant factor in the restoration, regeneration, and survival of Indigenous knowledge, and yet they are the most endangered.

The Blessed New Stories

With the realization of the necessity of constitutional reconciliation and transformative principles in the various UN conventions and declarations, and the emerging awareness of the demographic challenges of growing populations of Aboriginal peoples in Canada, some educational systems and universities across Canada have made Aboriginal education a new mission or a priority. One collaborative effort worth mentioning is the Canadian Association of Deans of Education that in 2010 developed an Accord on Indigenous Education. This Accord establishes an agreed upon mission for all deans of education across Canada and outlines the importance, urgency, roles, and responsibilities of the Colleges of Education in Canada to develop and pursue mechanisms and structures for improving Aboriginal achievement through the structures and mechanisms of education. Grounded in beliefs of social justice, collaborative and consultative principles with Indigenous peoples, multiple partnerships within communities and beyond, and the recognition of the value of Indigenous knowledge, the Accord urges transformative action in all areas of their responsibilities in delivering teacher education.

Many universities are now prioritizing Aboriginal education in many forms of engagement with communities and focus on Aboriginal students, although what this means has been a focus more on recruitment and retention of Indigenous students. What is significant in the Deans' Accord is the clear recognition and acknowledgement of the development of Indigenous knowledge. While the College of Education at the University of Saskatchewan has prioritized Aboriginal education in course content, student recruitment, and retention, research, and hiring Aboriginal faculty, they have also developed integrative programs that include Indigenous knowledges and methodologies.

Recognizing the interpretative monopoly that Eurocentric thought reserves for itself is the key to understanding the new transdisciplinary quest to balance European and Indigenous ways of knowing. This academic effort seeks to identify relations between the two generalized perspectives of Eurocentric modernism (and postmodernism), and Indigenous knowledge (and postcolonialism). The contradictions, gaps, and inconsistencies between the two knowledge systems suggest that the next step needed in the quest is a deeper understanding of Indigenous knowledge and how it is unique and not just different. To date, Eurocentric scholars have taken three main approaches to understanding Indigenous knowledge. First, they have tried to reduce it to categories such as art, religious practices, culture, or traditional ecological knowledge. Second, they have tried to reduce it to its quantifiably observable empirical elements, such as farming or hunting practices. And third, they have assumed that Indigenous knowledge has no validity, as it cannot be verified by scientific criteria. None of these approaches and issues, however, adequately explains the holistic nature of Indigenous knowledge, its fundamental importance to Aboriginal people, or its potential for new knowledge in the interface between the two knowledge systems.

Indigenous knowledge is inherently tied to the people's mutual relationship with their place and with each other over time, and through the common experiences of colonialism with an imperial might, whether arising from European explorations or subsequent colonial governments. Maori scholar Mason Durie notes that there are three most distinguishing features of Indigenous knowledge: "it is a product of a dynamic system, it is an integral part of the physical and social environment of communities, and it is a collective good" (2004, p. 5).

Indigenous knowledge is best protected by continuous usage within Aboriginal languages and traditions protected by Aboriginal treaty rights in s. 35 and the constitutional supremacy clause in s. 52 of the *Constitution Act, 1982*. Both provide constitutional grounds for Indigenous peoples to contest any abridgement of their rights.

Canadian common law does not offer any support or protection of Indigenous knowledge, as it protects individual or corporate knowledge under Canadian copyrights, trademarks, and patents as defined as intellectual or cultural property laws. These laws distinguish sharply between artistic works (with copyright and "neighbouring rights" to artistic performances), commercially valuable symbols (with trademarks), and useful scientific knowledge (with patents). For example, a patent, a trademark, or a copyright cannot adequately protect a ceremony that uses striking sacred-society symbolism to communicate empirical knowledge of medicinal plants. The medical knowledge may be patented, but the patent will expire in a matter of years. The text and music for a ceremony can be recorded (or "fixed") and copyrighted, but only the recorded version will be protected and only for the lifetimes of the performers plus fifty years. The symbols can be protected as trademarks forever, but their significance will be diminished when they are taken out of context. Modern law as defined by copyrights, patents, and trademarks thus does not protect the collective nature of Indigenous knowledges, as these are not acquired by individuals as their own creativity or imagination, nor can they be collectivized under a corporate theme.

Indigenous knowledge embodies webs of relationships within specific ecological contexts; contains linguistic categories, rules, and relationships unique to each knowledge system; has localized content and meaning; has established customs with respect to acquiring and sharing of knowledge (not all Aboriginal peoples equally recognize their responsibilities); and implies responsibilities for possessing various kinds of knowledge. In the context of the current education transformation, the dissemination of Indigenous knowledge should be targeted toward current First Nations students and to the next generation, ensuring that the study and development of Indigenous knowledge and the skills of their ancestors are valued and available in all institutions for learning and in the disciplinary areas of the sciences and the humanities. Young students must feel that it is rewarding to pursue careers based on the traditional knowledge of their forebears, and not just the kinds of knowledges that are developed outside their realm.

That said, however, all peoples have knowledge, but the group that controls the meanings and diffusion of knowledge exercises power and privilege over other groups. Those with control then link the diffusion of knowledge with economics, ensuring that some kinds of knowledge are diffused with rewards and other kinds of knowledge are not. For this reason, public schools are not politically neutral sites. Using sanctions, grants, and awards, governments tie knowledge to their own interests, using vague notions of "standards" and "public good" to control what counts as knowledge, how this knowledge is diffused, and who benefits from it. In all cases, those holding political power control knowledge, and have the power to exclude knowledge from curricula as it is regarded as being too local, particularistic, or unverifiable to be considered beside what is carried in schools and universities. Only recently have some ethno-botanists and some pharmaceutical companies begun to see the potential and value in buying or appropriating Indigenous knowledges, experimenting and patenting the results that were asserted by Indigenous peoples, and selling them back to them and others in the form of essences, medicines, and herbal remedies. This commodification of Indigenous knowledge occurs where knowledge, power, and economics intersect, which takes me to my next theme: the political voices and visions of Indigenous peoples.

A modern form of discrimination comes under the guise of state theories of cultural, rather than biological superiority, and results in rejection of the legitimacy or viability of Indigenous peoples' own values and institutions. Often, theories of both cultural and biological superiority are involved and interconnected in responses to Indigenous peoples; cultural racism is alive and well in the areas of intellectual and cultural property rights.

Discrimination is defined both internationally and nationally as any unfair treatment of, or denial of normal privileges to, persons because of their race, age, sex, nationality, or religion. When discrimination is effected through the machinery of the state, it can have mild to devastating impacts, ranging from students experiencing irrelevant or meaningless education, their leaving educational systems early, to deep psychological scars and eventually to racial and cultural genocide. For victims of discrimination, it matters little whether the damage is inflicted by invidious state action or by the less obvious application of facile neutral rules. The impacts are the same. Not only should nations not practice discrimination themselves, they must also identify ways in which they will protect their citizens from discrimination on both local and national levels.

The maintenance and protection of Indigenous knowledge should not be viewed solely as a benefit for Indigenous peoples, although access to their Indigenous world with its values and resources can deeply enhance their health, well-being, and ongoing livelihoods. These should be available to all peoples, regardless of affiliations and ethnicities. The potential benefit of Indigenous knowledge for all societies, however, is to draw on the vitality of Indigenous knowledge and its dynamic capacities to solve contemporary problems as well. Both scientists and Indigenous scholars who often reject each other's knowledge assumptions have contested the intersection of these diverse knowledge systems, methods, or conclusions based on the different contexts of parent knowledge systems. As Indigenous scholars enter the realm of university scholarship, they are both contesting the foundations of scientific objectivity as the sole methods for understanding the world they live in, as well as offering ways that Indigenous knowledges can be understood within different ontologies and epistemologies that embrace spiritual forces or phenomena. The Maori have been leading this work, particularly in the area of defining the terms for how Indigenous knowledge might prevail in modern times (Smith, 1999/2012; Durie, 2004). Some scientists are already beginning to understand the connections between the two knowledge systems, and are considering how their research might intersect with Indigenous peoples' ways of knowing. This does present the problem that has been cautioned by Indigenous peoples and scholars — that this new awareness and the need for further research on Indigenous knowledge should not be seen as the super highway for appropriation and misuse. There are many complexities involved in blending overlapping knowledge systems as Willie Ermine (2007) and Martin Nakata (2007) have raised. To start the process of investigating Indigenous knowledge requires respect, collaboration, and dialogue between Indigenous and non-Indigenous peoples as points of negotiation for how and what can be brought together. The Deans' Indigenous Accord (2010) and UN Principles and Guidelines for the Protection of Indigenous Knowledge (Weissner & Battiste, 2000) speak to these.

Both nationally and internationally, Indigenous knowledge is being revealed as an extensive and valuable knowledge system. Scientists, ecologists, and social justice activists are coming to understand the consequences to the world when Indigenous peoples, their languages and their knowledge are denigrated, dismissed or denied resources to retain them. Our ecology and environment, as many have come to know, are directly related to the people who either cultivate it for good or extract it for goods. It must be emphasized that the world's Indigenous peoples have been, and still are, cultivating 80 per cent of the world's natural biodiversity, and this is taking place within the cultural cultivation of their Indigenous knowledge. It is this inherent affinity between land and peoples that David Harmon (2002) is referencing as the linkages between biological and cultural diversity. All the world is at stake when contemporary reform toward uniformity, conformity, normativity, international connectivity and travel, consumerism, and globalization lead to the past and present losses to Indigenous languages, erosion of Indigenous cultures, and losses to the land bases on which Indigenous peoples cultivate their knowledges. Harmon aptly writes: "The essential nature of diversity combined with a looming threshold of irreversible diminishment justify the label 'crisis'"(p. 161). The list is long for the totality of losses that the world is currently undergoing. This has led to some groups around the world staking a claim for what is important to their activism. Indigenous peoples, the ecology, and social justice are three key themes that Paul Hawken (2007) addresses in his book *Blessed Unrest: How the Largest Movement in the World Came into Being and Why No One Saw it Coming*. These themes address the main issues needing to be resolved in order for us to manage the crisis that Harmon and others have raised about the losses of cultural, biological, and ecological diversity. The rate of decline among all cultures is large and growing, and at the current rate of decline, Hawken estimates that we can expect to witness half of our living cultural heritage disappearing in a single generation (2007, p. 94). He predicts, and I concur, that the world will suffer immeasurably with a loss of the "ethnosphere," which is the sum total of all the "aesthetic, intellectual wealth contained within the invisible folds of sound" (p. 94), leaving us as a people and a species, and Earth itself, deeply impoverished.

Thomas Berry (1998), author of *The Dream of the Earth*, suggests, "It's all a question of story. We are in trouble just now because we do not have a good story. We are in between stories. The old story, the account of how we fit into it, is no longer effective. Yet we have not learned the new story" (Berry, as cited in Suzuki 1997, p. 4). The recognition and intellectual activation of Indigenous knowledge today is an act of remediation, recognition of rights of Indigenous peoples and a renaissance among Indigenous scholars, social activists, and allies emerging in the past thirty years. The critical mass is felt in the many works of Indigenous scholars like Jo-Ann Archibald, Richard Atleo, Gregory Cajete, Willie Ermine, Laara Fitznor, Rainey Gaywish, Oscar Kawagley, Martin Nakata, Norman William Sheehan, Linda Smith, Graham Smith, Mason Durie, Tyson Yunkataporta, and many others on this continent and beyond.

The challenge continues for Indigenous scholars to restore and regenerate in younger generations the affirmation of the identities and cultural dignity of Indigenous peoples, where success has been found in affirming and activating the holistic systems of Indigenous knowledge, engaging elders, communities, and committed individuals and leaders. These practices reveal the utility, wealth, and richness of Indigenous languages, world views, teachings, and experiences to animate educational achievement. As Nuu-chahl-nuth scholar Richard Atleo (2004; 2011) reminds us, Indigenous knowledge is both theory and method. We learn from community narratives the theory of how to be and we process the theory in our actions with our doing as defined in our stories of how to be a good human. Once again in the struggle, language is the most significant factor in the restoration, regeneration, and survival of Indigenous knowledge.

To affect the needed reform, educators need to make a conscious decision to nurture Indigenous knowledge, its dignity, identity, and integrity by making a direct change in school philosophy, policy, pedagogy, and practice. They need to develop missions and purposes that carve out time and space, that affirm and connect with the wisdom and traditions of Indigenous knowledge, that are with the people themselves, their Elders and communities. They need to define what it means to teach in holistic ways and develop humanistic connections to local and collective relationships. They need to make educational opportunities for students that nourish their learning spirits and build strong minds, bodies, and spirits. One Cree student shares this analogy: if you have one arrow, it can easily be broken. But put six arrows together and it is difficult for any of them to break. Aboriginal students need a critical mass of peers, allies, and supporters who will help them reach their own potential and create their own successes.

In those few exceptional universities that have acknowledged the Indigenous knowledge issue, the struggle becomes developing "trans-systemic" analyses and methods, of reaching beyond the two distinct systems of knowledge to create fair and just educational systems and experiences. This is part of the ultimate struggle, a regeneration of new relationships among and between knowledge systems, as scholars competent in both knowledge systems seek to unite and reconcile them. Only when these analyses and methods in thought and behaviour are made can we create truly "higher" educational systems that are a place of connectedness and caring, a place that honours the heritage, knowledge, and spirit of every Indigenous student and contributes to the building of trans-systemic knowledge for all students.

CHAPTER 5

Animating Ethical
Trans-Systemic Education Systems

Indigenous peoples have the right to maintain, control, protect and develop their cultural heritage, traditional knowledge and traditional cultural expressions, as well as the manifestations of their sciences, technologies and cultures, including human and genetic resources, seeds,
medicines, knowledge of the properties of fauna and flora, oral traditions, literatures, designs, sports and traditional games and visual and
performing arts. They also have the right to maintain, control, protect
and develop their intellectual property over such cultural heritage, traditional knowledge, and traditional cultural expressions. In conjunction
with Indigenous peoples, States shall take effective measures to recognize and protect the exercise of these rights.

Article 31, *UN Declaration on the Rights of Indigenous Peoples* (2007)

CANADIAN EDUCATIONAL INSTITUTIONS ARE POISED to make (hopefully
major) changes within their institutions dealing with Aboriginal education,
building on several catalytic moments, some mentioned already: 1) the *Declaration of the Rights of Indigenous Peoples*; 2) pressure on the ministry of Aboriginal Affairs and Northern Development to improve the educational gap of
First Nations education in comparison with the Canadian average; 3) priority
setting established among the provinces and territories that affects both public schooling and university education in advancing Aboriginal education as
represented in the Council of Ministers of Education, Canada; and 4) the Accord on Indigenous Education of the Association of Canadian Deans of Education. Over the past 50 years, much research, writing, and intersecting traditions dealing with equality, human rights for minorities, cultural difference,
educational equity, cultural diversity and inclusion, anti-racist, anti-homo-
phobic, and anti-oppressive education have coloured or shaped the multiple
directions schools and educational institutions have taken. Some of the successes of these directions have been shared in multiple forums — for example,
Paul Martin's on-line Promising Practices in Aboriginal Education, and the

short-termed Canadian Council on Learning, which was also initiated under former Liberal Prime Minister Paul Martin's administration.

The past two decades of invigorated work in universities across Canada, have also ushered in many areas of leadership in improved Aboriginal student access to higher education, increased retention, and diversified programming of Aboriginal content in the institutions, and increased Aboriginal scholars, academics, and leaders in many colleges, disciplines, and units. My colleague, Cree educator Alex Wilson, and I prepared a report that outlined many Canadian examples of success (Wilson & Battiste, 2011). As well, in the last decade some disciplinary traditions in higher education and post-secondary institutions have responded to calls for inclusion of Aboriginal scholarship, which we have seen in conferences, workshops, research, writing, and output involving minorities, Indigenous, postcolonial, post-structural, and cultural studies that have largely supported the new directions and contributed to the critique of the older models. It has been a long trajectory of Indigenous, anti-oppressive, critical feminist theory, critique, and research in many disciplinary areas that has taken us to where we are today. But where do we still have to go, and what can we take from the past, and what needs to be rethought in terms of new directions? These models have neglected Indigenous knowledge and content. They exist within the dominating Eurocentric foundations, suggesting that every student starting from the same place could benefit from the same instruction, curricula, and materials, including instructors who were largely white and female in the early years, and white and male in the later years.

For the most part, my own scholarly work has grown from that seed of critiquing past and current systems and directing attention to the disciplinary omissions that perpetuate stereotypes and contribute to cognitive assimilation. My work has also been characterized as visionary, or imagining what can be as a result of informed ethical engaged effort. In this chapter I would like to consider several innovative areas of visioning forward with Indigenous knowledge, and in particular in two areas of the curricula, the humanities and the sciences. These are areas that have long histories and traditions in current educational institutions. These disciplinary traditions are grounded in Eurocentric assumptions, values, and methodologies that need to be discussed in relation to Indigenous knowledges and traditions.

At present, few universities have acknowledged Indigenous knowledges as being a foundation for disciplinary knowledges and traditions, although there are some excellent examples at present that we can learn from. Having been part of a university that is trying to make changes through strategic planning and priority setting at the macro and micro levels, I have witnessed many different approaches to bringing Indigenous students, knowledge, and partnerships into their units, departments, and colleges. Some of these approaches have been at the level of professional development of faculty and staff, others have been at committees attempting to bring Indigenous content into the curricula, while others have been at improving access, recruitment, and retention of Aboriginal students, the latter being the largest efforts at the post-secondary level. Many promising practices in Aboriginal education have focused on culturally inclusive curricula affecting attitudes, motivation, and retention of Aboriginal students, but until institutions also interrogate the existing cultural interpretative monopoly of Eurocentric knowledges, assumptions, and methodologies, the efforts will be band-aids on festering wounds. The institutions must move beyond the mere "culture" discourses tools for both analazying problems and offering solutions, for in these discourses culture gets attached to an othering strategy when institutions do not want to acknowledge the dominant cultural traditions that draw from cultural attitudes, values, and presumptions, and how these are applied to notions of culture of Indigenous peoples in forms of "difference." Difference gets read as aberrations from the normative Eurocentric cultural traditions, whether in gender, class, race, or sexuality, and Indigenous peoples. Difference marks Indigenous peoples as largely historical and local, but not contemporary and global, and their knowledge systems become minimized to local value. Thus, teachers and institutions can easily ignore Indigenous knowledge, peoples, and histories, rationalizing that there are too few or no Indigenous students in their class to make any reasonable effort for inclusion, and far more immigrant students whose cultures need to be included.

Bringing two diverse knowledge systems together needs some consideration of the assumptions underlying each foundation and where the points of inclusion or merging might seem advisable. The need then becomes one of developing "trans-systemic" analyses and methods — that is, reaching *beyond* the two distinct systems of knowledge to create fair and just educational systems and experiences so that all students can benefit from their education in multiple ways. Beyond suggesting that neither Indigenous knowledge nor Eurocentric knowledge systems can be the sole arbiter of the work involved, I am also suggesting that part of the ultimate struggle is a regeneration of new relationships among and between knowledge systems, which needs scholars competent in both knowledge systems to converge and reconcile these and other knowledges, ways of knowing, and systems. Such a practice has begun.

As these next sections take up aspects of Indigenous knowledge in the disciplinary traditions of humanities and sciences, I am envisioning areas where many of my colleagues have dialogued and supported Indigeneity and Indigenous teachings or knowledge as part of their scholarly work, and what is still emerging — and, even more so, still being resisted. This chapter then shares some of those foundations and the questions asked as well as those left to be answered. What is appropriate to include in curricula as Indigenous knowledge, or who should speak about questions of curricular content and pedagogy in educational pluralism? When educators consider "mainstream" education, who does the "main" belong to, and who is privileged, and who is "streamed?" What is stereotyped, represented, or imagined in the terms "Aboriginal," "First Nations," or "Indigenous?" How do we know the "other," and what methodology do we employ to talk with and about the "other?" What role does the "other" have in self-representing, defining their agenda, and speaking and being heard? What does the work look like after these issues have been addressed? In posing and answering these questions, I suggest we need to centre educational commitment to, and our responsibilities for, the enhancement of humanity and its infinite capacities. Each strategy taken to rebuild human capacity is a decolonizing activity that turns collective hope into insights, voices, and partnerships, not resistance, resignation, or despair.

Generating an Ethical Space for Decolonization

Education is a process by which a culture expresses its reality and values, processes its culture, and transmits it to each generation. The modern curriculum is the organized portion of education through which the state sanctions and standardizes not only what counts as knowledge but the ways of knowing they will adopt and prescribe. Largely, the elite in power chooses what language(s) will be used for this state network of education, and what content and methods will be sanctioned. In this way, the state has established one main stream, a culturally imperialistic stream that ignores or erodes, if not destroys, other ways of knowing or the accumulated knowledge of some groups. These processes occur in human science curricula as socially constructed. The interface between culture and education is essentially a communicative art, requiring decision makers in curricula design to be knowledgeable not only of subject areas but of the different cultural world views and realities from which the students operate. What we now know about students in Canada is that they are a diverse group, and represent a variety of experiences, traditions, histories, and knowledges.

What is apparent to Indigenous education is the need for a serious and far-reaching examination of the assumptions inherent in Eurocentric curricula currently divided into two main elements of disciplinary traditions, one the humanities, the other science. Modern educational theory and practice draw from these curricula foundations, and to envisage inclusivity, one must consider what is excluded. Current educational shortcomings may or may not be in the curriculum, or in finance, or in testing, or in community involvement, but no one will ever know this — or the changes necessary for improvement —

without a deeper philosophical analysis of modern thought and educational practices.

Selecting curricular knowledge requires that decisions made include the overriding issues of power, status, and legitimation, as well as racism, hierarchy, and normativity. These decisions entail questions about whose knowledge is included, whose languages are considered legitimate vehicles for carrying the knowledge, who are the people who make these decisions, how will their choices be made, and what governs those choices? What is the role of a critical education about the hierarchy of power embedded in society, and how can the inclusion of antiracist, anti-oppressive education support all students, not just Aboriginal ones?

Ethical space was theorized initially by Roger Poole in his book *Toward Deep Subjectivity* (1972), and applied by Willie Ermine (2007) to the two sets of intentions confronting the in-between space that connects Indigenous and Eurocentric knowledge systems. Ermine's inspiration came from the space that is created when Indigenous and Western thought are brought together. It is not a merge or a clash, but a space that is new, electrifying, and even contentious, but ultimately has the potential for an interchange or dialogue of the assumptions, values, and interests each holds. Adding ethics to this space then speaks to the harms and enhancements, and "entertains our personal capacity and our integrity to stand up for cherished notions of good, responsibility, and duty. . ." (p. 195). In other words, it makes one consider the limits of the boundaries one chooses, and reconsider how what one chooses may infringe on another's space or standards, codes of conduct, or the community ethos in each community. It is in this space that Indigenous and non-Indigenous peoples can begin to truthfully speak to the predicaments and issues that face them and the standards they speak for. It is an enabling space that needs to be a foundation for a first encounter between Indigenous and non-Indigenous peoples.

Unfortunately in Canada, and beyond, Eurocentric knowledge operates as if it is a depoliticized process of intellectual refinement, whereas Indigenous knowledge is treated as if it is a by-product of domestic politics among Aboriginal peoples, such as the history of treaties, constitutional issues, politics and policies of Indian Affairs, and continuing struggles Aboriginal people have with white settlers, including the effects of not implementing treaties as agreed to, forced acculturation and assimilation, and its dissonances in learning and teaching styles, and family socialization. Cultural relevance and inclusion in curricula are then unreflectively regarded as the cornerstones of some mainstreaming education, without attention to the ethical considerations that are defined within diverse communities of what is trans-cultural or trans-boundary in nature.

Cultural relevance and inclusion have been interpreted in many ways, largely managed as an additive approach to curricula, for the teachers' own assumptions and location are not interrogated and the curricula held as if it has no history, politic, or community significance, and is not complicit with the diminishing derogatory past. In "mainstream" or conventional schooling, teachers use approved cultural content and books, including resources and speakers from the communities, but often do so without having to consider the power dynamics involved or their lack of agency in repeating the serious past omissions. They do not pause and ask why Indigenous content was not included in the first place, or what biases they themselves bring to the lessons.

When social indicators illustrate the impoverished life of Aboriginal peoples across Canada, the narratives of residential school abuse, violence in families, high rates of incarceration and suicide of youth, there is a call to examine the role of education in society and to recognize the obstacles to some groups and thus the need to decolonize education. Critical education and anti-oppressive education begin with the unpacking of Eurocentric assumptions of education, the normalized discourses and discursive practices that bestow ignorance on students, while it bestows layers of meaningless knowledge on to youth that hide the social and economic structures of Eurocentrism, white dominance, and racism. Paulo Friere (1973/1993) calls this kind of additive education the banking concept of education. In this framework, youth receive an education in which the teacher talks about reality as if it were motionless, static, compartmentalized, and predictable. Or else he or she expounds on a topic completely alien to the existential experience of the students. His/her task is to "fill" the students with the contents of his narration — contents that are detached from reality, disconnected from the totality that engendered them and could give them significance. Words are emptied of their concreteness and become a hollow, alienated, and alienating verbosity (chap. 2 at http://www2.webster.edu/~corbetre/philosophy/education/freire/freire-2.html).

Students regularly are memorizing textbook content without critiquing its origins, its practices, its outcomes, and its inequities. Whiteness is hidden in this system, because it never looks at itself, only the perceived "different other." Norms surrounding whiteness then are the measure for success or failure, and rewards for whiteness are not critiqued for the benefit and rewards it gives to a few and the kinds of punishment and low outcomes it gives to those who are different in terms of skin colour, religion or non-religion, sexual orientation, abilities, age, or class status.

Colonialism as a theory of relationships is embedded in power, voice, and legitimacy. In Canada, it has racialized Aboriginal peoples' identity, marginalized and de-legitimated their knowledge and languages, and exploited their powerlessness in taking their lands. This imperialistic system of knowledge that is considered the "mainstream" functions like a "keeper" current in a rapidly flowing river or ocean. The keeper current drags a person to the bottom and then to the top, but if one fights against the current one usually drowns. Decolonization then is a process of unpacking the keeper current in education: its powerful Eurocentric assumptions of education, its narratives of race and difference in curriculum and pedagogy, its establishing culturalism or cultural racism as a justification for the status quo, and the advocacy for Indigenous knowledge as a legitimate education topic. It is the channel for generating a postcolonial education system in Canada and disrupting those normalized discourses and singularities and allowing diverse voices and perspectives and objectives into "mainstream" schooling.

Many literature reviews have been done in my research and in others' to identify the promising practices in education. The most effective strategies centre Indigenous knowledge, such as Indigenous humanities and sciences, as a shared education norm. Aboriginal students' success is not an issue of their own reclamations and identities reinforced in an unreflective Canadian society that masks systemic discrimination and practices of cultural imperialism within discourses of inclusion and respect. Their success cannot be achieved with research on Indigenous youth and their capacities as if their languages, their isolation from Canadian modernity, and the lack of parity in the systems they come from are the causes of their lack of achievement. Rather we, as educators, must determine when we are thinking about mainstreaming, whose is the "main" that is "streamed?" Whose experiences are normalized as centre? What is imagined within the terms "Aboriginal," "First Nations," or "Indigenous"? How do we know each other, and what methodology do we employ to acknowledge the cultural interface of the dialogue? How are the Indigenous multiple voices represented? What role does the "other" have in their own self-representing, in defining, as well as in speaking and being heard? What does the outcome look like after these issues have been determined?

Decolonizing Indigenous education first and foremost must be framed within concepts of dialogue, respect for educational pluralities, multiplicities, and diversities. It is about self-determination, deconstructing decisions about curricular knowledge, and re-energizing education and knowledge to the contexts of lives. Also, it is about deconstructing decisions about curricular knowledge and reframing education and knowledge to the contexts of people's lives, a *sui generis* or "one of a kind" education and learning. It is not a singular or total theory, but multiple theories, strategies, and struggles. Its outcomes must account for the imposed tragedies and indignities colonial education has placed on Aboriginal people, and the need for systemic awareness of everyone and the reconciliation and healing in educational systems. Aboriginal educators have embarked on a transformative journey, but this time it is not assimilative; it is a therapeutic education process of healing of the relationships within and among communities and drawing out the positive and enriched aspects of their lives and their teachings. They have always been there, but hidden by cognitive imperialistic English language education. It is also about restoring a balance in relationships and undoing the hegemonic authority over our lives. We are interdependent in our ecology and environment, and we will have to develop institutions, policies, and practices that go beyond signalling respect for cultural diversity and acknowledge their own interdependence with our place and the people of this place.

Decolonizing the Humanities

Inspiration for my research has come from many places, sometimes from my Mi'kmaw life experience, courses I have taken or taught, writing papers or speeches, or dreams. My learning spirit guides me to these "ah-hah" moments, which happen in the most unlikely times and places, especially when I am led to let go of thinking, drifting and edging on various states of relaxation, exercise, or alternate forms of consciousness when I am led to consider something new. My shift toward the Indigenous humanities started one day after receiving a brochure about an international conference on humanities which, I discovered, covered many of the humanities of the world: Asia, India, Europe, the many continents the world over. I was struck, however, with how absent Indigenous peoples and their humanities were, regardless of continent. Since then, I have been considering how the Indigenous humanities in Canada could be framed.

The history of colonization has so affected so much of Indigenous people's lives that today we must look beyond the modernity of reserve life, or the technology of the times, to ask what of our Indigenous selves and civilization remains and how is it represented and understood by the people themselves? Recalling the Jesuit journal written by Father Christian Le Clerq, the book I came upon so many years ago, I could see then, as I do today, beyond the biases and prejudices of the writer, the Mi'kmaw people and their values and attitudes that remain the same today and which have the potential to introduce an Indigenous humanity that is a rich resource for the world's humanities and in particular for Canada. Indigenous humanities are much more than just the small disciplinary corner of Native Studies carved out of liberal arts studies of religion, art, linguistics, and social sciences. It can, like the humanities emerging from Eurocentric philosophy so long ago, be a source of inspiration in a new time and in an old place.

When a team of allied scholars in multiple colleges found each other, it was at the 1996 International Summer Institute on Cultural Restoration on

Oppressed Indigenous Peoples, led by Blackfoot scholar Leroy Little Bear and funded by the Social Science and Humanities Council of Canada in their last year for the Summer Institutes. In 1996, the Summer Institute on Cultural Restoration of Indigenous Peoples became a strategic entry point at the University of Saskatchewan for what was to follow. Our discussions and camaraderie revolved around various themes of social justice, professionalization, and institutional hierarchies on which we built our collaborative, interdisciplinary, and trans-systemic theory and methods to achieve our intended research outcomes in curriculum design, teaching, interdisciplinary and Indigenous capacity building, cultural theory, and modes of dissemination.

No available theory or method was complete in helping to address the massive colonial and neo-colonial events in Canada and beyond, and to address the past and ongoing colonial challenges facing Indigenous peoples worldwide. We spent ten days discussing with some of the best minds among Indigenous peoples and non-Indigenous allies, drawing on ceremony and tradition within dialogue and story, on informal events that created community and enabled us to address the many layers of colonial history and contemporary challenges, and finally on our activism, our plans; our strategic alliances needed to move from where we were to new places we envisioned. The outcome of this exercise led to the book *Reclaiming Indigenous Voice and Vision* (Battiste 2000), which I edited and which continues to inspire many youth as they examine their own situations and outcomes in their communities. Many students have since shared with me appreciatively what they drew from these essays and how it carved out their own scholarly work.

The alliances and friendships over the years with my colleagues Lynne Bell, Len and Isobel Findlay, Mary Longman, Deborah Lee, and others have led to many other smaller and larger collaborations, among them further proposal writing and funded projects, collaborative writing, co-presentations at conferences, and sharing funds to bring in other Indigenous scholars and teachers. Bringing Maori scholars Graham and Linda Smith back to the University of Saskatchewan, together and individually, provided us with many opportunities to bring their experiences and lessons learned about transformative praxis from Aotearoa (New Zealand) to the attention of many (Smith, Battiste, Bell, & Findlay, 2003). Indigenous writers and other allied postcolonial authors supported the expansion of our students' awareness of the processes of domination, the awareness of their pain, the processes of healing and coping, and the visions of transformations of the colonized/oppressed.

By our collaborations and individual work, the colleagues with whom I worked sought to understand the various patterns of violence on people, the effects and struggles they were articulating in their communities, and their resurging hope and struggles for liberation. In 2008 the Truth and Reconciliation Commission was beginning a nationwide awareness campaign of the over 150 Indian residential s chools in Canada and the over 150,000 people who attended these schools, and the schools and universities that were complicit with the churches and government involved in the objective of removing the Indian from the child, and replacing it with their "superior" version of civilization. We also wanted to mark the geographical spaces marginalized in colonialism and imperialism, as well as consider the manner by which the local economies had created poverty and educational obstacles for youth. The task was great, and eventually it led to our efforts toward examining the ways in which we might project a visionary postcolonial university in a Social Sciences and Humanities Research Council of Canada (SSHRC) grant, that was to be a precursor to our project directed at "Animating the Mi'kmaw humanities."

Our initial search for university mission statements, priorities, or strategic planning around Aboriginal peoples was found wanting in 2002, with the universities being still stuck in the Eurocentric canon with the normal exceptions of the ongoing development of Native Studies, access programming for entering students at both undergraduate or graduate programming, and limited Aboriginal recruitment of faculty and staff in various departments. Ten years later, and after the provinces had made a commitment to prioritizing Aboriginal education and to addressing the gap between Aboriginal peoples and Canadians at large, many more universities are changing their strategic planning, priorities, and missions with regard to Aboriginal peoples, students, and contexts.

The ground was ripe for change and the engagement of new relations with First Nations and Métis peoples in the province and the experimentation of new initiatives that went beyond the access and retention programs. At the University of Saskatchewan, one of these initiatives that I particularly felt had potential was when the university began working on an Aboriginal foundational document which would guide all the colleges and units in the university in their priority setting with regard to Aboriginal initiatives in hiring, student recruitment, research, and programming. When it was finally initiated as one of the core foundation documents, I was delighted with the changes that began to emerge, programs that increased Aboriginal content in courses, Aboriginal hiring in colleges, and an Indigenous library portal that housed and accessed Indigenous research, scholarship, and collections. At the core of one of the SSHRC-funded projects with my colleagues Len Findlay and Lynne Bell, we recognized that, despite the attention to Aboriginal education, we really aspired to inclusive institutions where Indigenous peoples' knowledge, diversity, and engagement were embraced and honoured in multiple ways. Activating new relationships with Indigenous peoples and faculty necessitated that we openly face racism and complicities with power and dominance in the decision about what would be included or changed. We began to imagine what a postcolonial university might look and feel like. The project, Animating the Postcolonial University, sought to identify the existing mission statements and strategic planning given to support the access and retention of Indigenous peoples in Canadian universities, the kinds of programming stemming from those narratives, and exploring how decolonizing methodologies might be applied in our three disciplinary areas (education, art and art history, and literary and cultural studies) to drive our own teaching and writing as well as to raise the consciousness of what was possible in our disciplines over a three-year funded project that included archival and applied research, discourse analysis, community dialogues, pedagogical innovation, speaker series, and policy analysis and formation. "Animating" was a term we used in the SSHRC project to express an active, affirmative, ongoing focus of change needed for our work in the arts, humanities, and education. As teaching faculty, we also sought to identify the principles that would guide our own work so that it would inspire and transform the capacities, visions, and gifts of our students. This foundation led to the next step of our work, which was to take the project into a specific First Nations community to undertake a more thorough exploration of humanity and its implications for post-secondary institutions in their locales — thus, our project, Animating the Mi'kmaw Humanities.

In their rich theoretical work, Maori educators Linda and Graham Smith of New Zealand, have theorized that any Indigenous movement is going to be necessarily unique to each area, to its nations, to the colonial encounters in its territory, because context with colonialism has not been all alike, and these diverse histories and experiences would need to be addressed. Decolonizing these spaces, they assert, is also not a linear and tidy process. Rather, as in the case of making universities responsive to Indigenous peoples, women, minorities, or diverse knowledge systems, the sites of struggle for recognition, acceptance, and integration were going to require collaborative, interdisciplinary, participatory, and Indigenous research methodologies to decolonize educational institutions.

Following on that SSHRC project, we then prepared for the next proposal, Animating the Mi'kmaw Humanities, which was funded by SSHRC in 2010. In this project, drawing on the work where we left off, we knew we needed to move beyond the institutions to the communities themselves to engage Mi'kmaw voices and visions and use these as the foundation for growing new collaborations with the conventional educational institutions. We sought to explore specifically what aspects of Indigenous humanity in one context could be centred as a force of cognitive pluralism, identity reclamation, and self-determination. Our strategy was not unique, but contextualized to treaties and responsibilities that fell on Canada and its institutions as a result of the Constitution's affirmation of Aboriginal and treaty rights. We were also building on the rich work of the Royal Commission of Aboriginal Peoples' Report (RCAP, 1996), honouring that rich composite of research, analyses, dialogues, and consultation that brought the comprehensive research and recommendations to the centre, while identifying ways allied scholars, scholarship, and research supported those urgently desired outcomes. Invariably, the process would require continued dialogue among and with Indigenous peoples, identifying, honouring, and honing of the protocols of place, and adding to the promising decolonizing practices whose benefits we expected would be broadly felt.

This project focused more specifically on the Mi'kmaw humanities, and included involving interdisciplinary and collaborative work with partners from the Mi'kmaw communities on the eastern seaboard. In this work, the opportunity for me to work within my own Mi'kmaw communities came with the skills, experiences, and relations I had gained from being a former resident and member of the local communities of Potlotek and Eskasoni, and knowledge of my ancestral language. My long-term service within the community provided the entrance and knowledge of the ethical engagement of Mi'kmaq, as both my husband Sa'ke'j and I had done working on many continuing projects, including the treaty and Aboriginal rights in the Constitution of Canada, the Mi'kmaw language revival, Mi'kmaw teacher training programs, the development of Mi'kmaq Studies at the University of Cape Breton, Grand Council work, Indigenous Knowledge Protection (Battiste & Henderson, 2000), the *Declaration on the Rights of Indigenous Peoples*, and the Mi'kmaw Ethics Watch.

It was important for both Indigenous and non-Indigenous scholars to etch out the space for naming and examining the mechanisms of Eurocentric colonialism and not put those solely on the shoulders of Indigenous peoples. White allied scholars who know their own locations and complicities with colonialism are important collaborators, as Hunkpapa Lakota Sioux filmmaker, photographer and performance artist Dana Claxton points out:

> all of us who come to this continent, regardless of race and relationships to different colonialisms, are implicated in the imperial subjugation of Indigenous peoples. Acknowledging that we are implicated does not have to be a negative, stagnant place; it can be the springboard for action and consciousness. (as cited in Mather & Wong, 2011, p.117)

Our team members knew this well, for they had long committed themselves to various forms of critical consciousness and social justice, equality, and equity in the universities and social and political economies. Each of them in their disciplines had addressed stereotypes and racism, historical context and gender studies, postcolonial studies and First Nations, Métis, and Inuit advocacy and activism, carving out new scholarly areas and enhancing Indigenous capacity.

Every conception of Indigenous humanity begins from a consciousness in which a specific place takes prominence. This locality initially shapes an understanding of being and by experience in that place shapes and sustains the people, providing them an understanding of themselves and an awareness of their being at home in the world. Each child represents a micro ethnic group for which teachers need to become aware of their schemata that reflects their world view. So for us, our research works, protocols, collaborations, and listening drew first from the place of Mi'kma'ki, the seven districts home of the Mi'kmaq.

Our broad work began with community dialogues in local communities in several key sites in Mi'kma'ki: Potlotek, Sydney, and Halifax, Nova Scotia; Fredericton, New Brunswick; and Listigutj, Quebec. In preparing for these dialogue sessions with community leaders, educators, students, and elders, we followed local visiting protocols that preceded and followed the dialogues. In each visit, we shared our interests and commitments to the project while taking up whatever was on their agenda for the day. In one home, we sat down with tea and counted out the coins that came as donations for a particular cause, and in another, with community volunteers we packed raw salmon into bottles that were being prepared for elders and the needy. We listened, shared our own stories, offered tobacco, cloth, and gifts to the participants, as well as shared university protocols of informed consent forms offering clarification of our purpose, our project aspirations, and processes.

Indigenous humanities speak to the core of resilient humanity, the similarities and diversities of all peoples who develop from their ecological origins rather than from their cultural differences. Indigenous humanities are a new conception of Indigenous knowledge that was once embedded in notions of difference in culture, but is a concept seeking to live beside and in balance with the discursive Eurocentric categories and regimes of the humanities as knowledge. In the Eurocentric humanities, the core is understood as learned philosophers, who devise by design their legacy, a history based on relations among nations that led to supremacy of being. Their society comes into being through questioning the moral assumptions within the church and state, the settling of treaties among nations, the conquering of nations, the philosophical choices and consequences, and finally the emergence of a civilization of human beings with government, laws, and institutions. Played out in the educational arena, it becomes the grand narrative of constructing a serious white Christian heterosexual male version of achievement and presumed success.

However, to consider another humanity, such as Indigenous peoples, would require a different conception of humanity, one that rests its foundations on place and the ecological teachings and practices of what constitutes being human within a certain ecology. Ecology is the animating force that teaches by trial and error, and elders' guidance, how to live and how to be human. As such, it is not derived from theological, moral, or political ideologies. Ecology privileges no particular people or way of life. Like ecologies, Indigenous heritages or cultures can have a respectful place in education. They honour and nourish a respect for diversity rather than hierarchy and normative preferences. First Nations concepts of humanity relate a certain style of being human, of being present with the forces and energies — human, physical, natural, and spiritual — thus overcoming the forces of doubt and inertia. Action and sharing, rather than reflection, definitions, or categories best illustrate this concept.

Indigenous humanities, as a broad concept, bring together the core capacities of all societies and cultures. They operate locally and distinctively, but confirm constructs that characterize all human beings. These include the ability to communicate through language and art, to mark our place and progress across time and space, and to locate ourselves reflectively and spiritually in relation to each other, to the world we all share, and to the forces that lie beyond our understanding or control. As such, it is a study of resilience, resistance, and representation as defined with Indigenous concepts in the knowledge disciplines of secondary and post-secondary education.

Among the best examples of the Indigenous humanities in action is the work of many writers, poets, singers, and dramatists. Among these are singer songwriter educator Buffy Sainte-Marie, storytellers and writers Linda Hogan, Maria Campbell, Rita Joe, Thomas King, Dale Auger, and many others who offer voices that expand Indigenous artistry, creativity, imagination, and dreams. They understand concepts of humanities and creativity as performance or doing or living. Action brings humanity and creativity to life, and doing and being turn life into knowledge and wisdom.

As a postcolonial strategy toward better education, First Nations humanities have been functioning as critique and creativity, resistance and celebration. As critique, they work against the grain of "White" pretensions of racial supremacy. As creativity, they relegate new disciplinary traditions to the outskirts of Western discourses to offer an analysis that confronts the uniform and grand narratives on how the world operates. They consider not just the one civilization but include all students and all peoples, the diversities of cultures and knowledges, and solutions that are not universally owned, socialized, and acknowledged.

First Nations humanities are not synonymous with ethnic and class elitism, although they have been associated with versions of the "barbarian" or savage in order to authenticate and privilege Eurocentrism. By this characterization — and its pseudo-civilizing mission — First Nations humanities seem a contradiction in terms. By this categorization, too, the socially contrived primitive or uncivilized Indigene could not credibly lay claim to such knowledge in earlier centuries, and they may only do so now via imitation and assimilation because of the continuing misguided perception that there is no such thing as Indigenous knowledge and nothing to be learned from Indigenous peoples.

First Nations humanities have been systematically excluded in the Eurocentric narratives. Education from Eurocentric origins arose from Greek classical philosophers and evolved through modern scientific inquiry to have its roots in character, history, and the roots and politics of modern society. Educators must recognize the Eurocentric ideologies that have shaped educational curricula, and recognize different and legitimate ways of knowing and doing that are not currently part of the educational process.

The golden age of the Eurocentric humanities was the Renaissance in early modern Europe: the rediscovery of the ancient languages, disciplines, and texts occurred virtually simultaneously with voyages of "discovery" that were the prelude to modern colonialism. The golden age of Renaissance humanism was, not coincidentally, the first heyday of modern Euro-colonialism. The Eurocentric humanities are founded upon an oppositional binary of race. Through the rise of print and a literary public, a focus of interest was placed on the Orient and its peoples, who supplied an exotic variance to the ordinary common subject (Said, 1977). The Orient and its peoples lost their own subjectivity and awareness of self to be reinvented as the counterpart to a constructed civilized white identity, while Orientals as objects of scrutiny were regarded as an opposing and inferior construct by white writers. It was a creation of literature that bore the strategies of normalization of superiority and negation of the other.

As such, this tradition embedded in Eurocentric literature makes it difficult to introduce the Indigenous humanities into the existing curriculum guides, teacher's activity guides, and universities without similar comparisons being used and subjectivities lost. It recognizes the interconnectedness of scholarship and knowledge traditions that connect universities with elementary and secondary schools, and the importance of the Indigenous humanities in the public schools.

The great forgetting or disinformation replayed in educational pedagogy and curricula have dealt unjustly or inadequately with First Nations knowledge systems, their rights, interests, accomplishments, and potential contributions. Critical theorist Henry Giroux notes that we need

to develop definitions of pedagogy that admit new knowledge from subordinated groups, address the "production of knowledge, social identities, and social relations [that] challenge racist assumptions and practices that inform a variety of cultural sites, including but not limited to the public and private spheres of schooling. (Giroux, 2000, p. 196, in Klug & Whitfield, 2002, p. 155)

The First Nations humanities point toward a place for education to prosper, but only if Canadians agree to work under an authentic version of humanity that includes First Nations. This postcolonial educational strategy invites us back to sustainable teaching. An inclusive Canadian educational system is well placed to nourish and export the protocols of respect, collaboration, and creativity that achieve justice in education and lead to the revaluing and protection internationally of Indigenous knowledge and heritage.

Most curricula provide for the inclusion of local content beyond the prescribed guides, as in Saskatchewan, where approximately twenty per cent of elementary and secondary public schools curricula may be locally adapted. However, teacher candidates trained in Eurocentric education systems rarely have the prerequisite knowledge, skills, and community connections to develop curricula based on local Indigenous histories, knowledge, and contexts, and depend on their alliances with First Nations colleagues to gather what they need. The false assumption is that Aboriginal teachers, as experts, have been raised in and have had the requisite cultural, ceremonial, and knowledge experts available to them, and thus their formal and information education has provided them with ongoing connections with their Indigenous knowledge and traditions. Unfortunately, imperialism, colonialism, and racist policies that disallowed certain cultural practices, and the educational systems' lack of receptivity to cultural diversity, have led to many educated First Nations, Métis, and Inuit teachers having little knowledge of the traditions and languages of their ancestors. Indeed, many teachers' knowledge of Aboriginal communities and cultures is based on their limited experience with their own context and a singular Native Studies course. The lucky ones are those who may have taken more courses or who are themselves involved in spiritual and ceremonial work with elders. Pre-service teachers without Indigenous humanities teachings and materials rarely have the knowledge, skills, funding, and community connections to develop curricula based on local Aboriginal knowledge.

So who will be the teachers and the knowledge builders of the Aboriginal programs that many educational institutions are currently poised to develop? It is not enough to depend on Aboriginal faculty who are trying to develop their own areas of scholarship, although they must be engaged. It will not be Aboriginal teacher programs that achieve this, as many Aboriginal teacher candidates are still growing stronger with the help of inclusive curricula and understanding their own losses. The Indigenous humanities can become a tremendous step forward in advancing cognitive and knowledge pluralism and contribute to building a more informed base for all teacher candidates who understand what role they can have in building a more inclusive society.

In the next section, I examine how science has been framed from Eurocentric foundations and how it could be framed to make it a more effective force for good in the decolonizing of education.

Decolonizing Science

Native Americans could be the vanguard of a collaborative and cooperative scientific tradition. Yet, of the 23,279,000 scientists and engineers in the United States reported in 2008, only 93,000 were American Indians/Alaskan Natives (0.4 per cent), and of this percentage only 46,000 were female (NSF-Gov, 2008). While statistics like these are not present in Canada, they illustrate what is evident. In the past two decades, the achievement of Aboriginal students has consistently been reported as being far below national averages, and especially in areas involving the sciences.

Eurocentric science has ignored Indigenous science. The tipping point against Eurocentric resistance to Indigenous science came in the World Conference on Science for the Twenty-First Century: A New Commitment, assembled in Budapest, Hungary, from 26 June to 1 July 1999, under the aegis of the United Nations Educational, Scientific and Cultural Organization (UNESCO) and the International Council for Science (ICSU). More than 1,800 delegates representing 155 countries, twenty-eight intergovernmental organizations and more than sixty international non-governmental organizations; and approximately eighty ministers of science and technology, research, and education stated the innovative global consensus of the scientific community in the *Declaration on Science and the Uses of Scientific Knowledge*.

Section 35 of the Declaration stated that "[m]odern science does not constitute the only form of knowledge, and closer links need to be established between this and other forms, systems and approaches to knowledge, for their mutual enrichment and benefit."

Section 36 declared:

Traditional societies, many of them with strong cultural roots, have nurtured and refined systems of knowledge of their own, relating to such diverse domains as astronomy, meteorology, geology, ecology, botany, agriculture, physiology, psychology and health. Such knowledge systems represent an enormous wealth. Not only do they harbour information as yet unknown to modern science, but they are also expressions of other ways of living in the world, other relationships between society and nature, and other approaches to the acquisition and construction of knowledge. Special action must be taken to conserve and cultivate this fragile and diverse world heritage, in the face of globalization and the growing dominance of a single view of the natural world as espoused by science. A closer linkage between science and other knowledge systems is expected to bring important advantages to both sides.

In *The Science Agenda — Framework for Action*, participants agreed to the following guidelines and instrument for action to achieve the goals proclaimed in the Declaration:

84. Enhanced support for activities at the national and international levels on traditional and local knowledge systems should be considered.

85. Countries should promote better understanding and use of traditional knowledge systems, instead of focusing only on extracting elements for their perceived utility to the S&T [Science and Technology] system. Knowledge should flow simultaneously to and from rural communities.

86. Governmental and non-governmental organizations should sustain traditional knowledge systems through active support to the societies that are keepers and developers of this knowledge, their ways of life, their languages, their social organization and the environments in which they live, and fully recognize the contribution of women as repositories of a large part of traditional knowledge.

87. Governments should support cooperation between holders of traditional knowledge and scientists to explore the relationships between different knowledge systems and to foster interlinkages of mutual benefit.

The Declaration and Agenda were the results of Indigenous diplomacy, and another manifestation of the Indigenous renaissance. It established new global standards for scientists and science educators.

Professor Emeritus Glen Aikenhead, my colleague in education at the University of Saskatchewan, has for decades been leading research and critique about the cultural and equity issues surrounding underachievement among Aboriginal youth in the sciences. He points to, among other things, the consequential losses to economic, resource management, and sovereignty for First Nations, Inuit, and Métis communities (collectively, Aboriginal communities); the ethical problem of equity and social justice for the rest of Canada, as the underachievement further contributes to the disproportionately high level of poverty in Aboriginal communities; and the foreign nature of school science and mathematics for many (but not all) Aboriginal students owing to the inherent dissonance they experience when they move from their home culture to the Eurocentric culture of school science and mathematics.

In subsequent collaborations, Aikenhead has teamed with Herman Michell, a Cree science educator (Aikenhead & Michell, 2011) to support science educators in understanding the clashes of knowledge systems and world views. Their collaborations reveal Indigenous students' experiences and also guide teachers in building their own bridges between the various traditions leading to a culturally responsive science classroom. They further explain how conventional science programs build from Eurocentric theories, presumptions, and methodologies, and how these differ from Indigenous peoples' knowledge systems based on action and wisdom. They show how Cree science is based on holistic, relational, and empirical practices for understanding self in relation to nature. They illustrate how conventional Eurocentric science curricula have not nurtured Aboriginal students' identities or strengthened their resiliency, and contributed to Aboriginal students' lack of interest or achievement in these courses. The knowledge systems clash becomes a source of dissonance, leading to multiple forms of disengagement with sciences, the disciplines that lead to scientific career paths, and ultimately to students leaving school. Educators and teacher candidates preparing to work in schools with Aboriginal students need an understanding of this clash and the need for a decolonizing approach to the sciences. In this next section, I offer my understanding of the issues underlying the dissonance between Eurocentric science and Indigenous science and conclude with some curricula issues needing consideration in decolonizing the sciences.

Modern science and science education is a subset of Eurocentric knowledge. It is a way of knowing drawing on principles of inquiry about nature that certain people, historically initiated and dominated by white males, have deemed to be valid and reliable processes for acquiring knowledge. Like Indigenous knowledge, Eurocentric science draws from a complex array of experiences, ways of collecting, adopting, and sustaining old knowledge (oral and written), and gaining new knowledge (ceremony as experimentation). However, Eurocentric science, like Indigenous science, ultimately is socially constructed, meaning that it is contingent on variables involving language, values, thought, and reality. There is no neutral knowledge system. All knowledge about nature is socially constructed. Thus, science based on certain accepted methodologies and constructs such as reason, objective observation, and interpretation takes place in a context of contextualized assumptions, values, ideas, and beliefs, for which objectivity is not entirely possible. But there are more contingent variables.

The formal science curricula are as socially constructed as the social science curricula. Since the 15th century, Eurocentric knowledge has been put into a form of writing, which has been structured according to certain discourses and writing styles and normalized in certain languages and mathematical formulas passed on through formal teaching practices in schools in organized curricula, lectures, and programmed courses. Critical education theorist Michael Apple has argued that not only do schools organize curricula and confer cultural legitimacy on knowledge through certain textbooks, but they also organize the curricula in a nexus of other institutions — political, economic, cultural — that confer power in ways that are hegemonic. Furthermore, textbooks form particular constructions of reality, selecting and organizing the vast universe of possible knowledge into a selective tradition (Apple & Christian-Smith, 1991) that is then sanctioned through schools and universities.

Classification systems in Eurocentric science are not innate, but are chosen within linguistically and culturally specific scientific communities. These discourses are embedded in modernity's descriptive explanatory prose, often imparting a grand narrative by an all-knowing, distant, unnamed voice.

The inadequacies of Eurocentric science and science educators for diverse groups of students in Canada are as follows:

- The application of scientific principles is derived from studying an inadequate, limited, non-inclusive sample; Indigenous peoples and other nations have been virtually excluded from the canons of knowledge.
- The Eurocentric scientific method is largely based on the assumption that one can know the whole (the universal) by examining the parts. If the parts are incomplete, then Eurocentric knowledge is fragmented and incomplete.
- Eurocentric science seeks principles that are universal and, as such, can be applied anywhere and any time. Born of empirical observation, made sense of by hypothesis which can, in turn, be empirically tested, Eurocentric science contradicts the faith in its knowledge. In effect, it suggests that all information is open to be disproved, thus severing it from temporal and geographic specificity. In so doing, it loses its meaning to context, and as David Suzuki has offered, such "a story . . . has lost its meaning, its purpose and its abilities to touch and inform." (Suzuki, 1997, p. 19)

The decolonization of Eurocentric science can only be achieved when all voices are allowed to emerge, when we do not give up on all that others have come to know, or all the forms and techniques of thinking that have been developed, and we find ways to make use of whatever can help us to think not only within but also about the dominant tradition. To reject other knowledge systems is to subject students to selective silences and collective ignorance. The exclusivity of Eurocentric science must be transformed, not just corrected or supplemented. It requires that we understand how these traditions of hegemonic knowledge in science and the humanities gained power and prestige, how the terms and systems came to express and shape the curricula, and recognize that equality need not mean sameness.

Indigenous peoples understand the nature in which they live. They have a science derived from relationships with nature and with the energies within an ecosystem, including their relationships with each other and with their environment. The source of Indigenous knowledge, then, lies within the changing ecosystem, from which Indigenous peoples develop their awareness and their strategies of living within that ecology. This continuous relationship over time creates awareness and a world view in which one can look to the whole to see the patterns that develop. These patterns thus form specific cultural behaviours and ways of knowing. This world view flows from the same source: the relationship within the flux, a kinship with the other living creatures and life energies embodied in their land, and a kinship with the spirit world. Over time, the knowledge manifests itself in many other social forms and processes: stories, symbolic and creative manifestations, technologies, ways of being and learning, traditions, and ceremonies.

Shared relationships are interconnected and not separable, collectively developed and constituted, in which each person is a contributor, applying their individual idiosyncrasies to the whole, as well as holding to the collective ideals of the group to which they either maintain or change over time. This collective repository of knowledge also is the basis of defining appropriate behaviours within the context which derives from the knowledge system. This knowledge system is an internalized law of philosophy, customs, values, beliefs and morals which is understood broadly in terms of culture. Thus, Indigenous peoples act within their natural context according to a way of knowing, and their knowledge is largely connected to that local context.

While Indigenous knowledge is as encompassing as Eurocentric knowledge, the science of the Indigenous world view is founded upon an understanding of how humanity fits with nature. Indigenous science is not a collection of observations, facts, and measurements, but rather a dynamic, living process of watching, listening, connecting, responding, and renewing. Indigenous science embodies a holistic view of the world in which all human, animal, and plant life are perceived as being connected, related, and interdependent. All things are imbued with spirit and thus have energies that interact at both an earthly level and a spiritual level. In comparing Indigenous science to Western science, physicist David Peat notes that

Indigenous science does not seek to found its knowledge, as we do, at the level of some most ultimate elementary particle or theory, rather it is a science of harmony and compassion, of dream and vision, of earth and cosmos, of hunting and growing, of technology and spirit, of song and dance, of colour and number, of cycle and balance, of death and renewal. (Peat, 1994, p. 8)

Since Indigenous peoples have developed a physical and spiritual unity with their total environment and simultaneously with their cosmos, they have an obligation to act responsibly and ethically toward their environment and all elements in it. Traditional knowledge embodies those principles and practices which are enacted holistically in their ways of knowing and doing, in how they acquire their food and sustenance on the earth, in their rituals and ceremonies, in their beliefs and values, and in their language. Some anthropologists have called that "culture."

Indigenous science holds that all the world and life is in constant flux. Indigenous peoples have recognized that they have no control over that flux, but manage to live and adapt themselves to its variations. They have lived both in wealth and poverty and in each have developed an adaptive culture to accommodate richness or scarcity. Over time, Indigenous peoples became particularly attuned to the irregularities and regularities in the flux. They then had to accommodate and adapt, within an extreme range of diversities, their discerning observations, continuous participation, acculturation, and experiential learning, and their highly dependent intrapersonal, interpersonal, kinaesthetic, and spatial learning as expressed in oral language and involvement in the tribal culture to create a resilience that has provided the capacity to continue to survive.

The path of the constant flux has been marked with diversity and adversity. Indigenous peoples' science has not been passive, but active and dynamic and ready to meet the challenges of their environment and the social fabric. The highest calling for Indigenous people, then, is to teach succeeding generations about that knowledge. Yet within a hostile Eurocentric society that imposes cognitive imperialism in compulsory education, we are witnessing an ever-growing transition from First Nations, Inuit, and Méchif speakers to English, thus making it difficult for elders to pass on their wisdom, knowledge, and traditions.

Since the advent of Eurocentric influence over government and institutions, Indigenous peoples' science has been weakened enormously. No Indigenous group in North America or in the world has been exempt from the losses that threaten their livelihood and existence. Cognitive imperialism, or the whitewashing of Indigenous people's minds both subtly and overtly, has created irreparable language and cultural erosion and loss, and an overall diminishment of the significance among the youth of their elders, their culture, their knowledge, and their language. In this century and the previous one, almost all Indigenous youth have been subjected to the compelling and negative forces of Eurocentric knowledge and science through federal, residential, and public schooling that has been thrust upon them; they have come to distrust their own instincts and knowledge for finding meaning in their context and in shaping their future survival. Many youth today have lost the detailed knowledge and taxonomies, the elemental and subtle principles of their culture, because they do not have their language with which to express them.

The greatest gap between Indigenous knowledge and Eurocentric science is found in the differences in their traditions of privilege, prestige, and power. Despite the enormous, rich diversity in humankind today in terms of knowledge, skills, talents, and heritage, only one visible, powerful, and defining tradition of knowledge has been embraced, developed, conventionalized, and diffused throughout the world.

Conclusion

The content of Eurocentric scientific knowledge is thus an accumulation of acquired selected measurements, facts, and information, having no existence apart from the one who knows. Acquiring what another experiences with a minimal loss caused by cultural or subjective experience is thought to be achieved through measurable observation. This way of thinking leads one to conclude not only that experience can be accurately measured, but that these measurements are reliable and valid processes for describing reality. Objectivity in the Eurocentric mind is thus given a higher value over subjectivity, promising in its measured mathematical model to enable one to experience a universal truth that is independent of subjective experience, a tainted perception grounded in their particular social, cultural, and religious context. This trust in objectivity is based on a supposed value-free framework which is thought necessary to the search for laws of regularity and eternal truths (Peat, 1994).

Eurocentric science carries an aura of authority that has made the majority of its users believe that they can know and understand, as well as control and manage, their surroundings. When Eurocentric science is the official knowledge base, it operates from a position of power, a position that is also relegated to the highest order and thus to receiving priority in funding by the state and national organizations. Eurocentric scientists receive the greatest amount of financial, emotional, and publication support for their inquiries using the conventional methods in the tradition. Those who are recipients of this knowledge base come to believe in the strength and power of that knowledge, as well as in the tradition that creates its power.

Eurocentric knowledge's privileges have been revealed, and in it has been revealed the use of that knowledge to oppress others while it accumulates power, wealth, and economic benefit for a few. Educators must now reconceive what we thought we knew. We must remove our conceptual lenses, learn to immerse ourselves in systems of meaning that are different from ours, think through and challenge invidious hierarchical monism, and examine terms and systems that express and shape hegemonic knowledge (Minnick, 1990). This requires a new and innovative ethical space in the curricula.

Eurocentric content, methods, and approaches are but a limited sample of what is available for students. As globalization, technologies, and other influences usher in variations from afar, and as student engagement and motivation and identities still are considered important factors for increasing student potential and capacities, the exploration of Indigenous knowledges, whether in the humanities or sciences, in conventional curricula can be valuable. One of the most important reasons for this is that contemporary content in schools increases being in the world, but disengages the student from themselves, their locales, and values that support humanity. Generating an ethical space in the curricula requires animating Indigenous humanity and science to engage students in their own histories, their own complicities with the dominating forces of the past, to give them a new sense of awareness of holism, connectedness, and grounding of their own power to activate change in themselves and others and ultimately the future of humanity.

CHAPTER 6

Confronting and Eliminating Racism

Convinced that any doctrine of superiority based on racial differentiation is scientifically false, morally condemnable, socially unjust and dangerous, and that there is no justification for racial discrimination, in theory or in practice, anywhere, . . . Resolved to adopt all necessary measures for speedily eliminating racial discrimination in all its forms and manifestations, and to prevent and combat racist doctrines and practices in order to promote understanding between races and to build an international community free from all forms of racial segregation and racial discrimination. . . .

International Convention on the Elimination of All Forms of Racial Discrimination (1965, in force 1969)

TALKING ABOUT RACE AND RACISM is a difficult topic for teachers and students, as well as for anyone unwilling to consider their complicity with this country's long history of racism. Yet confronting and eliminating the false concept of racial superiority is a necessary initial process in developing a decolonization consciousness in Canadian education. The difficulty begins in part because Canada has generated in its self-narrative a description of a generous, liberal, and progressive society that has overcome its earlier bigotries and prejudices. The 70s ushered in formal bilingualism and multiculturalism and human rights, the 80s acknowledged Aboriginal and treaty rights in the new Constitution of Canada, the 90s brought a new, largely Inuit-populated territory that would formally recognize Indigenous languages as core languages in the territory, the Crees in Quebec would help hold on to the country by refusing separation from Canada, and the turn of the century would see the growing technological revolution that would buttress the economies in Canada and beyond.

Race has long been debunked as a constructed category that justifies dominance and privilege and other forms of oppression. Yet, racialization is well known to all those targeted under the imaginary line of social justice. Whiteness and privilege are less evident to those who swim in the sea of whiteness and dominance. Confronting racism, then, is confronting racial superiority and its legacy, not only in history but also in contemporary experience.

Back in 1995 when I had just started teaching at the University of Saskatchewan, a review of the undergraduate program in the College of Education revealed a need to address educational inequities among Aboriginal and other marginalized students in Saskatchewan, as well as to address the curricular omissions regarding Aboriginal peoples and their relationships with Canada that most Saskatchewan schools had neglected. Most Saskatchewan students came to university with little or no understanding of the treaty relationships that their ancestors had negotiated and benefitted from, and little understanding of how Aboriginal peoples had suffered. When the College of Education agreed that all teacher candidates enter their training with a required course in Native Studies, it was thought that this would enlarge their awareness of the historical past and the foundations of colonialism that had prevented First Nations, Métis, and Inuit peoples from benefitting equally in Canada. They would be prepared for a cross-cultural education that would reveal how inequities were further created in the social construction of knowledge, how relations of power and privilege were linked to all inequities and sustained in government policy, practice, and the discourses of society. What the course revealed to those who taught it was that understanding how racial superiority in Canada was constructed and maintained created tensions in students, and these feelings needed to be understood and managed effectively if there was to be a transformation of thought. Teacher candidates were comfortable to discuss cross-cultural differences because they had a perception and position from which to view differences and the "other" — largely negative caricatures learned in social discourses in their families, among relatives and friends, and in the media. What they did not realize was how they themselves sustained the dominant discourses of difference and reproduced a sense of superiority embodied in whiteness that marginalized, diminished, and reproduced inequities among students who were different. They did not have to consider how their own privileges were gained through the normalization of their ideas, values, and beliefs to the detriment of others. Such is the core issue in confronting cultural and cognitive racism.

The normalization of the status quo and the transmission of content that reflected this perspective have been the core issues in what my research in diverse literacies revealed about cognitive imperialism which continues today in many sectors in society. Students have absorbed one aspect of the term of equality, thinking that it means that everyone was equal to receiving all services and education in Canada, but have little understanding of what equity means in relation to the different processes required to ensure everyone has an equal starting position. Most entering students coming from Saskatchewan schools did not have an understanding of the ideologies and economics embedded in their own histories. Therefore, it was not unusual that their attitudes reflected common understandings of the day about Aboriginal peoples, women, gay and lesbian students, students with diverse abilities, and the economics of poverty, which were negative, blaming the victims for their disadvantages and asserting that equity provided unearned privileges for minorities in affirmative action programming.

As most of my students were white, they rarely questioned the whiteness of the university, their classes, the employment of people in Saskatchewan, the divided city solitudes of east and west, the high rates of incarceration of Aboriginal youth, the media's negative depictions of Aboriginal peoples, and the overwhelming racism endemic to this province and country. When asked to consider these issues, cultural difference was ultimately their answer, meaning it is about them, not me, as the source of the inequities

So the required course Cross Cultural and First Nations education gradually moved from Canada's responses to difference to a course in anti-racism and anti-oppressive education. This was not an easy course for anyone. Racism is one of those topics that is provocative and often contentious. Students were uncomfortable and incredulous that the roots of racism and concealed racial superiority lay in the structures of their own society and were embedded in their socialized ways of knowing, and could be traced in their ancestors' beliefs, values, and judgements, and in their own familial decisions and political actions taken in Saskatchewan. They knew that there were differences between Aboriginal people and themselves — differences in school outcomes, in employment and education rates, as well as in levels of poverty, incarceration, social maladjustments, and suicide — but they saw these from the perspective of character flaws, cultural misunderstandings, or maladjustments by Aboriginal people themselves to modernity. Public discourses had put Aboriginal people naturally and justifiably at the bottom of a socially and culturally constructed hierarchy in Canadian and Saskatchewan society.

It was interesting to note that the colour of faculty members was an important factor in how well students could accept social constructions of their location. One white teacher who taught this course found fewer issues when she could unpack her own investments from her white location, and how much easier it was for students to consider their locations and privileges. This unpacking of the social and political ideologies of racism has required a delicate mix of teaching strategies and approaches, including critical autobiographies, essays on diverse visible and nonvisible minorities and groups, theorizing the social constructions of power, knowledge, and the politics of knowing within institutional curricula and hierarchy; reflective pedagogies and writing, and lots of directed discussion and dialogue in small and large groups. It has been especially gratifying to have many antiracist scholars, such as Beverly Tatum,

Christine Sleeter, George Dei, Verna St. Denis, and Carol Schick, to name but a few, conducting research and helping us understand and confront racism and anti-oppressive pedagogies that work as we are guided through these contesting constructions.

The Confrontation with Racism

Why is racism such a difficult topic to understand and absorb as a nation? Haven't we been talking about equity, diversity, and inclusion long enough? While it is true that legal confrontation of racial discrimination by governments has occurred, it has not yet affected the power of racial supremacy in Canadian society. Indeed, more evident than ever during the Idle No More Movement of Aboriginal peoples is the power of racial supremacy.

The Idle No More movement emerged from a grassroots campaign to make people aware of Canadian government's proposed bills that were being discussed and approved without Aboriginal peoples' consultation or consent. The effect of these bills, presented as an omnibus bill, would greatly harm Indigenous nations' rights within Canada, rights recognized by treaty relationships with the Crown affirmed in the Constitution of Canada and upheld by many court cases. The bills discussed in Parliament and unilaterally passed by the Conservative government were the source of the roar activated by social media that stormed the media at large across the globe. As Indigenous people by the thousands took their protests into the streets, shopping malls, Parliament, and other places throughout Canada and the world, Idle No More became a social media insignia of strength and determination. Not since the 90s when Canadians watched the blockade at Kahnawake, Quebec, had there been such a flood of Aboriginal people in the media. Idle No More was first characterized by gatherings with few if any speeches, most discontent embodied in drumming, round dances, and messages framed on placards, with the media picking up on the masses, the children, and the elders. Facebook and Twitter brought people en masse, with the key message being that we are a presence and we will be heard. People of all nations and diverse origins showed their support with social media broadcasting support, while many other Canadians unleashed virulent hate, disgust, and racial discourses against Aboriginal peoples and their peaceful protest. Anti-Indigenous sentiments circulated everywhere on the Internet in blogs, Twitter, and Facebook, largely fuelled by national newspapers, radio talk shows, and television whose coverage of the events was found biased and misleading as it had been fuelled financially and administratively from a Conservative campaign in the federal government. One national tribal newspaper aptly wrote:

Success in maintaining the anti-indigenosity enterprise depends not upon day-to-day racism, but rather upon vigilant maintenance of a convincing historical narrative which justifies the taking, which implies that "native people" didn't "own" the land and resources which nourished their survival, while at the same time glorifying the virtues of "ownership of private property" within the settler society. It is a principal theme in Canadian education. Canadian law is based on it and reinforces it. (Four Arrows Treaty Eight First Nations of Alberta News Summaries, 2013, p. 8)

While events are still unfolding as to the outcomes of the Idle No More movement — many other government bills are being considered without Aboriginal peoples consultation — at another level, the confrontation of racist discourse in Canada has led twenty chiefs to take their complaints regarding the racialization discourses to the international stage, accusing the Harper government of violating the human rights of their people and of failing to take action against "racist" media reports. Their complaint is making its way to the United Nations Committee for the Elimination of All Forms of Racial Discrimination. This committee was formed from the United Nations *Convention on the Elimination of All Forms of Racial Discrimination* (1965), that solemnly affirmed the necessity of eliminating racial discrimination in all its manifestations throughout the world, and of securing understanding of and respect for the dignity of the human person. In 1966, the United Nations declared March 21 the International Day for the Elimination of Racial Discrimination.

The *International Convention on the Elimination of All Forms of Racial Discrimination,* adopted by the UN General Assembly in 1965, came into force in 1969; it is legally binding on the states that ratify it. Canada ratified this convention in 1970, agreeing to implement its principles to eliminate all forms of racial discrimination and to report to the General Assembly regularly on their progress toward eliminating racism. In strong language, the *Convention* affirms that any doctrine of superiority based on racial differentiation is scientifically false, morally condemnable, socially unjust, and dangerous. It further affirms that there is no justification for racial discrimination, in theory or in practice; that the existence of racial barriers do not support the ideals in any human society of the principles of the dignity and equality inherent in all human beings. The *Convention* reaffirms that all human beings are born free and equal in dignity and rights; that everyone is entitled to all the rights and freedoms set out therein, without distinction of any kind, in particular as to race, colour, or national origin; and that all human beings are equal before the law and are entitled to equal protection of the law against any discrimination or incitement to discrimination. The *Convention* recognizes that discrimination between human beings on the grounds of race, colour, or ethnic origin is capable of disturbing peace and security among peoples and the harmony of persons living side by side, even within the same state, and is an obstacle to friendly and peaceful relations among nations. States must then report on their government's initiatives to the General Assembly, which Canada does every five years.

In 1983, the General Assembly of the United Nations called on all states and organizations to participate in a program of action to combat racism and racial discrimination. Twenty years after the UN declared March 21 to be the International Day for the Elimination of Racial Discrimination in honour of African citizens killed in the Sharpeville Massacre, Canada joined the world to fight racism. In 1986, the Prime Minister of Canada, Brian Mulroney, encouraged Canadians to join together and extend their efforts to "ensure the rapid eradication of racism and racial discrimination and the realization of mutual understanding, respect, equality, and justice for all Canadians" (as cited in Décoste, 2013). In 1989 Canada instituted a national March 21 campaign through the Department of Canadian Heritage entitled "Racism. Stop it!" to eliminate the existing legacy of racial superiority and discrimination. These efforts underscored the fact that racism was still alive and had to be corrected.

Cognitive Construction of Racism

Few Canadians understand the cognitive operation of racism, how it came to be a dominant force in the history of Canada, and how it justified policies, practices, and outcomes that Canadians have come to accept as neutral and even just. The idea of racial superiority is widely condemned by our collective experience and governments because it is tied to the perpetuation of violence and human degradation. It is outside the realm of the protected privileges of one people.

One of the most significant features of Canada is its foundation by settlers based on treaties with the First Peoples of Canada. These people, as a collective, were initial signatories of treaties with the Crown that allowed for the settlement of European immigrants, and in return the government would provide provisions as stipulated in the treaties and other subsequent agreements. These treaties set a different relationship with First Nations peoples as to why they received certain provisions such as subsidies, reserve lands, and why their education and their health and welfare are outside provincial responsibilities. Few Canadians understand that their ancestors' entrance into Canada is tied to the treaties. More commonly, people view First Nations, Métis, and Inuit peoples as a race, likened to immigrants coming to Canada. They believe that Aboriginal and treaty rights are "racial" rights built on equality principles, rather than constitutional rights that give them rights to settle, buy lands, and pass them on to their descendants. Though race has been disclaimed as a valid category of analysis, racialization or proclaiming racial inferiority for certain people or all members of a target group is a common experience worldwide that has denied the personhood of the target-group members in their countries or regions. There is a strong push to replace the term "race" with the term "ethnicity." The horror of race is its biological implication, and the association with biological heritability and immutability. The fixed nature of race is countered by the mutable notion of ethnicity, a changing cultural identity that is more fluid and under greater personal control. There is merit in the notion of ethnicity, but it will take more than a semantic end run to eliminate race from Canadian minds and hearts. This requires that we know more about this term, "race."

Race is a social or cultural construct of European consciousness. Race is not something that resides in the blood or genes of a group of people as characterized in biology. It has no biological source, like the colour of the eyes. Race is created in the social attitudes and beliefs of society. It was not created in the streets but rather was created by social scientists at universities, as a product of the "Enlightenment" in the German universities, part of a particular rational and scientific project to understand the nature of the world and human nature. As voyagers to different continents brought back new information, the European interpretation of the difference produced an unprecedented project to classify and rank the diversity of the world's plants, animals, and humans. To compare Europeans and their descendants with the peoples of the New World was to examine not only the social, political, cultural, and physical attributes of these bodies, but to find out how they compared with European bodies, minds, and spirituality.

A theory of scientific racism established by scientists then provided a coherent account of observed differences and originated a comprehensive theory of European superiority over other peoples. Superiority could be viewed in experiments that compared one group to another, from the size of the skull to the size of the penis. There was difference; they were marked as inferior, and that inferiority and its counterpart superiority had its consequences. Racial difference and superiority became the ideological handmaidens of European slavery, imperialism, and colonialism. The English and French languages' use of the concept of race in scientific analysis as "natural selection," "eugenics," and in public policy as survival of the fittest (or social Darwinism), have been used as justification for policies of assimilation, or as common values for the greatest common good. Research and more informed publics have led scholars, science, and the UN General Assembly to reiterate that there is no scientific justification for differential treatment of people based on race.

The significance of race rests in its cumulative influence on the psyches and social arrangements of colonization and our nationhood. We cannot isolate and segregate its influence in a given era, a given belief, or a given person. However, race is a term whose use and impact has been used in Canadian history and policy, having dire consequences on certain groups in Canada, Aboriginal peoples being just one of many who have received treatment that has discriminated against them. Social psychological research clearly shows that ignoring race in a race-neutral or "colour blind" way may do a disservice to the targets of racial bias as well as to those who presume themselves to be free of it.

Given its terribly divisive and denigrating nature, and its scientific utility, a critical question for Canadians is why is the construct of race allowed to persist? The typical answer is that race persists because it has a meaningful and prominent place in our cultural history. Race helps Canadians to make sense of who they are and who they are not, where they have come from, and even where they are going. But the meaning of race is constructed from what we do, say, and think as a society. Just as we have created race by our actions and deeds, we can un-create it or de-legitimize it.

Racism remains the theory, while intolerance, prejudice, and discrimination remain its integral practice. Although race is a false category, theories of racial superiority and discrimination continue to circulate, and critical cultural studies are only one of the many ways disciplinary knowledges are unpacking, acknowledging, and hopefully terminating racism. Many writers have sought to unpack the various conceptualizations of race, racialization, and racism.

One of my inspirations in understanding racism is Albert Memmi (1969), an Algerian writer of Jewish ancestry living in Tunisia, where an independence movement emerged, thus provoking in him an awareness of how racism is created from human situations of social origin, embedded in power, and choice. His early writings were fiction, although his first book was largely autobiographical, revealing the disquieting aspects of being Jewish in a country that was at war with anti-Semitic countries. When Tunisia finally won its independence from France, he and his wife left the country for France, fearing reprisals from the new Muslim government.

Most significant of his writings was his first book of essays, *The Colonizer and the Colonized*, that captures a theory or logic of colonization by examining the social constructions of difference that embed in social situations. Memmi (1969) captured the nature of the cognitive construction of racism in this definition:

Racism . . . is the generalized and final assigning of values to real or imaginary differences, to the accuser's benefit and at his victim's expense, in order to justify the former's own privileges or aggression. (p. 185)

Within this definition he identifies four strategies which have been used to maintain colonial power and which are significant in examining the situation of Indigenous peoples in Canada and beyond: (1) stressing real or imaginary differences between the body of the racist and the victim; (2) assigning values to these differences to the advantage of the racist and the detriment of the victim; (3) trying to make these values absolute by generalizing from them and claiming that they are final; and (4) using these values to justify any present or possible aggression or privilege (p. 186).

The colonialists, mostly of European heritage, viewed the continent as unoccupied land. The Indigenous inhabitants were considered a wild, untutored, and ignorant race given to strange customs and ungodly practices. They would, it was presumed, in time, through precept and example, come to appreciate the superior wisdom of the strangers and adopt their ways — or, alternatively, the inhabitants would be left behind in the march of progress and survive only as an anthropological footnote (RCAP, 1996).

The concepts of racial superiority, discrimination, and racialization have been an integral part of the tactical strategies and tools of colonialism, the defining ideology of Canadian education. Sociologist John Warnock (2004) writes:

> Racism is an ideological argument used to legitimize inequality between two groups of people. In this situation, a dominant group will identify another group by a variety of biological and/or cultural characteristics in order to justify unequal treatment. (p. 157)

As a collective ideology or artificial construct, racism asserts a belief in an intellectual or moral superiority based on the skin colour or biological characteristics of a constructed category called "race." Typically, this pathology teaches a willingness to discriminate, segregate, or deny rights to other groups based on the perceived biological or cultural hierarchy of superior and inferior "races." It is a mode of thought that professes to explain superiority and thus legitimize power based on the alleged or presumed legitimacy of intrinsic or innate biologically distinguishable races or groups. Many manifestations of tactical strategy exist as intolerance, racial discrimination, xenophobia, and violence, and are reflected in governmental policies, such as apartheid, segregation, or separation, as well as bad faith or betrayal.

From the earliest thoughts about colonialism, the racialization of Indigenous people has preoccupied Europeans, and it continues in contemporary social situations. Historical approaches to defining Indigeneity focused on the need to survey and control socialization, mobility, and biological reproduction, while contemporary constructions of Indigeneity are primarily concerned with attributing the cause of Indigenous inequality to the deviant and "othered' Indigene. The breadth and depth of systemic racializing practices have created extraordinary ill health contexts and conditions among Indigenous peoples. How this is achieved was well described in research conducted in public health research that implicates racializing of Indigenous peoples as causes of their ill health, both historically and to the present day.

Social work policy analyst Juanita Sherwood (2010) conducted her research on Australia's public health research and policy to conclude that Australia's Eurocentric attitudes and policies not only contributed to Australian Indigenous poor health status but directly created the conditions, attitudes, ideologies, and policies that have ensured that Australian Aborigines have the worst health in Australia. She demonstrates how scientific positivistic research is achieved through the social constructions of the "other" as deficient Indigenous peoples who would develop assumptions that would bias their questions, methods, analyses, and conclusions, including their recommendations and resulting policies. The derived recommendations would not address the situations that Aboriginal peoples live with, created by the othering and diminishing of them, but would problematize Aboriginal peoples as the cause of their own ill health and develop policies based on the inferiority theme. She points to examples of multiple national research projects that were used to develop Aboriginal policy and practices. In these, researchers, most of whom do not understand or have no sensitivities to Aboriginal communities, based health policy on their assumptions and presumptions that further subjugated the Indigenous peoples. Most significant in this research are two kinds of processes: one that is positivistic in its approach, and the other developed from Aboriginal principles of respectful dialogical research of how different the questions, processes, analyses, and conclusions might be based on the researcher assumptions, values, sensitivities, and connections with the communities they are researching. Sherwood's research demonstrates that the Western model of defining determinants of health are the result of the economic and social exploitation of Aboriginal peoples, with governments complicit in their production of social gradients of health and the social conditions and factors influencing those health outcomes. This dissertation is significant as an example of how government and institutional denial, omissions, policy, and strategies working outside Aboriginal community contexts contribute directly to continuing negative health outcomes. This is not just relevant to Australia, but is a worldwide phenomenon.

Racism should be conceptualized as one of the many indicators of oppression that Indigenous peoples have had to endure. It is an ideology about essentializing people to groups based on phenotype, ancestry and/or culture, and creating differences between groups that are embodied in attitudes, beliefs, behaviours, laws, norms, and practices. This cognitive process is called racialization, and covers unconscious systemic forms, and intentional acts.

Cree Métis educator Verna St. Denis (2002, 2007) aptly showed how the racialization of Indigenous peoples was achieved through many strategies rooted in colonial history and Canadian politics, particularly in the legislation of the *Indian Act* that shaped ideas and practices of constructing an Indian, including who belonged, who did not belong, how one would belong and whether one could belong (2007). These identity politics continue to create a bi-cognitive ambivalence that has been both affirming and destructive, depending on where one is positioned and what colour skin and visual ethnic cues one holds. Critical race analysis, she suggests, is then a strategy for helping to understand how the processes of racialization developed within racist ideologies and politics, and helping to understand how Indigenous youth have come to understand themselves in certain ways damaging to their self-concept and self-identity.

False premises have been created in the *Indian Acts* and residential schools. As a result, Aboriginal people have been removed from their homeland, their nationhood suppressed, their Aboriginal and treaty rights ignored, their governments undermined, and their identity and cultures smothered. The legacy of the colonial history of Canada bears heavily upon Aboriginal people in the form of culture stress. It also distorts the perception of non-Aboriginal people (colonial immigrants), sustaining false assumptions, and a readiness to relegate Aboriginal people to the margins of Canadian society as its remote, historical past (RCAP 1996). No wonder the movement not to take it any more has resounded so forcefully among Aboriginal peoples the colonial world over in the Idle No More protests.

There is danger in Canada's thinking of itself as a fair and just society. The fact that many notions of racism are no longer formally acknowledged does not lessen their contemporary influence in Canada and in the policies that are still unfolding. They still significantly underpin the institutions that drive and constrain federal policy on Aboriginal peoples. They are the foundations of meritocracy in a classed society that thinks whiteness is privileged because the people represented in this social construct worked hard and earned what they have. Whiteness, like race, is but another social construct that is connected with the privileges of the elite from which they come. It is not real, except for its power, privileges, and hegemony.

While racism has been officially disavowed in Canada and beyond, as the Royal Commission on Aboriginal Peoples has argued, it does not end the capacity of political institutions to devise new forms of discrimination and exclusion. Racism continues to remain integral to constructed Canadian consciousness, enforced by education and governments, and entrenched in public media. Canada remains a racist society. It is racist in the sense both of its residual cultural and biological superiority, and in subtle and systemic forms;

it is still deemed an appropriate category in legal and social analysis. As law professor Richard Delgado (1990) commented, "There is change from one era to another, but the net quantum of racism remains exactly the same. Racism is neither created nor destroyed" (pp. 105– 106).

Canadian society has failed to rid itself of this founding construction of racism wrapped in colonialism and Eurocentrism; it remains the deep structure of Canadian thought and contexts. While it began with certain groups like the colonists, it is not singular but involves many groups, their histories, and their successes and achievements, or lack thereof. Past and present education systems that have attempted to forcibly assimilate Indigenous peoples to colonial modes have generated new, multi-generational oppression and traumas. These processes of cognitive assimilation have generated many forms of violence directed at Indigenous peoples, and soul wounds and diseases within them. Evidence of the effects of forced education of Indigenous peoples in residential schools and other institutions are well known to be a substantial contributor to the current high level of suicide, substance abuse, incarcerations, children in care, and family violence.

In a study of the experiences of Aboriginal teachers in Saskatchewan public schools, I worked with my colleagues Verna St. Denis and Rita Bouvier on a study of Aboriginal teachers working in the public schools of Saskatchewan (St. Denis, Bouvier, & Battiste 1998). When we asked them to prioritize their key issues, they noted race and racialization as being the most significant factors in the work they do in schools and in their relations with others in the school, as reflected in other teachers' and administrators' expectations of them, in work performance, in assumptions of their motivation and aspirations (working with Aboriginal issues), and in the system's evaluation of them. White teachers in schools disparage Aboriginal parents in ways that continue to assume that these parents have created their own situations of poverty by their lack of effort, and their alienation and resignation are the result of laziness and other social disorders. In other words, they were the creators of their situation. Their students' resistance to school was their parents' fault, or the fault of their language or culture. It was the same litany of discourses that had been reported in the past century. Several contemporary reports on First Nations, Métis, and Inuit education continue to reveal racism as the ever-present issue in schools rather than to examine the oppressive and discriminating systems that Aboriginal peoples must live in (CCL, 2007; Canada, Senate, 2011; Ireland, 2009; Saskatchewan Joint Task Force, 2013).

The goal of eliminating racism cannot be achieved if we continue to use and rely on the concept of "race." Educators, teachers, and researchers must challenge the typological methods used to create the false concepts of race. Just as the anti-slavery movement of the nineteenth century delegitimized and eventually banned servitude, the antiracist movement of the twentieth and twenty-first centuries are unpacking racial superiority and racism, and in their public critique raising new questions about racialization and racial identity. Today, many stand strong to their experience as being a marker of resilience, and racial identity is now understood as a marker of social relationship rather than as an unalterable individual trait (Lopez, 1994; Zuberi, 2001). By exposing the social, political, religious, and legal underpinning of racism, these movements have raised the consciousness of the world's people and attempted to overcome by law the destructive effects of racism and racial discrimination.

Manifestation of Hate Ideologies

Racism is part of an overarching hate ideology in Eurocentrism. Indigenous peoples continue to live in a persistent climate of hate, disparagement, diminishment, and discrimination that has been projected on them by racism. Systemic change cannot come without concerted efforts to understand hate ideologies, without anti-racist education, and without improving the human rights and social justice of Aboriginal peoples.

To be hated, despised, and threatened by other humans is the ultimate fear of all human beings. Such experiences create numerous and overlapping psychological and physiological distresses in Aboriginal peoples. The most enduring distress is the idea of race itself and the related, abhorrent idea that racial inferiority holds some truth. In its modern form, racism is encoded as a false but controlling category. International and Canadian law continually renounce colonialism, racism, racial discrimination, hate propaganda and crimes, and other forms of violence, yet Canada remains tolerant of certain forms of racism, especially covert and systemic discrimination and sanctioned and sanitized actions and words that damage the Aboriginal spirit.

The union of hate and racism has created tragic outcomes. It has created the socio-historic reality of violence, colonization, cultural and cognitive imperialism, forced assimilation in education, specialized racialized poverty, systemic and individual racism, and residential schools, all of which affect how these statistics of deficiency are created and sustained.

Although racism and oppression has been discussed since at least the 18th century, oppression-related stress is a relatively new concept. Oppression is an old concept; however, stress is a relatively new idea. Psychosocial stress has now become one of the most ubiquitous concepts in scientific health and contemporary discourses. Since the 1960s, a plethora of disciplines including psychology, psychiatry, nursing, medicine, sociology, anthropology, and pharmacology have studied psychosocial stress (Mulhall, 1996).

The symptoms of racial oppression are diverse: poverty, substandard housing, water, and sanitation, increasing health concerns like diabetes and cancer rates, high-risk maternal care, birth defects with FASD, youth disabilities, children in care, unemployment, high stress levels and low coping skills leading to trauma, violence, incarceration, and suicide. Aboriginal peoples face persistent barriers that far exceed those facing non-Aboriginal Canadians. The statistics associated with these categories and Aboriginal peoples are staggering. Under such situations and growing indifference by the federal government and Canadians, a continuum of oppression has led to fragile consciousnesses, poor health, socioeconomic disadvantage, resource alienation, and nihilism among Aboriginal peoples. Similarly, cultural alienation and nihilism have also been recognized as an important cause of poor health (Duran & Duran, 1995). The only reliable resource to combat nihilism is decolonization of the Indigenous experience with Indigenous knowledge.

Educators and teachers must recognize the nature of language as meaning-making from within a particular racial location that is always sliding and changing, floating in a sea of signifiers. Race is a signifier and racism is lived reality, seen in its effects in institutions and systems on individuals and collectivities. We read genetic codes as differences of colour, hair, and bone, and read it as a code of race, a text we can read. The consequences of the system that constructs race and racializing characteristics are evidenced in Aboriginal people being grossly underrepresented in higher education, professions, businesses, government decision-makers, and social institutions, and overly represented in social agencies, courts, youth correctional institutions and penal institutions, and in their incidences of depression and suicide. It is also interconnected with all forms of oppression, including patriarchy, homophobia, ableism, and classism, for in each will be found the core social constructions of superiority and inferiority, of perceived normal and abnormal, and the diminishment of the "other" they appear to represent. Like colonialism, racism is violent, ongoing, and traumatic, and reaches everyone in some form, although it is still denied, uncomfortable to talk about and often creates anger and guilt. It is also difficult for Aboriginal students who have to contend with stresses involving white discursive denial practices or rationalizations that continue the violence on them while also having to live in violent situations of bias, prejudice, discrimination, powerlessness, and racialization that are normalized in society.

Racism is more than race hatred or prejudice; it is about power to oppress and subordinate. It is the structural subordination of a group in society based on the idea of racial inferiority that establishes a hierarchical power relationship. But racism as a learned or acquired set of behaviours can be unlearned, and the law is one of the means by which the nation and government historic-ally have provided incentives for changes in behaviour and attitudes.

In confronting these problems, we need to critically examine and under-stand the false logic of racism. What is the connection between people and their bodies? These connections are social constructions, not biological. Lit-tle exists biologically between people, except male/female or colour of eyes and blood type. Anything else is perceptual. All people are various shades of brown. How can these variations in features add up to justifying discrimina-tion and racism? Any classification is a social system of meaning used to im-pose a value on a characteristic and to give it meaning, such as how it interacts with intelligence, performance, human capacity, and morality. Most scientists and scholars say it should not matter, but within a colonial system, which has created the characteristics and values of the "other," race has been determined to matter greatly. At one end are "short distance" factors, such as the continued use of a false concept of race and genetics in the scientific and health commun-ities that masks impacts of oppression on their bodies. At the other end are "long distance" factors, including health consequences arising from situations, government policies, colonial values and lifestyles, and standards of living.

Mi'kmaw elder Kji Keptin Alex Denny persistently relayed an important precept to educators, teachers, and students: "You can't be the doctor if you are the disease." Aptly, he was addressing using racial categories and other Eurocentric cures in the fight against the disease of racism. Unless Eurocentric education systems eliminatee their racial and cultural paradigm and began to rely on Indigenous knowledge, they remain the disease. Unless Canadian education can be reformulated in a manner in which Indigenous science, hu-manities, and treatment strategies can flourish in an integrated trans-systemic synthesis, the educators will continue to be the disease. Yet, this is only part of the experiences. The statistics do not tell a story of resilience, creativity, and community sharing of love and resources with each other through multiple layers of crises that strike families daily. This is what keeps communities feel-ing committed to be where they are. The next chapter will examine the need for displacing the cognitive imperialism of Eurocentrism, which is based on racism, in the decolonization of existing education.

psychosocial stressors

social status
respect
self-worth

Chapter 7

Respecting Aboriginal Languages in Education Systems

THE RICH AND DIVERSE CHARACTER OF CANADA is represented in First Nations, Inuit, and Métis peoples across Canada speaking some fifty-three to seventy-three Aboriginal languages (depending on how language varieties are categorized) in eleven different language families, as well as French and English (AFN, 1990). These languages inform and animate their knowledge systems. They are essential to exercising their Aboriginal and treaty rights as part of the supreme law of Canada (s. 35 and 52(1), *Constitution Act, 1982*). The Canadian Charter of Rights and Freedoms protects the right to Aboriginal languages as understood as Aboriginal rights. The Charter provides that "[t]he guarantee in this Charter of certain rights and freedoms shall not be construed so as to abrogate or derogate from any aboriginal, treaty or other rights or freedoms that pertain to the aboriginal peoples of Canada" (s. 25). While the Charter provides expressly for the English and French languages, it also provides: "[n]othing in sections 16 to 20 abrogates or derogates from any legal or customary right or privilege acquired or enjoyed either before or after the coming into force of this Charter with respect to any language that is not English or French" (s. 22). In addition, Canada has affirmed the language right of minorities. Article 27 of the *International Covenant on Civil and Political Rights* (1967) states that: "In those states in which ethnic, religious, or linguistic minorities exist, persons belonging to such minorities shall not be denied the right, in community with other members of their own group, to enjoy their own culture, to profess and practice their own religion, or to use their own language." Article 2 of the *International Covenant on Economic, Social, and Cultural Rights* (1967) prohibits discrimination on the basis of language in guaranteeing all such rights, which include such areas as education and freedom of expression, discrimination on the basis of language. Canada acceded to these covenants on 19 August 1976.

Regardless of these constitutional protections of Aboriginal languages and the affirmation of the human right to languages, these concepts are basically the unexplored, suppressed territory in contemporary education, no longer considered as primitive as in colonization, but not yet understood as containing the vast knowledge systems of this continent and its ecosystems and beyond.

Aboriginal peoples as a whole represent a young, growing population in urban areas, reserves, and isolated northern villages. One third of the Aboriginal population is under the age of fourteen years (Avison, 2004, p. 2). This demographic is so widely advanced as to its implications for the future of Canada that it has stirred the Canadian Council of Ministers to move Aboriginal education to a higher level of priority, recognizing that they need to build a skilled and highly qualified workforce in Canada. However, success in provincial schools has meant Aboriginal students having to submit to more assimilative paths, compromising their ancestral language and identities connected to their place, and the continuity with elders and communities as schools have been homogenizing and normalizingh Eurocentric experiences. These then create other problems for Aboriginal peoples, among others.

When First Nations children start compulsory school in a public school, now as in the past, many may experience difficulties, most notably in language arts. This is not unique to any province; it has been found nationally that the academic performance of Aboriginal children remains considerably below majority norms. With 68.7 per cent of all First Nations students in Canada reported in 1996 to be in public schools (RCAP, 1996), the ministers of education and the ministries across Canada have a lot at stake to reduce the Aboriginal student gap, resulting in many important initiatives by provincial governments and school boards to effect modest gains, such as has been occurring in British Columbia. With their emphasis on reporting and on locally based, culturally based activity, British Columbia now leads the provinces in gains in Aboriginal education. Largely the reason for these gains are that most students are already in public schools, and fewer in band-operated schools, thereby reducing the transitions loss between schools and the disparities in funding First Nations schools have had to endure.

This has not gone unnoticed. Many school authorities have taken action through advancing new policies and practices. Across the nation, nearly every territory or province has issued a policy statement and developed action plans and have begun implementation of teacher training and in-service programs, developing an inclusive curriculum, initiating new inner-school programs which enlist teachers and parents in a new, cooperative role.

After more than a century of public schooling among Aboriginal peoples in Canada, the most serious problem lies not only in the failure of public schools to liberate the human potential among Aboriginal peoples, but also in their limiting of diversity of thought to cognitive imperialistic policies and practices. These continue to deny Aboriginal peoples access to and participation in government and policies. They deny the use and development of their own world views and thought through the suppression of Indigenous languages and cultures in schools, and confine education to Western methodologies and approaches which undermine a balanced view of the world and threaten the global future.

In 1983, Saskatchewan Education put forth its philosophy and rationale for Aboriginal and Métis Education in their Five Year Action Plan, and from 1985 through 1995, all school districts that had Aboriginal student enrolments of over fifteen per cent were required to submit Equity Plans each year to be assessed by the Saskatchewan Human Rights Commission. These schools were given five principal areas in which they were to address their progress. They have responded affirmatively, offering a multitude of ways in which they have responded to the issue of raising the educational achievements of Aboriginal children in their district. Although they have been limited by financial resources, they have also restricted their efforts to curricula and program development, with few mechanisms for effective accountability to Aboriginal people and the involvement of parents (RCAP, 1996, p. 441). Much of the early instructional remedies, as was reported in the Equity Reports of the Human Rights Commission in Saskatchewan, ignored the languages of the children, the differential power issues, and the racism in the system.

In this chapter, I shall offer an examination of some insights regarding Aboriginal students and the significance of Aboriginal language education. In addition, I will seek to explain the research available regarding second language learning and English language teaching, and apply these to Aboriginal learners in order to address the incongruities of schooling approaches to meeting the needs of Aboriginal second language learners.

Aboriginal Language Learners

Every child born learns at least one language. In many countries, children learn many languages, both within their own families and in the local schools, making the norm not just bilingualism but multilingualism. This fact stands in stark contrast to the failure of education systems in the Western world to teach second or third languages. Language researchers Mary Heit and Heather Blair (1993) have identified an evolving spectrum of Aboriginal language proficiencies and use that have occurred as a result of the history of Aboriginal peoples in Canada. Educators can expect students to have any of the following diverse language characteristics: be monolingual in an Aboriginal language, be monolingual in English, speak a dialect of English, be bilingual in an Aboriginal language and English, speak an Aboriginal language and some degree of English, or speak English or a dialect of English and some degree of an Aboriginal language. These continua of language capacities are shaped from local conditions evolving from a history of the peoples, and their experiences with settler communities and with government schools. This broad range of linguistic variations will also affect the students' needs for instructional programming, the type of language program chosen (Heit & Blair, 1993, pp. 104–106), and their achievement and success. While linguistic imperialism in colonial languages has eroded Aboriginal languages persistently, there are still many Aboriginal communities in rural and northern areas where students begin school speaking primarily, if not exclusively, their own Indigenous language. On the other side of that spectrum, there are communities where students enter school speaking English or an Indigenous dialect of English, such as Miklish, which is combined English and Mi'kmaq. In almost all of these cases, the English spoken is a non-standard variety of English, which derives from the Indigenous language as it makes a rapid transition from the encounter of English within a Native language community.

When placed in schools, most teachers who do informal assessments of students will be inclined to put Aboriginal students in regular routed classes where English is invariably the language of instruction. While there will be many First Nation, Inuit, and Métis students who appear to have a handle on social English, it should not be assumed that they can manage the same literacy and writing tasks as first language English speakers. Without a recognition of their limited second language understanding and the deep knowledge they carry with their first language, these students will show their disadvantages early, demonstrating increasing difficulty with academic English, in all modes of written and spoken English.

The evaluation of social English skills among First Nations students is fraught with problems because of what is now known about how long it will take Aboriginal students to learn a second language. Language researcher Jim Cummins (1981, 1989) has offered the following observations: second language learners immersed in a new language begin functional language learning in spurts, and over a five-month period will be able to handle the daily patterns of interaction, and the necessary requirements to be part of a group, but they will not have acquired much of the language. I recall working in Eskasoni when teachers would find that after a few months, second language learning Mi'kmaw students seem to be more alert to the nuances of the English language and function better in routines, although for many of the events in school, active English language use may play a very small part, whereas listening and responding are more common. As time goes on, Cummins notes, second language learners begin to learn some idioms, common question-and-answer formats, and may be able after approximately two years of intensive interaction to have acquired enough social language to approximate a conversation that is largely comprised of teacher questions and the child's short, halting answers. Although a child may arrive at this social level of English, he or she has not mastered the many different functions of the language, depending on different topics, places, or speakers. This conversational functionality does not suggest that students are ready for the cognitively demanding tasks of academic English, which research has shown will take approximately five years to develop (Cummins, 1981). It will take eight to ten years before a second language learner is able to think in that second language. This latter point is astonishing to educators who do not understand the implications for second language learners who are in high school, where they are subjected to high levels of language complexity and discourses for which they are still doing mental translations back and forth with the language with which they are familiar.

In my classes, I often ask students if there were any who spoke a language other than English growing up, and if they could recall thinking in English. To other English speakers' surprise, many students say either that they continue to think in Cree or that they recall thinking in English at some point in high school. Thinking in a language, then, does not occur with the second language for many years, if it does at all. This has major implications for students who are processing English language lectures, and must make some translation into a First Nations language, and be taking notes as well. I have had some students who do not take notes at all, choosing rather to listen and try to comprehend the subject matter, as the logic of what they are hearing is their first concern. This memory work is further taxed when the language is particularly complex, or the student is unfamiliar with the new vocabulary, the disciplinary discourses or idioms in the language. Add a professor with a variant dialect of English and the student goes into overload, frustration, and despair.

The Language Crisis and Planning for Change

In Canada, every Aboriginal language is endangered. While as many as 300 Aboriginal languages were recorded in North America (Cook, 1998), Canada has now fifty-three to seventy-three Aboriginal languages within eleven distinctive linguistic families (AFN, 1988). Ten of these language families are First Nations languages, while the others are spoken among the Inuk or Inuit. Over half of these languages, or thirty-eight languages, are spoken in British Columbia (ALTF, 2005). Few surveys have been initiated to access the language loss among First Nations under previous policies, and Statistics Canada had attempted to keep details of this information. With the current trend in statistics to ask for less information, detailed and accurate language data and the state of Aboriginal linguistic vitality in Canada will remain uncertain. What is common knowledge is Aboriginal languages are in decline and are being lamented by most Aboriginal politicians and by the language communities.

In 1988, the Assembly of First Nations (AFN, 1990) studied the state of Aboriginal languages. Their report, entitled *Toward Linguistic Justice for First Nations*, was derived from a survey of 151 out of 600 First Nations in the mid 80s. The report found that two-thirds of those communities surveyed had endangered or critical loss of Aboriginal languages. Endangered languages meant that the older adult population was fluent, with few or no speakers in younger age groups. Critical languages meant fewer than 10 speakers existed. The report found only one third had "flourishing" Aboriginal languages (over 80 per cent of all age groups fluent in their native language) or "enduring" (60 per cent of all age groups). However, these First Nations had a generation gap. While more than three quarters of the older age groups were fluent, among the youth the proportion was rapidly dropping to less than ten per cent. The resiliency of Aboriginal languages was surprising, considering the fact that, as children, many had experienced discrimination when their languages and cultures were denied them in schools. English language instruction was made compulsory in 1920 in all First Nations schools (AFN, 1990). The report noted every First Nation shared similar problems in operating Aboriginal Language Programs (ALPs) due to lack of funds, a shortage of trained language instructors and materials, a lack of support from the community, or lack of continuity in the languages among generations.

Since 1996, Canada has attempted to ascertain mother tongue and languages use in the home using census surveys. Census Canada asked how many households and persons in families spoke other languages outside the official languages. Census Canada reported only 24 per cent of the total population of Aboriginal peoples surveyed reported being able to carry on a conversation in an Aboriginal language (Norris, 2008, p. 316). This was a drop in mother tongue speakers from what was reported as twenty-nine per cent in 1996 (p. 19). Significantly, in the 2001 census, there was a rise in the number of speakers, illustrating that while mother tongue speakers were down, second language speakers were on the rise, giving credence to the impact of second language instruction. In 2006, Inuit were the most likely to have an Aboriginal language (Statistics Canada, 2010) at seventy per cent. First Nations people living on reserve were more likely to be able to speak a First Nations language (fifty-one per cent), whereas only twelve per cent of urban Aboriginal dwellers had knowledge of at least one Aboriginal language, and the Métis were least likely (four per cent) to speak their ancestral languages (Statistics Canada 2010, chart 8). One may conclude, as have the authors of the reports at AFN and Statistics Canada, that there is a clear erosion of capacities of Aboriginal peoples to speak their ancestral language, and, as such, each Aboriginal language exists in a state of endangerment, whether they were considered in 1988 to be flourishing or not.

Additionally, many First Nations educators and authors have reported the devastating consequences of language loss to their identities, their development of self-esteem and self-confidence, their connections with their elders and families, and the losses to their cultures and communities (Grant, 1996; Johnston, 1988; Knockwood, 1992). Elders and educators note that each Aboriginal language should be viewed as endangered, and efforts made to ensure they are stabilized, revitalized, or maintained.

The Canadian data are consistent with international data. Linguistic human rights activist Tove Skutnabb-Kangas (2000) reports the ill health of world languages is attributed to systemic linguistic genocide by the states. Natural forces are not the source or cause of the elimination of Aboriginal languages, she notes. Without the recognition of and appreciation for Aboriginal languages in state policy or practice, Skutnabb-Kangas asserts the world's Indigenous languages will surely vanish from neglect, hegemony of power relations over languages, and official support for other languages.

Stabilizing Aboriginal Languages: The Challenge

Indigenous languages are the most significant factor in the survival of Indigenous knowledge and culture. Indigenous languages in their symbolic, verbal, and unconscious orders structure Indigenous knowledge. Where Indigenous knowledge survives, it is transmitted best through Aboriginal languages. Where Aboriginal languages, heritages, and communities are respected, supported, and connected to elders and education, educational successes among Aboriginal students can be found (Wilson & Battiste, 2011). The first principle of any educational plan constructed on Indigenous knowledge must be to respect Indigenous languages, not just because students have difficulty learning without their first language, but because each language represents a knowledge system that holds a depth of knowing that has not yet been tapped for contemporary education and the future of sustainable development.

Modern educational policy in Canada has focused almost exclusively on English-language instruction, with regional concerns for the retention of French. Without the internal structures and functions of Aboriginal languages that value direct learning, however, Indigenous knowledge will struggle to survive. Elders often speak to the important role language plays in building strong communities, of the importance of relationships with the land, and in storing the collected wisdom and knowledge that enables Aboriginal people to survive and flourish. Ceremonies and rituals help communities and individuals learn the relationships and values manifested in language.

The comprehension of the inherent structure of the language as a model for understanding both how Aboriginal consciousness and rationality function and how they are manifested and renewed in Aboriginal knowledge, heritages, and relationships are the fundamental prerequisites for language education that contributes to saving Aboriginal languages. This is more than learning to speak or read in an Aboriginal language. Aboriginal language education cannot be considered merely a transitional approach to learning English or a token integration of culture to bolster self-esteem.

Educational reforms need to redefine literacy to affirm Aboriginal languages and consciousnesses that are connected to place, for it is place where Aboriginal identity resides. This connectedness and holism are reflected as well in Jeanette Armstrong's comment that the Okanagan word for their language is also the word for "our place on the land," and in her comments of situating land as the teacher: Armstrong (2006) has situated language as a drawing from a relationship with the land.

> The way we survived is to speak the language that the land offered us as its teachings. To know all the plants, animals, seasons, and geography is to construct language for them. . . . We also refer to the land and our bodies with the same root syllable. This means that the flesh that is our body is pieces of the land that came to us through the things that this land is. The soil, the water, the air, and all other life forms contributed parts to be our flesh. We are our land/place. (Armstrong, 2006)

Complexity and Complementarity in Finding Solutions

Since children's oral language is well established as the foundation of literacy, children need to have school activities that build on the home experiences and their home language. This should entail a recognition and acceptance of the ancestral languages and the varieties of English that Aboriginal children bring with them that have been learned in the social context of their relations and networks of home, school, and community. Aboriginal English has been shown to be more than just a non-standard dialect of English. It is a language variety that has been developed and transmitted through many generations from within unique situations when two languages merge in social relationships and networks of home, community, and school. "These structures, regular, fully functional and adequate, continue to serve their social, familial, and community communication needs and are the language form that students bring to school" (Battiste, Kovach, & Balzer, 2010, p. 5). What we have found is that these once thought of as "non-standard dialects" have a much wider appeal in contemporary literature, film, and poetry and can now be illustrated to youth as being a fully functional language system that has been raised in popular literature and pop culture.

Schools that attempt to eradicate Aboriginal Englishes through the privileging of standard English do a disservice to their students. Rather, the need is to embrace and support the diversity of languages currently held by students, and find ways to share the multiple ways communities shape, function, and transmit their languages. Youth can benefit from the study of languages, as well as a study of the standard hybrid form of English, which is not a singularity but rather another hybrid that has gained prestige and thus has been placed in a social power hierarchy with other languages and dialects. Every language meets the vocabulary and communication needs of the people who speak it, and when this language is accessed for further instruction, it provides the base on which all other learning develops, and becomes another source of learning and not a source of shame.

Aboriginal languages, when possible, should include the languages of instruction, through their school years, especially in the elementary years, transitioning into more extensive ESL at the senior levels. Several types of educational language program may have been used for teaching endangered languages: bilingual education, single subject language courses, and immersion programming. These types have different goals, benefits, limitations, and results (Hinton, 2001, p. 182). In communities, where the Aboriginal language is in various stages of erosion, immersion programs at the early childhood level can buttress Aboriginal languages in language shifting status. Bilingual education programs can provide another option for children to learn from the rich knowledge base within Aboriginal languages and to reconnect them with their elders and communities that had their languages driven from them through colonial policy. Several second language learning program options are now available for optimally preparing and transitioning first language speakers to English programming, such as bilingual programming or English as a second language programs. The least effective among these are the early English transitional programs, whereby children are given early but limited support in their first language to exit after kindergarten into full English programs.

Educators must recognize that many second language students are at a disadvantage because they are being taught in a second language and often are being tested in their second and most often least competent language. When the resulting scores are compared to the English-speaking norms in Canada, they are labeled "at risk," "slow learners," or children targeted for "resource" programs. The tests do not adequately assess student competence and knowledge, but are often judged on the extent to which the child has acculturated himself or herself to English structures, vocabulary, and norms that they have not been taught or have not yet acquired. This is often the source of teacher expectations which students have either to live up to or fail. Determining what skills each person must have in order to develop progressively through the education system, and making these the foundation of the curricula within the context of the experiences and knowledge bases of the students, appears to be a far-reaching goal, but one that approaches the current context-based learning.

Different cultures have different styles of learning and knowing. Consider these two statements: "If at first you don't succeed, try, try again" (English). "Watch and listen and do it right, watch and listen and do it right" (Mohawk). The teacher's task is to help students discover the information and ways of knowing accessible to them through English, as well as to recognize the insights their mother tongues have given them (Leavitt, 1995).

The more we accommodate the learning environment to the learner while holding high expectations and accountability to the learner, the more meaningful and successful the learning experience will be for them. Building, then, on the educational and personal experiences they bring to school will prove beneficial. These cultural and language experiences can and should form part of the foundation for every learner and not just be the privilege of the elite.

Learning a language means, among other things, to learn to use a language to socialize, to learn, to query, to make believe, to imagine, and to wonder. In order for students to be allowed and encouraged to continue the development of their cognitive and academic growth while developing the second language, they require continued experiences, growth, and dialogue in their first language. Language programs that provide multiple experiences and connections, beyond conversation and dialogues, become important knowledge building bases for students. For students in a classroom with non-Aboriginal teachers, the situation seems more difficult. However, a non-Aboriginal teacher can and should encourage the dialogue among language groups without having to know the language. Some teachers may see this, at first, fraught with risk, but allowing children to explore the boundaries of knowledge in their first language will build bridges to their knowledge and oral traditions and encourage the cultural milieu and acceptance of different cultures within the school environment. Viewed as an asset, Aboriginal languages and the knowledge embedded in them can create the bridge between the oral and written traditions and be a valuable complement to students' English.

Almost all North American Aboriginal languages fundamentally operate from a view of the world as interrelated and in flux, signifying these relations in highly descriptive prefixes and suffixes with the verbs. Some might even say these are verb-based languages, although this is not to say English could not operate without verbs, or that Algonkian languages do not have nouns. This is significant to current public education and First Nations learners because most school curricula and experience is focused on noun-based learning. Any elementary program is fraught with classifications, categories, and components of all kinds that are developed in all aspects of the curriculum. Names are given to everything and dictionaries expound that every noun has a meaning. Vocabulary development of objects is thus set out very early for children. In many Aboriginal languages, however, the preverbs and suffixes provide a wealth of possibilities, and therefore the names of objects are secondary to knowing how to put multiple combinations together.

In addition, as has been found to be the case among Aboriginal first language students, they appear to have greater ease with social language, and more trouble with academic English language that focuses on these certain discourses, and structures such as noun agreement, prepositions, and complex phrasing that are not translatable forms from their Aboriginal languages. Being aware of the differences that verb- and noun-based languages have within world views can help many educators to understand something more about Aboriginal world views, thought, and consciousness, while addressing a major cognitive gap in learning.

Much innovative Aboriginal language education, development, and research has been pursued in both First Nations and public schools. Yet, due to the sparse curricula available in Aboriginal languages, many programs have focused primarily on language as a subject. When the Aboriginal language is taught in a school, it is taught as an object within a subject area focusing on verbs, vocabulary, grammar, or even conversation. Children are taught the numbers, colours, and names of objects, and not the wealth of diversified knowledge embedded in the rich stores of collective epistemology. Much Aboriginal language instruction neglects the social nature of learning language and the cognitive processes that are part of the language learning. Language is communication among peoples, building on the interrelated interests and connective cognitive links of the learners, not just grammar, structure, syntax, morphology, and phonology. Therefore, core Aboriginal language instruction should not be solely focused on language itself as object, but on the knowledge embedded in that language and the interrelationship formed in the learning, from animals, plants, spirit guides, and the ecology. Learning in Aboriginal languages about the world of knowledge, understanding, and philosophy will do more to enlighten the child to the Aboriginal world than trying to make transitions between Aboriginal languages to English.

Finally, if all the school can do is provide English as a Second Language (ESL) with an English-speaking instructor, let not ESL become equated with another acronym, ESC = Exchange for a Second (and better) Culture. The view held toward English language has historically been imperialistic, and is largely if not solely Eurocentric. Aboriginal children have a rich and varied history and culture for which their leadership has found the political measures to assure its continuity.

The educational system has historically devalued difference and has used difference as a defining element of racism and oppression among First Nations peoples.

We have a long way to go, however. The negative legacy of the Indian Affairs policies on Aboriginal languages represents a significant educational challenge and a crucial test of the resolve of many educators, policymakers, and First Nations people who need to be part of this dialogue and action to affect different outcomes from the past. Understanding and remedying this failure of education has been challenging for many agencies, federal and provincial.

Aboriginal peoples who have lost languages due to assimilation policies are presented with a great challenge, for language loss has been shown to be not purely linguistic, involving sounds and sentence structures, but involves much more, including the socialization of language and knowledge, ways of knowing, and nonverbal and verbal communication.

Diverse program goals, methodologies, frameworks, and resource capacities affect the outcomes of these language efforts. But with the diversity of Aboriginal languages in Canada, there are no standardized measures for these languages and their users. Teachers and program planners must then initiate alternative indicators for demonstrating their successes. Some programs seek to illustrate their effectiveness by demonstrating the scaffolding capacity of Aboriginal languages and students' cognitive flexibility as they test the transferability of skills from one language to another. Toward this end, programs then demonstrate how well their students can achieve in standardized English tests or English content areas. The positive outcomes of these kinds of tests reflect the theory that Aboriginal languages offer a cognitive foundation that allows students to transfer knowledge gained in one language to the second language without interference. This kind of result, then, is viewed in the positivistic evaluation tradition as especially impressive, such as those of the Navajo Rock Point Program and the Puna Leo Hawaiian Language Immersion Programs. These kinds of results appear to create much interest among educators, although whether the students can remain at these levels or whether this makes for added capacity for Aboriginal languages is unknown.

Aboriginal language program successes are tied to many factors and indicators. In successful school language programs, strong grassroots activity is evident and community members are actively involved in the planning, organizing, and implementing of the programs. The success of programs that engage community and parents is built on the extension of education, not just in the school but also within the lives of the students. When parents and community members are engaged in a program, everyone wins. The students are more apt to be involved in their education as well. Parents are in the schools, being connected to their child's teachers and staff, and teachers and staff can expect the students to be more well behaved, more engaged with school, and have multiple opportunities to extend their daily school life into the home and community.

The kind of language program that is selected for the children will depend on several factors: what language is used by the youth; if the community or some adults have a speaking and literacy capacity in the Aboriginal language, what goals are sought among the parents in terms of language skills and capacities, and what kinds of resources the school has. The most effective programs for developing language fluency in an Aboriginal language have been found in total immersion programs.

In Eskasoni, after ten years of immersion language, students were found to have had gains in levels of fluency and identity formation; the year after leaving the program, they were found to be consistently in the top of English language arts. The study, conducted by two of the teachers of the immersion programming, showed in both qualitative and quantitative methodologies that student gains in learning continued after they left the immersion programming, transitioning the skills learned in one program to the next (Paul-Gould, 2012; Sock, 2012).

Immersion is a program that has been aimed primarily at students who are English speakers, although in the case of Eskasoni, many of the students came from dual-language homes. For these latter students, some variation of bilingual education for transition, maintenance, or enrichment would be preferable for developing their language gains and English and/or French language and literacy capacities. Immersion programming offers a proven process for regaining a language that has moved to an endangered category, and where there are some committed adults remaining who are fluent in the language and can act as models, monitors, teachers, and activists in language revitalization.

Student assessments are then best tied to personal performance outcomes, where the teachers can monitor student activity and outputs. There are multiple suggested activities that can be monitored and many provincial documents offer these as part of conventional literacy and subject content assessments. It is, however, more difficult to assess cultural understandings and knowledge as well as values, attitudes, and motivations. Some teachers may note that student attendance or interest has improved, as measured by rates of attendance, questioning, engaging teachers in dialogue, and so on. Other tests determine student's mastery and achievement after Aboriginal language lessons, again more difficult to measure since they involve a teacher's mastery of the oral and written language, skills that are not well established in most Aboriginal communities.

What is possible to assess is found in students' interaction in a cultural and social context. How they perform in communicating and conversing on diverse topics, with different people of many ages, over different locations, and involving many contexts can help establish how capable a student has become. Teachers should keep in mind that learners need to be tested in the language of instruction, not in the dominant language of the school, which is usually English or French. While language proficiency is a targeted goal, each language program will have to decide at what level they construct measures of language capacity to signal "success." Allowing elders and parents to have a role in the evaluation seems important, as well as having students be part of the goal setting.

As diverse language programs have evolved in several countries, testing for language proficiency has taken many diverse processes, and many measures have been used; as well, there has been much criticism offered regarding these measures. For example, some tests are based on adult expectations of what children should be able to produce linguistically; however, students or speakers of Aboriginal languages tend to overestimate or underestimate the students' understanding and emerging language skills. Many programs offer multiple means by which evaluation for language programs can be conducted, including testing oral performances, attitudes and interest, participation, work completed, such as assignments, responses, teacher observations, and teacher-pupil conferences.

Whatever method of language programming that is used, additive bilingual environments ensure learning a second language is accomplished at no cost to the first language. The transitional model of bilingual education operates from the assumption that the minority language student will move toward mastering the English language over time in combination with their first language. Again, the objective is English language proficiency, which many older models of "submersion" programming attempted to achieve. But without the support of knowledgeable teachers trained in second language acquisition, the outcome may lead to students losing their first language, a case of subtractive bilingualism, meaning that in time the student would develop better English and over time would not continue to use and develop their Aboriginal language. Teachers knowledgeable in second language acquisition theory and practice do help establish positive additive environments, and thus teacher training and in-service must remain a strong feature of program planning.

While research has been positive about the result of immersion programming and more recently with Mi'kmaw immersion programming, more research is needed in evaluation, for little is known about Aboriginal cognitive schemata and how Aboriginal languages create diverse ways of knowing. In the early years of language education, academic success also depended on community attitudes and involvement and on the knowledge and training of language professionals. Toward this end, much literature has been offered of the features of language planning that effect the success of these programs. To summarize:

- Assessment strategies should be appropriate for and compatible with the purpose and context of the assessment.
- Students should be provided with sufficient opportunity to demonstrate the knowledge, skills, attitudes, or behaviours being assessed.
- Procedures for judging or scoring student performance should be appropriate for the assessment strategy used and be consistently applied and monitored.
- Procedures for summarizing and interpreting assessment results should yield accurate and informative representations of a student's performance in relation to the curriculum outcomes for the reporting period.
- Assessment reports should be clear, accurate, and of practical value to the audience for whom they are intended (Nova Scotia, 2003, p. 50).
- Individual progress is assessed based accordingly on a continuum of learning, especially in the area of personal development.
- Tie student progress in language ability to their use of language in social and cultural activity.
- Assess student progress continuously, rather than only as the summation of a unit of study.
- Share the results of assessments in a holistic manner, rather than as a mark or letter grade alone.
- Involve students in the assessment of their own learning.
- Involve Elders in developing authentic means of assessing student progress.
- Use the data from student assessments to continuously evaluate and enhance the program. (Western Protocol, 2000, p. 119)

The educational models must move beyond the traditional models of teaching that focus on the learner, the teacher, and the linguistic/language content to focus on "experiential, situational, task-based and problem solving components; cultural and intercultural awareness; strategic competencies; interpretive, interactionalist, symbolic and spiritual uses of language and constructive approaches to culture as part of collective identity formation" (p. 88).

Conclusion

This review of the literature on Aboriginal Language Programs (ALP) illustrates a lack of consistency or compatibility in measuring outcomes of ALPs. This is partly due to the innovation of ALPs and the need to develop the capacity of Aboriginal language communities, teachers, schools, and methodologies in a deep learning cycle. This dissonance needs to be resolved. The key factor in the literature of ALPs is the process of generating and sustaining a community that fosters learning, and reconnecting with the younger generations that ALPs serve. This is a nested activity, notable for its complexity. Also, it requires a school that embraces its connection to the community and its desires. Both community and staff need to recognize that the school is not the only organization with responsibilities for children.

1. Measuring outcomes

While the students' language change is ultimately the impact sought for ALPs, the process for achieving those goals comes in many forms and processes, and teachers and administrators need to focus on training their stakeholders in the benefits of ongoing monitoring and evaluation. Language outcomes may be viewed as changes in students' identity and language use, the clarity of their questions and answers, the number of their questions and engagements, their reading skills or behaviours, their attendance, and so on. This literature review identified programs with diverse measures, but none that could account for success in an ALP.

2. Success of Immersion

Communities and educators have long assumed that the language loss of a generation generated an inevitable path of language loss. They assumed little could be done to stop language loss. Structural approaches involved in creating official language policies and school programming were criticized for not being able to restore languages, as it was assumed that languages must be transmitted as a first language from generation to generation.

Immersion programming in ALP, however, among many Aboriginal communities in Canada and beyond, have demonstrated that language erosion does not have inevitable negative consequences. Rather, immersion programs introduced in many communities have successfully been restoring languages among younger generations, and then among their parents and the larger community, while also contributing to their transition to English and their successes in reading in that second language. The Mohawk Kahnawake Immersion Program and later other immersion programs, such as the Cayuga Immersion program in Six Nations Reserve, to the Ko Hunga Reo and Kura Kaupapa Maori programs in New Zealand, and the Aha Puna Leo Programs in Hawaii, have all illustrated that immersion programming does work for arresting the erosion of Aboriginal languages and reconstructing language in communities. Tricia Longboat notes, "Total immersion programs have proven to be the most effective way to promote fluency in a traditional language. Partial language programs seemed not to work as well as one hundred percent language instruction. This was a fact proven by other Iroquois community education programs in the past; such as language programs in Akwesasne and Kahnawake" (Longboat, 2005, p. 112).

All immersion ALPs report that the success of their programs comes from their most important feature: parent and community engagement and involvement. Longboat (2004) noted that, "When a child goes to school, it does not end the parental influence or responsibility; but it begins a partnership with educators and those involved in the education system. There should not be a time or place when parents are not cognizant of their child's lives" (p. 109). The strongest voices of support in successful ALPs came as the parents and community struggled to achieve new directions for the school, urging and rekindling the fire of commitment among parents to change conventional schools to immersion schools. When engaged, their commitment yielded active support and a direct role in education. The success of the Maori, Hawaiian, Mohawk, Cayuga, and others drew from a base of support that alerted parents to the need for political activism, and ushered in a new resolve to take up their language in new ways, developed incentives to parents and familiarized them with the process and practices that required their cooperation and support. Without community and parental support, these programs cannot have success. Successful schools also enlist elders, and draw on their wisdom and knowledge, and in so doing, reinvigorate the customary role of elders as transmitters of traditional knowledge.

3. ALP planning

ALP requires clarity of roles. The animate roles must be comprehensible in providing direction and administration of the programs — including the roles of parents, community, principal, boards of education, and teachers. Early and continuous communication and dissemination of information to the community and parents ensures successful aspects of program planning, as well as the engagement of parents from the beginning. Successful development of a language plan includes:

- Program visibility in the school system through administrative policy development and implementation.
- Development of a strong supportive school environment.
- Involvement of committed community resource people to monitor and guide the process of development for one year.
- The participation of parents.

- Creating general community awareness and support for the plan by the Band Council.
- Financial resources to hire persons to develop, maintain, and expand the program once [it is] set in place (Hill, 1985, p. 11, as cited in Longboat, 2004, p. 53).

Students are not just passive recipients of the language programs but are active learners and activators of learning and respect in schools. Students must be treated with respect, be given choices, and be valued for the knowledge they bring. Likewise, ALP students demonstrate respect for others, act as mentors and guides for substitute teachers, and are often the best behaved among the students.

ALPs achieve success in many ways. Fluency is the least likely factor to be able to assess, as there are no reliable fluency measures for Aboriginal languages. While fluency is a desired outcome, research in ALPs has confirmed that a program must be activated for as long as six years before fluency is achieved. Thus, it may be unproductive to attach too much meaning to results that are attached to fluency. Enlisting elders and community members to assist with determining student capacity and skills may be more useful, for it is in the intergenerational transmission of language that language be generated and restored. Teachers may use a multitude of methods to assess student capacity, interest, motivation, knowledge, and skills, although the least valuable among these is attendance rates, which may be related to factors other than the program components. While some ALP noted that attendance had increased with language programming, not all could show this result.

4. Ongoing systematic evaluation

Evaluations have long been associated with dread and fear, as any weighing of the merits of a program or school is threatening to those being evaluated. Negative reactions to evaluations can be reduced when the community and school staff are involved early in creating benchmarks and processes that are continually monitored and evaluated. These may be in the form of ongoing data collecting from parents, students, and teachers and staff. This process-based evaluation is effective in informing stakeholders of the progress of the program and the ongoing accountability of the work toward achieving the goals of the program. Evaluations take time, money, energy, planning, and skill — all of which are taxing on a new program. Evaluations must be ongoing, planned early in the program, and engage parents and the community.

CHAPTER 8

Displacing Cognitive Imperialism

Displacing systemic discrimination against Indigenous peoples created and legitimized by the cognitive frameworks of imperialism and colonialism remains the single most crucial cultural challenge facing humanity. Meeting this responsibility is not just a problem for the colonized and the oppressed, but rather the defining challenge for all peoples. It is the path to a shared and sustainable future for all peoples. . . .

Dr. Erica Irene Daes, United Nations Working Group on Indigenous Peoples at the UNESCO Conference on Education, July 1999

IN 1980, AT STANFORD UNIVERSITY, I took a course from Professor Martin Carnoy called Cultural Imperialism in Education, which was one of the most important courses for aiding my insights into the politics of knowledge production and dissemination. A labour economist with a special interest in the political economy of the educational system, Carnoy specialized in comparative analysis, and in this course on an examination of educational development in India, Africa, and South America. The manner and effect of that educational history gave me an entrance to the hegemonic economics of the Western world that took over the systems in those countries, thus affecting how their educational systems emerged and the priorities that were fostered. From these comparative analyses of many countries and the common themes that emerged, I got my foundational "ahah" moments.

Graduate students are constantly emerging with these moments of insight. They helped me see beyond the educational systems to the larger features of a system that carves out its strategies ultimately in and through colonization, and the manner by which education embeds the colonial apparatus in structures and discourses of education, particularly through policy, priorities, curriculum guides, and teacher training. These self-sustaining systems are created by state laws for public education, and delegated to professionals who ensure the curriculum fits the outcomes. Assessments are made to ensure the curricula, goals, and resources are appropriate, the teachers are fitted to the tasks, and institutions are coherent in their procedures and financially responsible for the funds given. On the face of it, such activities appear to be a benign and valued set of actions from which both the citizens and the nations benefit, as they are fitted to societal goals for the political, social, and economic outcomes sought for the nation — in this case, responsible citizens prepared to work and live together effectively.

What was made clear to me was that education, like the institutions and societies it derives from, is neither culturally neutral nor fair. Rather, education is a culturally and socially constructed institution for an imagined context with purposes defined by those who are privileged to be the deciders, and their work has not always been for the benefit of the masses. Education has its roots in a patriarchal, Eurocentric society, complicit with multiple forms of oppression of women, sometime men, children, minorities, and Indigenous peoples. As a cultural manifestation of society, education in North America is hegemonically distributed within raced, classed, and gendered systems. In the last century, multiple-voiced resistance to and calls for transformation of these systems have created a wealth of scholarship of a wide array of issues dealing with cultural studies, postcolonial and post-structural studies, anti-oppressive education that reveals different kinds of theories and practices that underscore the uneven politics of knowledge and learning. Framed in multiple theories, we have become aware of the great losses to the human spirit and capacity when not all sectors of society have gained or benefited from the culturally exclusive, patriarchal educational system.

Despite the fact that all peoples have knowledge, the transformation of knowledge into a political power base has required the control of the meanings and diffusion of knowledge. Elite groups in society use knowledge and the control of knowledge to exercise power over certain economic and cultural interests, which are decided by politicians in collaboration with interest groups, the amalgamation of interests in political parties, and in power interests, such as lobbies, corporations, and organizations. Such have been the controlling agents of education, and the rewards are the outcomes of working within that economy. Cognitive imperialism then generates knowledge legitimation, production, and diffusion, thus positioning some knowledge connected to power, and others marginalized, dismissed, or lying in wait until they are found useful to the outcomes needed in society.

While all of humanity's knowledge bases are drawn similarly from experience, perception, cultural transmission, and experimentation, not all peoples equally value those experiences, nor do they put their faith equally in their perceptions. Science was not always valued as a knowledge foundation, but was welcomed when it could show that it was a method for thinking and not a danger to the Catholic Church's teachings about the centrality of God. As such, method has become more of an ideological way of knowing than an understanding of self in the world. Both religion and philosophy serve the same purpose of coming to know one's place in the universe, although they have had different trajectories from science.

Approximately 600 million Indigenous people in the world exist in various landscapes and ecologies. Indigenous peoples around the world have lived in their ecologies, acquiring, developing, and sustaining relationships with their environments. Each generation has passed this knowledge and experience to succeeding generations through its language. The teachings have created the foundation for their knowledge, culture, and heritage — in Indigenous peoples, in particular, in their knowledge as well as of their relationship with natural resources. Indigenous peoples have a science or way of knowing, but it is a concept that has embodied a way of life, an intimacy and directness with nature. Indigenous knowledge is what directly links knowledge to place and to the relationships within that place. It thus refers to the complex set of knowledge and technologies existing and developed around specific conditions of populations and communities Indigenous to a particular geographic area.

Like all peoples, Indigenous peoples and settler colonialists have explored and continue to explore their environments for the insights and discoveries they bring. In some ways they have used similar tools and strategies to know, and arrived at similar thoughts about their place. But for Indigenous peoples, who have attempted to access the deeper order hidden in the ecologies where they live, this is not just about land ecology. Cree educator Willie Ermine explains:

> The year 1492 marked the first meeting of two disparate world-views, each on its own uncharted course of exploration and discovery for purposeful knowledge. The encounter featured two diametric trajectories into the realm of knowledge. One was bound for uncharted destination in outer space, the physical, and the other was on a delicate path into inner space, the metaphysical. (1995, p. 101)

Indigenous peoples continue this path of discovery of the inner space that provides an implicit order of reality and its sources to comprehend life, residing in various outcomes such as the Cree call *mawatowisowin*, "the capacity to connect to the life force that makes anything and everything possible" (p. 110) or *netukulimk* meaning, in Mi'kmaq, a lifestyle that protects the whole and seeks well-being. Such knowledge, facilitated by ritual, ceremony, tradition, language, and senses, enabled the greatest discoveries in their land, their spirituality, and their purposes. Inner space discoveries of the spiritual connections to all things were necessary foundations for pursuing and maintaining *mawatowisowin* or *netukulimk*. These required deep introspective learning and attention, not only to the teachings of elders and to the ancestors, but also deep connections to how one is present with one-self. Because both of these foundations were important learning, it required maximum non-interference in one's life journey, allowing each person to develop naturally into their giftedness and wholeness. Teaching, then, was nonintrusive and subtle, and reflected the cultural values and well-being of the community (Little Bear, 2000). This way of knowing continues to be cultivated in and through multiple traditions, ceremonies, intuition and re-flection, and deep connections to the universe manifested in another way of knowing that has been crucial to Indigenous peoples' survival, how their ancestors came to know, and how they continue to enrich the lives of the people. This kind of knowing, while similar to and different from science methods, is a foundation for a knowledge system that recognizes wholeness and connectedness and the benefits to humanity when one is attuned and connected to this awareness.

Cognitive imperialism is a form of manipulation used in Eurocentric edu-cational systems. Built on damaging assumptions and imperialist knowledge, educational curricula and pedagogy are built on a monocultural foundation of knowledge, and privileges it through public education (Battiste, 1986). Cog-nitive imperialism relies on colonial dominance as a foundation of thought, language, values, and frames of reference as reflected in the language of in-struction, curricula, discourses, texts, and methods (Apple, 1982, 1997; Bear Nicholas, 2008; Farmer, 2004). As a result of cognitive imperialism in educa-tion, cultural minorities in Canada have been led to believe that their poverty and powerlessness are the result of their cultural and racial origins rather than the power relations that create inequality in a capitalistic economy.

Despite the rich diversity in humankind today in terms of knowledge, skills, talents, and heritage, only one visible, powerful, and defining tradition of knowledge has been embraced, developed, and diffused throughout the world. This tradition has largely been led by men in the hierarchal society of Western society and based on the Eurocentric tradition, particularly in its understand-ing of the knowledge of the humanities and sciences. As diverse as Aborig-inal peoples are in Canada and beyond, so also are their ways of knowing and learning. Their stories of Creation and their psychological connectedness to their cosmology play a determining role in how Aboriginal peoples envision themselves in relation to each other and to everything else. Knowledge is not secular. It is a process derived from creation, and, as such, it has a sacred pur-pose. It is inherent in and connected to all of nature, to its creatures, and to human existence. Learning is viewed as a life-long responsibility. Knowledge teaches people how to be responsible for their own lives, develops their sense of relationship to others, and helps them model competent and respectful be-haviour. Traditions, ceremonies, and daily observations are all integral parts of the learning process. They are spirit-connecting processes that enable the gifts, visions, and spirits to emerge in each person.

Creation endows people with sacred gifts that emerge in different stages of their lives, enabling them to find their place in the cosmos and in their national traditions and ethos. Individual development is not predetermined, or based simply on cause and effect. Rather, inherent talents and capabilities are animated when people are faced with life decisions and situations. One Saulteaux Ojibwa story holds that when people are born, their spirits are in shock from leaving their loving world to come to this world, and they remain suspended until they receive nourishment from this life (Knight, 2001). People must know their own gifts and capabilities, strengths and weaknesses, interests and limits to be able to develop their self-esteem and concept of self. Self-knowledge and transmitted teachings are equally important, and people cannot effectively learn their purpose and actualize that purpose unless they receive both.

The history of education among Indigenous peoples has been strikingly similar. Education has been used as a sword of cultural imperialism to assimilate Native North America into a hegemonic system, not so that they might take their rightful place in the market economy after their economies were destroyed, but to be held hostage to systems of economy created outside the Aboriginal context. Cognitive imperialism is not just symbolic cultural assimilation, but wholesale cognitive whitewashing, working through the loss of Aboriginal languages that themselves inform the perspectives and values and world views of the peoples. As a result, success has been closely associated with Aboriginal students' losing their languages and cultural connections; many often do not see the merit of holding to Aboriginal language systems, cultures, or world views, nor understand the wealth of knowledge within their own systems. This self-doubt, coupled with racism, continues to sabotage their expectations for their own futures. The government of Canada and religious groups have used schools and their curricula as the swords of cultural transmission; they impose a cultural and political hegemony built on superior/inferior relations. Boarding schools for Aboriginal children are a legacy of Canadian society's intolerance toward Aboriginal society, language, culture, government, and social and spiritual beliefs. Their experiment has failed Aboriginal peoples, and other Canadians as well.

Education is a process by which a culture expresses its reality and values, processes its culture, and integrates its culture into it. The interface between culture and education is primarily a communicative art (Cajete, 1986), and the first colonial agents in English and French in Canada have created the frames for communicating their colonial histories, languages, and knowledge legacies, as well as influence the trajectories of knowledge production for their institutions of health, education, governance, and law.

For Indigenous students, this education has been partial, fragmented, alienating, and disrupting to the inner wholeness that their education trajectory has been. Aboriginal peoples have not participated in Canada's political creation, its socio-cultural transformations, and its goal setting. If it were not that the Indigenous peoples of the world held the original land for the institutions and were the original creators of potatoes, rice, and corn, as well as the standard staples of the global food chain, and have cared for the biodiversity of the world, Indigenous peoples would be minor players in all of its configurations.

Today, the critically important postcolonial quest for Indigenous peoples is to bring their knowledge and practices fully into their children's lives. Reclaiming, recovering, restoring, and renewing Indigenous peoples' rights, which includes Indigenous knowledges and languages, is a revisionist educational project of great magnitude. It is clearly a project that many Indigenous peoples have taken to their sites of work and study, whether in the political activism of blockades and protests in and over the waters, in the courts, and in schools and classrooms. Teachers and students everywhere need to be aware of its significance.

While there are many features of the current systems of knowledge, knowing, teaching, and learning that have undergone multiple changes under a narrative of educational equity, the education of Aboriginal students remains Eurocentric in its structure and content, in its exclusion of Aboriginal cognition, knowledge, and ways of knowing. What a new curriculum must do is replace the failed Eurocentric educational practices with a more equitable and broader theory of education that informs, includes, and builds with Canadian pluralities and identities. This educational transformation must conform to the new constitutional vision of Canada as a nation in its own right rather than a derivative British colony. This new theory of education is just one part of the global transformation toward a fair and just postcolonial society.

While the federal government has adopted the policy of Indian Control of Indian Education, since 1972 efforts have been made to develop Aboriginal-adapted curriculum locally within these First Nations schools and communities, although little if any of this adapted cultural curriculum has been taken up by provincial public schools and teachers. As a result, schools have translated the transition of First Nations students into the public schools as requiring a culturally assimilative process, using the provincial curricula for their own schools as the base. Educational equity and other social justice initiatives have ushered in some policies of cultural inclusion, through the adaptive dimensions of curriculum, but Aboriginal content has been so marginalized, fragmented, and delivered from a Eurocentric perspective as to have not much effect on students. Education continues to be driven by Eurocentric foundations of education, on the pretext that it is universal, necessary, and effective for achieving success.

The provinces have been the constitutional agents of teacher education and training as well as of assessments and standards-setting. What First Nations first received with the policy of Indian Control of Indian Education was managerial control over schools in the hiring of teachers, control over the finances they received as a formula devised by Indian Affairs, and management of the procedures devised for them from federal departments in charge of Indian affairs. Many schools developed a school board or committee, drawing from their local communities, but control mechanisms remained outside these committees. For the most part, the provinces authorized the training and certification of their teachers, and largely educational innovations came from universities and the collaborations they engendered, and curricula were developed and authorized by the provinces. This was not control, but mere management of the administration of a school.

In 1998, Canada's statement of reconciliation with Aboriginal peoples acknowledged:

> Sadly, our history with respect to the treatment of Aboriginal people is not something in which we can take pride. Attitudes of racial and cultural superiority led to a suppression of Aboriginal culture and values. As a country, we are burdened by past actions that resulted in weakening the identity of Aboriginal peoples, suppressing their languages and cultures, and outlawing spiritual practices. We must recognize the impact of these actions on the once self-sustaining nations. . . . In renewing our partnership, we must ensure that the mistakes, which marked our past relationship, are not repeated. The Government of Canada recognizes that policies that sought to assimilate Aboriginal people, women and men, were not the way to build a strong country. We must instead continue to find ways in which Aboriginal people can participate fully in the economic, political, cultural and social life of Canada in a manner that preserves and enhances the collective identities of Aboriginal communities, and allows them to evolve and flourish in the future. (Canada, Statement of Reconciliation, 1998)

First Nations peoples have been highly critical of control under the Indian Affairs regime. So have studies such as those by the Auditor General of Canada (2000, 2004, 2010) and the Senate Report of the Standing Committee on Aboriginal Education (2011). The Senate Report calls on Canada to develop a First Nations Education Act that would provide sufficient resources to develop an education system with second- and third-level structures that would be optional for communities to accept. The Senate committee found multiple problems with current funding mechanisms, and urged the federal government to address this in statutory form and to take account of the diverse locations and demographics and to fund among other things language revitalization and language preservation. These are minimal changes that need to occur.

At present, following on the several reports that have criticized the federal government's lack of a system of education for First Nations, the federal government is poised to initiate new legislation that would bring First Nations education under a singular education system. The diversity of First Nations, Métis, and Inuit peoples must be considered in any change, including their participation and voice, considering their unique situations and locations, and involving their leadership and elders. Once again, however, the government has been responding reactively rather than proactively, developing the rudiments of this legislation in consultation with policy analysts rather than with Indigenous stakeholders in an appropriate consultative process. To achieve a system that meets the needs of diverse peoples in diverse locations with differential resources and different histories requires more than a few months of investigation and discussion with chiefs, parents, and educators. As a new minister of Indian Affairs has been announced, the urgent need for this minister and any further changes in bureaucracy to revisit the analyses and recommendations of the RCAP, as this document resounds as one of the most significant documents of the last century regarding studies done with Aboriginal peoples.

RCAP's comprehensive research spans five volumes that fill the gap in knowledge, most notably in their methodology. Over a period from 1990 to 1996, their extensive collaboration and consultation with Aboriginal people throughout Canada involved extensive travel and face-to-face encounters with thousands of Aboriginal people in formal and informal hearings, meetings, research, reviews of documentation, and reports, along with thousands of pages of transcripts. They reviewed policy, literature, and research addressing these most comprehensively, and the historical relations of First Nations, Métis, and Inuit from a holistic, academic, legal, and cultural perspective, taking into account the totality of experience Aboriginal peoples have had with other people, societies, governments, and institutions, and their desires, challenges, and obstacles that future policy would have to address.

The RCAP's original mandate was to unravel the effects of generations of exploitation, violence, marginalization, powerlessness, enforced cultural imperialism, and racism among Aboriginal peoples. In addition, they were to make recommendations to Canada on how to make effective changes and reform that would make a significant change in the lives of Aboriginal peoples. Their voluminous reports and written documents offer the most current understanding of the nature of the colonial problem as well as the continued aspirations of Aboriginal people for their children and future. The information is a wealth of comprehensive historical records, together with currently tried solutions and their ongoing effects on Aboriginal peoples. These understandings and recommendations represent the largest research project ever undertaken in Canada, and its recommendations are foundational to this century's mandate in all aspects of Aboriginal peoples' lives.

The Royal Commission *Report* concludes that the painful legacy of colonial history bears heavily upon Aboriginal people in the form of cultural stress, and that the time has come to correct false assumptions, especially in education. What this means is that it is not just in First Nations education that transformation will occur, but in the education of Canadians at large. Federal boarding schools and the push to assimilate Indians through urbanization are policies that cannot be initiated without the partnership of federal, provincial, and First Nations governments. Aboriginal peoples saw a reformed education providing a key to escaping poverty and the conditions that poverty and assimilation policies created, such as the negative impacts and consequence of losing Aboriginal languages and cultures. Out-dated policies must be reconciled and new partnerships established to revitalize Aboriginal people, languages, and cultures. For every educator, our responsibility is making a commitment to both unlearn and learn — to unlearn racism and superiority in all its manifestations, while examining our own social constructions in our judgements and learn new ways of knowing, valuing others, accepting diversity, and making equity and inclusion foundations for all learners. As Parker Palmer (1980) suggests, "we don't *think our way* into a new kind of living; *we live our way* into a new kind of thinking" (p. 188). Further reconciliations need to be found with the Aboriginal languages in Canada, the subject of the next chapter.

CHAPTER 9

Recommendations for Constitutional Reconciliation of Education

> It is only through the decolonization of our minds, if not our hearts, that we can begin to develop the necessary political clarity to reject the enslavement of colonial discourse that creates false dichotomy between Western and Indigenous knowledge.
>
> Donaldo Macedo (1999), as cited in Semali & Kincholoe, 1999, p. xv.

AS EDUCATORS AND TEACHERS BEGIN to confront new schemes of Indigenous knowledge and learning in reconciliations that create ethical, trans-systemic educational systems, they will need to identify new processes. These include raising the collective voice of Indigenous peoples, exposing the injustices in our colonial history, deconstructing the past by critically examining the social, political, economic, and emotional reasons for silencing Aboriginal voices in Canadian history, legitimating the voices and experiences of Aboriginal people in the curriculum, recognizing it as a dynamic context of knowledge and knowing, and communicating the emotional journey that such explorations will generate.

Creating a balance between the two world views is the great challenge to modern educators. Yet, it is also in creating the balance that the real justification for Indigenous knowledge is most needed. Educators are witnessing throughout the world the weaknesses in the knowledge base of human science and technology. No longer are we able to turn to Eurocentric science and contemporary technologies to rid us of modern society's mistakes of the past or to clean up our planet for the future of our children. Not only have those in modern society found that they need to make new decisions about their lifestyle to heal their body and maintain the planet, but also we are becoming increasingly aware of the limitations of modern knowledges that have placed our collective survival in jeopardy.

As Aboriginal peoples, we have experienced and generated knowledges of how to survive and flourish in our homeland. Our stories of ancient times tell us how, and our language provides those instructions. The Creator gave knowledges to all peoples, but it is not clear what those instructions are in the languages of the modern world. But it is known the modern world is experiencing problems in finding the means and the knowledge to sustain the earth and its creatures.

Canadian administrators and educators need to respectfully blend Indigenous epistemology and pedagogy with Euro-Canadian epistemology and pedagogy to create an innovative ethical, trans-systemic Canadian educational system. At present, without supports for the Indigenous languages of this land, Aboriginal epistemology is being allowed to die, and another world of knowledge that could help sustain it. To deny that tribal epistemology exists and serves a lasting purpose is to deprive Aboriginal children of their inheritance as well as perpetuate the belief that different cultures have nothing to offer but exotic food and dances or a shallow first chapter. As Nisga'a Rod Robinson has noted,

> Today the Aboriginal people and other Canadians stand on opposite shores of a wide river of mistrust and misunderstanding. Each continues to search through the mist for a clear reflection in the waters along the opposite shore. If we are truly to resolve the issues that separate us, that tear at the heart of this great country . . . then we must each retrace our steps through our history, to the source of our misperception and misconception of each other's truth. (As cited in McGregor, 2013, p. v)

The pedagogical challenge of trans-systemic education is not just reducing the distance between Eurocentric thinking and Aboriginal ways of knowing but engaging decolonized minds and hearts. (Visano & Jakubowski, 2002)

With the development of the First Nations education legislation with the *Mi'kmaw Kina'matnewey* in Nova Scotia, and the First Nations University of Canada, First Nations are well on their way to making a difference with advocating and administering their own schools, organizations, and boards. In each instance, they have resolved to involve the elders and Indigenous knowledges in their development of education and learning, building on key partnerships with the federal government and provincial officials and school districts where they are located. Thus, in this way, are they are initiating a more balanced spectrum of education that they were denied under earlier federal policies. The issues have yet to be resolved. First Nations schools do not have the same funding formula for their schools as provinces do, and with needs sometimes very different, First Nations schools have not been able to develop on a par with provincial schools. Furthermore, provincial authorities have not decided how to reconcile Aboriginal knowledge, ways of knowing and learning, making room within a school schedule for the additions these would require. Teacher professional development is needed, and content standards and guides across ✕ the multiple grades, to name just a few areas of concern.

While several provinces and territories have attempted to articulate standards for teaching Indigenous heritage in the classroom, few have articulated standards for teaching Indigenous knowledge. In provincial and territorial educational systems, blending Indigenous knowledge into the curricula involves three processes: respecting the diversity of Indigenous knowledge's protocols, preparations, and purposes; understanding the multi-levels of preparation and purpose in transmitting Indigenous knowledge; and developing constitutional and ethical responsibilities for those researching Indigenous knowledge.

All teachers have been educated in Eurocentric systems that have dismissed Indigenous knowledge and pedagogy. Similarly, Aboriginal language teachers have been trained to analyze Aboriginal language structures according to Eurocentric linguistic structural models instead of according to the epistemological foundations of the language itself.

The University of Saskatchewan's College of Education faculty embarked on a three-year teach-the-faculty program in 2010 aimed at providing a series of speakers, modules, experiences with elders and ceremonies, and dialogue with Aboriginal faculty to help faculty and staff understand their role and responsibilities in advancing Aboriginal education. This experiment is still unfolding, but it has at least commenced a process for educating the educators and finding ways to include Aboriginal content, learning, Indigenous knowledge, and anti-racism in the teacher training program at both elementary and secondary schools.

Elders, knowledge keepers, and workers are indispensable to the process of appropriate Aboriginal language education in schools and in teacher training institutions. The preparations, ceremonies, and rituals required for teaching certain parts of Indigenous knowledge will confront the existing tension about teaching religion in secular public schools. Public schools today seek to balance church and state over issues such as teaching evolutionary theory and disallowing prayer or spiritual ceremonies in the classroom. The preparations required for teaching some parts of Indigenous knowledge represent a categorization dilemma for administrators or educators. If they approach Indigenous knowledge as a way of knowing, this problem may be resolved. If they approach it as religious content, this will create obstacles to the dissemination of Indigenous knowledge in the public school system.

Recent losses to Indigenous knowledges, heritages, and languages caused by Eurocentric methods of research and categorization are very real. Before further research is done, ethical guidelines on research practices must be set in place. Vetting research on Indigenous knowledge, either through a constitutional and legal duty to consult or through a generalized central ethics committee, is a necessary prerequisite to protecting Indigenous knowledge for the future. The way that Indigenous knowledge is presented in the school system must also be subject to ethical guidelines. Even though the commodification of knowledge in books, marketing, and institutions is a seemingly normal aspect of education, the commodification of Indigenous knowledge without consent, consideration, or compensation is another form of exploitation and marginalization and must be avoided.

Recommendations for Constitutional Reconciliation

Several minimum requirements are needed in order to create a decolonized, ethical, and balanced trans-systemic educational system based on reconciling Aboriginal and treaty rights within the various educational provisions of provinces or in a federal First Nations Act. Some of the most important principles or guidelines are as follows.

1. Affirm Canada's Commitment to Indigenous Knowledge

Canada should affirm that Indigenous knowledge is an integral and essential part of the national heritage of Canada that must be preserved and enhanced for the benefit of current and future Canadians. Indigenous knowledges should be viewed as a constitutional right that has to be reconciled with the federal and provincial education systems. Canada, the provinces, and territories should work together to ensure that Indigenous knowledge is respected and promoted in all funded education programs, and in an appropriate range of documents and contexts.

2. Recognize and Affirm Aboriginal and Treaty Rights as Creating Constitutional Educational Jurisdictions

The Aboriginal and treaty territories should be recognized and affirmed as constitutional educational territories under s. 35(1). Similarly, for the Aboriginal peoples who entered into treaties with the King of Great Britain, the treaty boundaries should operate as constitutional educational territories. The geographic or territorial boundaries of either Aboriginal or treaty rights should be the primary units of administration of education for these peoples. This constitutional concept for the delivery of an appropriate education for the beneficiaries is distinct from the existing political boundaries of the provinces and territories. These new educational jurisdictions should operate in the same way as provincial boundaries, and be the source for encouraging Indigenous knowledges and languages in the school systems. In case of overlapping boundaries, power should be constitutionally reconciled.

3. Affirm Aboriginal Lifestyles and Intergenerational Use of Indigenous Knowledge

Canada, its provinces, and territories should recognize and affirm that Indigenous knowledge requires the protection of the lifestyles that permit intergenerational use of the lands, traditional ecological practices, and the maintenance of cycles of interaction with species and land forms in a traditional lifestyle of hunting, fishing, trapping, planting, and gathering foods and medicinal plants. Most teachings that Aboriginals pass on to their children comes through daily living, like making baskets, drying salmon, hunting caribou, berry picking, and other seasonal activities particular to place. Indigenous knowledge, then, requires the protection of the land, the water, the forests, and the ecological environment for these generations and those to come.

[handwritten marginalia: "?] really?"]

4. Affirm Aboriginal Teachings of Next Generations within Place

Canada, its provinces, and territories should affirm that First Nations, Métis, and Inuit children are invaluable sources of intergenerational transmission of traditional knowledge. Education, therefore, needs to encourage the development and survival of that knowledge within educational sites as sources of knowledge for environmental sustainability, which also needs to be supported by school structures and distance education to enable families to continue their traditional lifestyles.

5. Develop and Support Indigenous Knowledge Innovations in Educational Institutions

[handwritten marginalia: "? roles & extent"]

Canada, its provinces, and territories should develop effective and enriched First Nations, Métis, and Inuit education to provide a choice to parents and children, using multiple approaches and customized interventions related to First Nations, Métis, and Inuit language, knowledge, learning, and heritage. This might include identifying targeted "model" schools that are fully funded, and developed in a model similar in theory to the Kaupapa Maori schools of New Zealand. This calls for developing a "promising and tested best practice models" approach, and creating the examples for other schools to follow.

6. Develop Opportunities to Learn in Order to Teach

Canadian teacher preparation institutions need to ensure all teachers have opportunities to learn and acquire Indigenous knowledge in appropriate contexts and in multiple ways. They should be able to explore and develop Indigenous knowledge in a rich, dynamic educational context that combines both Indigenous and other knowledge systems. The University of Saskatchewan's land-based master's degree for teachers provides a model at the graduate level where teacher cohorts spend several weeks in an Indigenous site learning from elders, in ceremony and on the land, while they also take core courses leading to a master's in education.

7. Create New Certification and Standard Setting for First Nations Schools

First Nations schools need to develop their own standards and certification requirements for their schools that embrace national and local competencies in Indigenous knowledge. Provincial certification builds typically on two levels of academic specializing and professional skill building. First Nations schools should identify standards for their schools that target academic and informal learning as well as appropriate core knowledge and skills for teachers working in their schools that should be respected by the provinces and territories.

8. Encourage Research and Innovations in Classroom Work

First Nations schools, Canada, its provinces, and territories should identify teachers who are Indigenous knowledge holders and provide support through financial incentives for creative and innovative work, as well as working with centres of excellence such that they may form a working network among these teachers and with other educators for collaborative work, research, development, and support in their classrooms. Teachers should be eligible for awards to support creative and innovative work by way of reduced teaching loads, travel, dialogue, workshops, and internet communication systems to assist others in developing and sharing best practices and new programming.

9. Adopt Principles and Guidelines for Respectful Protocols

Canada, its provinces, and territories, in collaboration with Aboriginal peoples, should accept the principle that any social, cultural, or educational initiative for First Nations students that is proposed to use, develop, or support Indigenous knowledge be accompanied by signed authorities or otherwise appropriately acknowledged Aboriginal and treaty signatories who accept and sanction the use of those traditional practices and protocols. At minimum, Canada, its provinces, and territories should adopt the United Nations Working Group on Indigenous Populations' *Principles and Guidelines for the Protection of Indigenous Heritage* (Wiessner & Battiste, 2000) as foundational to current and future use of Indigenous knowledge.

10. Implement the UN Human Rights Covenants and the Declaration on the Rights of Indigenous Peoples

Canada, its provinces, and territories, in collaboration with the Aboriginal peoples, should implement existing human rights covenants and the *UN Declaration on the Rights of Indigenous Peoples*, establishing a set of priorities, protocols, and processes for undertaking this work.

11. Implement the International Convention on the Elimination of Racial Discrimination

Canada, its provinces, and territories should enact measures to ensure the elimination of racial discrimination in all government programs, education goals, practices, and outcomes. The Canadian Commission on UNESCO and the Canadian Race Relations Foundation are two important assets for schools and educators to address racism in curricula. The United Nations is the other international institution that is setting ethical standards of conduct on a large scale. Women, children, minorities, Indigenous peoples, refugees, and disabled people are among the many groups that have now been recognized for the rights they carry and the responsibilities we all have to ensure peace, dignity, and respect are accorded to them in a civil society.

12. Protect Indigenous Knowledge and Heritage

Canada, its provinces, and territories, in collaboration with Aboriginal peoples, should review its legislation on the protection of intellectual property to ensure that First Nations, Métis, and Inuit interests and perspectives, in particular collective interests, are adequately protected. At present, property — whether it is books, papers, artefacts, film, music, theatre, and creative performances or objects — are protected only under individual or corporate protection laws and do not include the protection of collective ancestral products that have come from learning and living in collectivities, including songs, dances, chants, creative designs in baskets, rugs, tipis, or wherever Aboriginal peoples put their designs.

13. Support First Nations' Capacity to Oversee Use of Indigenous Knowledge

Canada, its provinces, and territories, in collaboration with Aboriginal peoples, should provide development funds to First Nations schools to support dialogues in accordance with their own local protocols among elders and knowledge keepers that will have as their outcome the development and dissemination of local protocols, practices, and procedures for accessing and disseminating First Nations knowledge for schools and universities, as well as for researchers seeking Indigenous knowledge for other research purposes. Mechanisms for overseeing the vetting of research proposals must be developed. As well, research proposals must be developed in consultation with First Nations peoples and supported with appropriate funds for administering this process over time.

14. Develop Research and Capacity Building in Indigenous Knowledge and Pedagogy

Canada, its provinces, and territories should support First Nations centres for Aboriginal knowledge to develop pedagogy; conduct language research; review, produce, and disseminate educational materials; and provide technical support for the production of materials to First Nations communities. At minimum, seven centres should be established across Canada and positioned in proximity to the major Aboriginal language families — e.g. British Columbia, the Prairies, Central, Eastern, Atlantic, and two in northern territories for Inuit and Dene nations. Drawing on the innovations of Alaska's Indigenous Network at the University of Fairbanks, these centres may establish priorities for their areas, but capacity building can be staggered over a period of time to ensure each objective and priority has had sufficient time to develop its capacity.

CHAPTER 10

Possibilities of Educational Transformations

Each generation must out of relative obscurity discover its mission,
fulfill it or betray it. . . .

Frantz Fanon (1963, p. 206)

EDUCATION IS THE BELIEF IN POSSIBILITIES. It is a belief about knowledge systems. It is a belief in the capacities of ordinary humans. We as educators must refuse to believe that anything in human nature and in various situations condemns humans to poverty, dependency, weakness, and ignorance. We must reject the idea that youth are confined to situations of fate, such as being born into a particular class, gender, or race. We must believe that teachers and students can confront and defeat the forces that prevent students from living more fully and more freely. Every school is either a site of reproduction or a site of change. In other words, education can be liberating, or it can domesticate and maintain domination. It can sustain colonization in neo-colonial ways or it can decolonize.

Teaching is the unlimited potential of practical problem solving and the transmission of knowledge and values. It is creating a path of practices of learning and innovation, depending on skills and cooperation. Teaching is the psychology of hope, and hope is a cause and a consequence of action. It prefers participation to observation, and it believes that vast problems can yield to several small solutions. Teaching creates the infrastructure of the art of the impossible.

No book that criticizes the faults of an educational system can end without consideration of what concerned and sensitive educators can do to effect positive outcomes for those affected by this flawed system. For many educators, the issue of what should we do is a compelling question that energizes and motivates us to actively seek solutions. Much research and study of Aboriginal language education and teaching, as well as research in teaching English as a second language, have offered solid insights to help address this question. As usual, however, there is not one solution to the complexity of the issues facing educators that would account for all levels of success. But there are clearly some elements that must necessarily be part of the remedies for taking Aboriginal second language learners out of risk. I offer some as have been proposed by the literature and are implied by the myths of English language teaching.

In the work of the Nourishing the Learning Spirit bundle with the Aboriginal Learning Knowledge Centre and the Canadian Council on Learning, one of the projects we funded was to discover what worked for Aboriginal learners within schools across Canada. To start, it is important that teachers see Aboriginal students as the diverse learners they are. They do not have a single, homogenous learning style, as generalized in some teaching literature from the 1970s and 1980s. Teachers must use a variety of styles of participation and information exchanges, adapt their teaching methods to Aboriginal styles of learning, and avoid over-generalizing Aboriginal students' capabilities based on perceived cultural differences. To maximize participation of Aboriginal students in the educational process, teachers need to experiment with teaching opportunities to connect with the multiple ways of knowing these students have, and the multiple intelligences (Cleary & Peacock, 1998).

In the review of further documents on Aboriginal learning, the Aboriginal Learning Knowledge Centre also found that the successful programs held to more than one of following practices:

- Considered the lifelong learning of Aboriginal individuals (First Nations, Métis, and Inuit) and respected their *diverse learning styles* in a *holistic* manner based on their spiritual, intellectual, emotional, and physical selves;
- Legitimized the voice of all Aboriginal people (First Nations, Métis, Inuit) through *place and culture*, including the circle of learning and respecting how one generation passes knowledge and culture on to other generations;
- Encouraged a *transformative* approach to learning which embraced Indigenous knowledge, experience, and knowing while respecting mainstream knowledge and experience, and including both a formal and informal approach for learning programs that reached all ages;
- Supported learning within the *community* by linking and encouraging the involvement of parents, elders, and community in order to build a successful learning continuum and healthy resilient communities;
- Normalized Indigenous knowledge as subject matter and ways of knowing and learning; and
- Clarified program or school's goals, practices, and expected results and how successes were to be measured or monitored.

Combined with antiracism, anti-oppressive, decolonizing, and reconstructing of Aboriginal education, the constitutional provision for affirming Aboriginal and treaty rights offers Aboriginal Affairs and Northern Development Canada and provincial and territorial education systems a framework for renewing First Nations education in Canada. It establishes a respectful education reform. Article 1 of the 1966 UNESCO *Declaration of the Principles of International Cultural Co-operation* offers an inspirational principle: "each culture has a dignity and value which must be respected and preserved." This prime postcolonial principle in education is the assertion of Aboriginal and treaty rights in education and a principle for constitutional rebuilding and reclaiming of the First Nations heritage and languages in Canada. These rights offer a practical and theoretical foundation for First Nations education.

In practical terms, this means that in the constitutional framework First Nations people must be involved at all stages and in all phases of education planning and future governing. Each First Nations treaty area can offer an opportunity to Canadians to rededicate themselves to protecting First Nations knowledge and heritage, redressing the damage and losses of First Nations peoples from their language, culture, and properties, and enabling First Nations heritage and knowledge to offer Canada and the provinces a chance to create an authentic educational system which comprehends an inclusive view of humanity. Many educators have recognized the assumptions and sources of the damage done to First Nations students by culturally oppressive curricula, and many remain committed to an education that is meaningful, relevant, critical, practical, and progressive.

Postcolonial, post-structural theory and methods have offered researchers some hope in how to position Indigenous people's voice in a process for transforming cognitive imperialism, although scholarship in Indigenous theory and methodology has evolved to the extent that no longer are researchers confined to postcolonial or anti-oppressive theory and practice for critique and solutions to the content, pedagogies of schooling, and recognition and respect of diverse identities. The affirmation of Aboriginal and treaty rights in the Canadian Constitution creates a theoretical and practical place to address educators' complicity in the devaluation of First Nations peoples and take an active role in repairing the damage. Unfortunately, current media focus on First Nations social problems, partly derived from failed educational strategies, has deflected the focus on reconciliation with treaties of First Nations peoples. While these social issues cannot be minimized or disregarded, each educator has a role, if not a responsibility, in changing her own and her students' conceptions about First Nations students, their heritage, and their contributions to society. Constitutional reforms have given Canadians responsibility for understanding educational harms, and education can reshape the order of the world here and beyond.

Whatever changes occur in schools, it is clear that contemporary educational transformations must flow from the agreement made in principle in 1973 with the federal government when Indian Control of Indian Education sought access, control, resources, and accountability for the people who benefit from that education.

If we are to educate in the spirit of the agreement, we must develop a critical perspective of the historical context that has created fragmentation and diminished perspectives. Understanding dominance and superiority within the context of history and their continued dominance in contemporary knowledge is foundational to change. We must also understand Aboriginal learning and learners, their holistic theories of lifelong learning, how to nourish the learning spirit, and the epistemologies that provide a stronger foundation for learning. We must understand how they can be transmitted in structured learning systems (i.e., K-12 schools, post-secondary institutions, alternative schools, in health and wellness, in the workplace, and in reformative and restorative justice), and how they continue through lifelong learning. We also need to examine current knowledge of the most promising of innovations together with the knowledge of Aboriginal learning so as to inform institutions, training programs, and policy makers. What is well accepted, however, is that where Indigenous knowledge survives, it is transmitted through Aboriginal languages. Where Aboriginal languages, heritages, and communities are respected, supported, and connected to elders and education, educational successes among Aboriginal students can be found (Willett, 2001).

Aboriginal languages are irreplaceable resources in any educational reforms. Modern educational policy has focused almost exclusively on English-language instruction, with regional concerns for the retention of French. Without the internal structures and functions of Aboriginal languages that value direct learning, Indigenous knowledge will struggle to survive. Elders speak to the important role languages play in building strong communities of social relationships and in storing the collected wisdom and knowledge that enables Aboriginal people to survive and flourish.

Training and education cannot focus on building the skills and capacities of individuals who will be forced to leave their communities to find employment and opportunities elsewhere. Rather, it will focus on building community strength and capacity so that they will have the choice to remain in their communities and contribute to building collective successes. Ensuring the complete and accurate transmission of knowledge and authority from generation to generation depends not only on maintaining ceremonies, which Canadian law treats as art rather than science, but also on maintaining the integrity of the land itself.

The distinctive features of Indigenous knowledge and pedagogy are learning by observation and doing, learning through authentic experiences and individualized instruction, and learning through enjoyment. Indigenous pedagogy accepts students' cognitive search for learning processes they can internalize, and Aboriginal teachers allow for a lag period of watching before doing. Indigenous knowledge is both empirical (that is, based on experience) and normative (that is, based on social values). It embraces both the circumstances people find themselves in and their beliefs about those circumstances in a way that is unfamiliar to Eurocentric knowledge systems, which distinguish clearly between the two. As a system, it constantly adapts to the dynamic interplay of changing empirical knowledge as well as changing social values. Caution is therefore advised before petrifying, oversimplifying, or mystifying Indigenous knowledge systems by stressing their normative content or "sacredness."

Indigenous knowledge may be embodied in songs, ceremonies, symbols, and artworks that have commercial value in their own right, separate from the empirical models of the world they represent. Values are so deeply embedded within Indigenous knowledges that it is difficult to distinguish the empirical content from the moral message. Stories about animals are sometimes not about animals at all, but about proper human behaviour, and the most uproarious tales about the foibles and misdeeds of animals often contain wise insights about community ecology. Many stories are proprietary to particular families, clans, societies, and tribes. Gardening, for example, is associated with tobacco, which is a sacred society concern. Grazing animals also belong to a sacred society and may be associated with a number of landmarks spread over several hundred square miles of a particular tribe's territory. The specialized knowledge of water and water creatures is associated with ceremonial bundles. Individual elders and knowledge keepers carefully observe changes in their landscape and formulate hypotheses about how things are changing. The long-term ecological history of the land is a cloth woven from the threads of stories and ceremonies provided by many different members of the community.

The representation, renewal, and legitimation of Aboriginal languages and knowledges involve changing the nature of instructional activities. In the past, reading and writing in educational systems centred skills primarily on decoding, spelling, grammar, and literal comprehension. They were treated as mechanistic processes instead of as active, constructive processes. Among students, especially Aboriginal students, this approach to language made direct experience irrelevant, caused critical faculties to retreat, and suspended creative thought. Today, students are encouraged to find meaning in the text by relying on their prior knowledge and experience.

There are many benefits for Aboriginal students in this learning model. First, making meaning helps students with the critical thinking and action-based skills they need to solve their own problems and the problems facing their communities. Second, it recognizes that literacy is not abstract but embedded in social contexts, and that underlying meanings are to be found in the social world of individuals, families, and communities. Third, it teaches that people read and write because they are motivated to do something with print, which allows students to explore the functions of literacy. This means that the content used to develop literacy must be rethought as an inclusive realm in which Indigenous knowledge and learning are integral elements. Fourth, literacy taught from constructivist models allows students to pursue literacy through highly individual paths. Finally, the constructivist model calls attention to the important roles that different life experiences and cultural schemata play in the process of making meaning.

Recognizing and Affirming the Learning Spirit

The history of Aboriginal peoples' experiences with education is a compelling story of the coercive relations of power and the ethical responsibility of educators to acknowledge and expand student identities, challenge those power relations that continue to diminish or challenge students' thinking about themselves and their futures, and bring the lives of Indigenous peoples more fully into their education. As the process of educational reform continues, it is imperative that educators understand the structure of doubt the Canadian educational system has generated among Aboriginal people. Aboriginal students have been contaminated by an educational system built on false colonial and racist assumptions that target them as inferior, and create self-doubt among Aboriginal students.

No educational system is perfect, yet few have a history as destructive to human potential as Canada's with its obsession with assimilation. In this coercive system, more than three out of four Aboriginal students fail to graduate. The achievement of the few who do succeed, however, does not directly relate to success in life, nor in parenting, nor in caring for others, nor does it mean the end of learning for them, for most continue to find other ways to continue their learning and earn diplomas and degrees. The racism inherent in the system drains students of their capacity for achievement in all aspects of their lives. It is time to change the educational outcomes for Aboriginal youth by fully integrating their knowledge and heritage into an educational system that values and respects Indigenous ways of knowing and allows Aboriginal students to embrace and celebrate who they are instead of making them doubt themselves. Indigenous knowledge is not a singular concept.

All learners are diverse, and when we consider the cultural realities in which each has to navigate to feel like they belong and are nourished to succeed, one can see why some students succeed and others don't. Learning itself is complex as well, in that it is not just about institutional contexts and outcomes. Learning is also a process that is "active, attuned, and intentional observation and listening of the visible environment and of the spiritual dimension. In this perspective, learning is a multidimensional process and it required knowing the visible (physical) and invisible (spiritual) aspects of oneself and of creation" (Ottmann & Pritchard, 2009, p. 12). What we together learned in the Aboriginal Learning Knowledge Centre with the Canadian Council on Learning (2007) from First Nations, Métis, and Inuit leaders, educators, and elders was that Aboriginal learning had many unique characteristics:

- Learning is holistic;
- Learning is a lifelong process;
- Learning is experiential in nature;
- Learning is rooted in Aboriginal languages and cultures;
- Learning is spiritually oriented;
- Learning is a communal activity, involving family, community, and elders; and
- Learning is an integration of Aboriginal and Eurocentric knowledge.

beliefs

Learning is then a lifelong enterprise eventually yielding to a self-directed path. It is also found in collectives, schools, and communities where a sense of vitality, energy, vision, and purpose prevail; when it is nourished, the difference can be seen in the hope, inspiration, and purposeful activity it generates. As teachers, we can provide the learning contexts in which students can unfold their own learning spirit and connect consistently to the inner forces of that self that can improve their chances for living authentically and optimally on their life journey. As they connect to themselves, to their community, and to their unique heritage, they "will create their own spiritual, intellectual and emotional fire" (Denton & Ashton, 2004, p. 34).

Culture comes in all forms and multiple patterns, and although the term is not found in most Indigenous languages, culture, heritage, and nationhood all help to develop a social and spiritual dimension in our lives that connects to those things that give life and meaning to our learning. It is the relational content for the stories, poetry, or literature we read or share; it is what gives meaning to the relationships within a web of mothers and fathers, grandmothers and grandfathers, and daughters and sons. It is how we struggle for justice, on behalf of others or ourselves, and inspires us to work against racism, to heal from the pains of our past, and it connects us to higher powers. First Nations' search for the inner knowledge that came from the connections they had made with those physical and metaphysical elements in their territories has become the source of the knowing that remains at the core of Indigenous knowledge and the foundations of personal development and Aboriginal epistemology.

Some see it as spiritually activated, although, again, spiritual should not be seen as narrowly religious.

The learning spirit seeks to share an understanding of the ways to increase the connections to it in order to improve learning, whether it is in structured formal schooling or informal learning. It is also about how to engage those inner capacities of the self to improve engagement with learning events, teachers, other learners, and to put these in the context of the education. This can improve the evidence of successful lifelong learning. Many diverse ways enable us to strive to be human, to find inspiration, motivation, clarity, coherence, and peace of mind. Each of us has found many ways to do this. For some, it is in prayer and ceremony, meditation, Yoga or Chi Gong, walking the dog in quiet places, driving or running mindlessly, listening to music, writing poetry, painting or doing crafts, or in quiet moments just before we sleep or as we wake. There are many more ways each one of us has explored. In each of these, there is a way of releasing the focus of the mind, and through relaxation and de-stressing, it opens the mind, body, heart, and spirit to a peace of mind, a place that infuses in-spir-ation, or spirit connecting moments that brings health benefits. These moments also bring clarity, and coherence, answers to our questions about life, our purpose, or solve our troubles. Willie Ermine relates how the experience with sweat lodges creates another way of knowing:

> The Cree sweat lodge ceremony has a tradition of responding to the basic dilemma of the human need to know. Broadly speaking, the mission to uncover the unknown of our human existence is consistent with our personal need to search for soul and spirit. The experience of the sweat lodge teaches that uncovering the sacred resources and giftedness that we each possess may be the way to our knowing. This may to the language and message in the silence of the stones. (2002, p. 194)

Spirit-gravitating experiences contribute to learning in significant ways. And they have a place in education and in lifelong learning. The silence on First Nations spirituality in the classroom, even in denominational schools, has left a gap in learning which reduces education to the mind and skills, and removes the factor that fuels our passion for our work, love, and meaning making. Yet, terms like spirit and spirituality are not used freely in nondenominational schools, for there is the notion that these are not compatible discourses for public schools. These become compartmentalized to practices conducted in private or in public community gatherings like churches. What, then, is learning spirit? And what does this mean in relation to our life journey connecting with the learning spirit?

Spirituality is a contemporary hot topic. Maybe it is its transformative possibilities that create human need for strength in troubling times. Parker Palmer speaks of the pain of education that is the "pain of disconnection" and kinship with subject matter, noting that institutional conditions create "more combat than community" (1993, p. x). bell hooks' (1994; 2003) notion of "engaged pedagogy" is about teaching that includes the mind, the body, and the spirit. She asserts that we are starving our students by only speaking abstractly of the mind, arguing that students want an education that is healing to their uninformed, unknowing spirit. They want knowledge that is meaningful, and for hooks, this examining of spirit is about healing, about union, and about community. It is about recognizing the complicated nature of the self, appreciating the mind *with* the body and *with* the spirit (2003, p. 24). Most Aboriginal people's lives are rooted in spirituality and practiced as individuals seek their own balance, healing, or inner strength. It is what is called *pimatisiwin* — a Cree word for good living is about, and *netaklimk* in Mi'kmaq — living well.

Whether we call this "engaged pedagogy," "teaching from the heart" (Denton & Ashton, 2004), holistic learning, or Aboriginal epistemology and pedagogy (Ermine, 1995), the foundation of this teaching resides in, first, acknowledging that each person has a unique and personal journey that will yield to their learning so that they find a way to express fully their own purpose, vision, and journey. bell hooks challenges her readers to "teach in a manner that respects and cares for the souls of our students . . . to provide the necessary conditions where learning can most deeply and intimately begin" (as cited in Denton & Ashton, 2004, p. 24). And in every part of the life journey, we are moving toward understanding, learning, and always self-improving as we operate from that core of our revealed self. This is what is understood by "authenticity" — that is, that each of us is operating "more from a sense of self that is defined by one's own self as opposed to being defined by other people's expectations" (Tisdell, 2003, p. 32).

Culture, language, and community serve to fashion or model the kinds of expressions we use to express and explore our meaning making. It is "the dynamic field, within which Spirit is shaped, formed and directed" (Owen, 1987, p. 121, as cited in Williams, 2006). And when it is brought into the school it provides the tone, the milieu, and atmosphere of the institution. Culture exists everywhere, but there are multiple cultures, and these need to find a place in the school through reciprocal relations with those communities.

Attending to spirit is always present in our learning environments- and is simply about creating an environment or space where people bring their whole selves, their stories, their voice, their culture, their symbols, and their spiritual experience to their learning. Ottmann and Pritchard (2009) recommend four ways in which teachers can enrich the experience of Aboriginal students, focusing especially on their affective development, including a teacher expectation to know students; enhancing student self-concept; facilitating positive interpersonal communications; and humanizing social studies (p. 22). Tisdell (2003) calls it a "spirited epistemology" (p. 42). These serve to infuse inspiration and imagination. These expressions come as forms of "insight" and then unfold in the manner that the culture provides and from which each person's connections to their wholeness emerges. Therefore, "when one engages the cognitive, affective, and the symbolic domains of learning, learning becomes more holistic, thereby increasing the change for learning to be transformative" (Tisdell, p. 43).

Achieving this level of engagement with spirit can be a pedagogical challenge, especially if it comes to indigenizing the curriculum. One research project conducted among seven teachers in elementary, middle, and secondary schools on storytelling offered a viable approach. The focus and the results of this project revealed that storytelling is a way of indigenizing the curriculum, building the socially constructed context of prior learning and meaning making into their lessons to be culturally responsive to Indigenous students, as well as offering non-Indigenous students an experience that brought new, interactive ways to represent their own experience and sharing meaning with new content (McLean & Wason-Ellan, 2006). Teachers and students all have memories, feelings, families, communities, and cultures that give them a distinctive voice. When the teacher cedes power to the students through encouraging shared listening and witnessing of storytelling experience, the students can build layers of new meaning into their own experiences. As their stories are shared and honoured, they come to appreciate and understand other storying processes that are embedded in the oral traditions of First Nations and Métis peoples. Such pedagogy, as characterized in the classic work of Nell Noddings's (1984, 1992) concept of "authentic caring," is about building respectful relations among the teachers and students and among the students themselves with each other in safe, caring environments of trust, kindness, and empathy. Storytelling is also the most important way of sharing the experience of Indigenous peoples, who locate their identities in an alternate knowledge system built within different ways of learning. The symbols, analogies, stories, and experiences of Indigenous peoples are reflected in their everyday lives, yet build upon deep layers of knowledge that cannot be accessed by books or grand narratives:

> Education and training programs that offer pan-Aboriginal curriculum content or essentializing about Aboriginal peoples in an effort to be culturally sensitive are flawed because they fail to appreciate the heterogeneity of over 605 different First Nations in Canada, each with their own particular history, language, dialect, culture, and social organization. (Ball, 2004, p. 5)

Some of these add-on materials are general and intended for integration in all curricula, and some, such as those dealing with integrating Aboriginal knowledge into the sciences or legends into literature, are specific. Few of the provincial initiatives taken so far have integrated the expertise of the Aboriginal peoples in ways that are truly transformational (Tymchak, 2001).

Canadian educational institutions should view elders, knowledge keepers, and workers who are competent in Aboriginal languages and knowledge as living educational treasures. These individuals comprise a functioning Aboriginal university based on Indigenous knowledge and pedagogy. Just how their experience can be adequately conveyed and appreciated as expertise that should be included in education is the challenge at the heart of this book. In some regions across Canada, their expertise has become an important resource for the development of educational materials. Elders have contributed their knowledge to and conditionally endorsed its development in some curricula, audio-visual materials, and books directed at improving the success of Aboriginal students in school and life.

Postcolonial Post-Secondary Education

The decolonization of Eurocentric thought in education is already under way in the works of many scholars; however, the experiences of Indigenous people engage decolonization in a distinct manner. Maori educator and scholar Linda Tuhiwai Smith, one of the leading theorists of decolonization in New Zealand, clarifies the nature of the task when she writes, "Decolonization is about centring our concerns and world views and then coming to know and understand theory and research from our own perspectives and for our own purposes" (1999/2012, p. 39). The interrelated strands of scholarship and experience intersect to weave solutions not only to decolonize education, but also to sustain the Indigenous renaissance and to empower intercultural diplomacy. Renaissance and empowerment are two essential features of the postcolonial movement. Postcolonialism is not about rejecting all theory or research of Western knowledge. It is about creating a new space where Indigenous peoples' knowledge, identity, and future is calculated into the global and contemporary equation.

Decolonization has both a negative movement and a positive, proactive one. The negative movement has been clearly articulated. As Dr. Daes noted at the UNESCO Conference on Education in July 1999,

> Displacing systemic discrimination against Indigenous peoples created and legitimized by the cognitive frameworks of imperialism and colonialism remains the single most crucial cultural challenge facing humanity. Meeting this responsibility is not just a problem for the colonized and

the oppressed, but also rather the defining challenge for all peoples. It is the path to a shared and sustainable future for all peoples. (Daes 1999: 1)

What is clear is that any attempt to decolonize education and actively resist colonial paradigms is a complex and daunting task. Educators must reject colonial curricula that offer students a fragmented and distorted picture of Indigenous peoples, and offer students a critical perspective of the historical context that created that fragmentation. In order to effect change, educators must help students understand the Eurocentric assumptions of superiority within the context of history and to recognize the continued dominance of these assumptions in all forms of contemporary knowledge.

Those who are researching Indigenous knowledge must understand both the historical development of Eurocentric thought and the Indigenous contexts. A body of knowledge differs when viewed from different perspectives. Not only will interpretations or validations of Indigenous knowledge depend on the researcher's attitudes, capabilities, and experiences, but they will also be based on the researcher's understanding of Indigenous consciousness, language, and order. Depending on the Eurocentric reductionist analysis used, Indigenous knowledge may be segmented or partial, utilitarian or non-utilitarian, or both. Indigenous knowledge needs to be interpreted based on form and manifestation, as the Indigenous people themselves understand it.

Every university discipline, and its various discourses, has a political and institutional stake in Eurocentric diffusionism and knowledge. Yet, every university has been structured to see the world through the lens of Eurocentrism, which opposes Indigenous perspectives and epistemes. The faculties of contemporary universities encourage their students to be the gatekeepers of Eurocentric disciplinary knowledge in the name of universal truth. Yet, Eurocentric knowledge is no more than a Western philosophy invested in history and identity to serve a particular interest. When it approaches Indigenous issues or peoples, its research methodology is contaminated with multiple forms of cognitive imperialism.

This is why postcolonial, Indigenist, and Indigenous frameworks cannot be constructed unless Indigenous people accept that their own world views, environments, languages, and forms of communication have value for their present and future, and understand how they can help to reclaim and restore them, or to benefit from them through supporting others who still have their languages. They need to have a strategy for examining their notions of success, reclaiming their resources for reconstruction of what was lost, and re-examining how all these elements combine to construct their humanity, as it was in the past, how it is remaining today, and what needs to be held for tomorrow.

Newly empowered Indigenous people and their non-Indigenous allies are providing critical frameworks for addressing these issues while acknowledging excellence through the proper valuing and respectful circulation of Indigenous knowledge across and beyond Eurocentric disciplines in postcolonial universities (Battiste, 2000; L. Findlay, 2000; I. Findlay, 2003; McConaghy, 2000). Indigenous people are seeking to heal themselves, to reshape their contexts, and to effect reforms based on a complex arrangement of conscientization, resistance, and transformative action. Through collaborative work with scholars in Canada and beyond in Australia, New Zealand, and the United States, Indigenous scholars and leaders are demonstrating the strength of the postcolonial movement by constructing the multidisciplinary foundations essential to remedying the acknowledged failure of the current system. They are achieving this transformation in multiple sites, where diverse problems engage multiple strategies, strategic goals, and broad political agendas.

The United Nations has produced a number of declarations and covenants embracing or urging the adoption of standards to protect women, children, and cultural minorities. Indigenous diplomacy has changed the International Labour Organization and the United Nations Education Science and Culture Organization, and the work of the Permanent Forum of Indigenous Peoples and the *UN Declaration on the Rights of Indigenous Peoples* (Henderson, 2008). The Indigenous renaissance has shifted the agenda from recrimination to rebirth, from conflict to collaboration, from perceived deficiency to capacity. It is also witnessing the early shifts in university thinking from a defensive/assimilative story to a receptive/transformative story which accepts that benefits to Aboriginal peoples are a benefit to the entire academic community and the multiple publics who look to elite institutions to lead and to listen. Innovation from diverse sources can lead to beneficial change for all.

Indigenous Self-Determination

It is hoped that Eurocentric scholars and institutions will recognize the urgent need to respect and promote the inherent rights of Indigenous peoples as affirmed in constitutional reconciliation and the 2007 *UN Declaration of the Rights of Indigenous Peoples*, which derive from their Indigenous institutions, Indigenous concept of belonging, and from their knowledge, heritage, cultures, spiritual traditions, histories, and philosophies. Aboriginal scholars are pushing the Eurocentric universities, their disciplines, and their scholars and students to honour the international law that affirms Indigenous knowledge to create a better environment for trans-systemic literature, institutions, and citizenship.

The self-determination movement inherent in the Indigenous renaissance has displayed the depth and power of a small portion of our humanity, its noble commitment to empower the powerless and dispossessed to lead better lives and overthrow the chains of racism, assimilation, and Eurocentrism. The renaissance among Indigenous peoples is carrying the dreamers, the workers, and the professionals as they build creative, effective institutions and programs for their people. They generate visions of the future and foundations for hard line front workers in schools and institutions, ensuring our Indigenous knowledge and Indigenous rights are respected and addressed. They embody the horizon of potentiality, possibility, and hope to which I and countless other Indigenous peoples and non-Indigenous allies hold tenaciously as we do our work.

Some First Nations, such as my nation, the Mi'kmaq, have acquired new choices in education — choices built on their ancient rights to an education of their own making and vision. Historically, Mi'kmaw people have held the right to educate their children, and have done so in their choices of what they felt was important as a family and a community their children should know to be productive and flourishing members of society. Colonial history imposed on that right, however, with forced assimilation to a culture, religion, and lifestyle that was not theirs. Their resistance is evident in their continued maintenance of their language and culture, although many other aspects of modern living have taken over most Mi'kmaw communities. But underlying that "look," there is the Mi'kmaw spirit, language, world view, values, and traditions that make us unique, that we acknowledge as being Mi'kmaq. This is a legacy that is passed on to our children in many ways, and in particular through education. The inadequate education of our past has done much damage to the Mi'kmaw spirit, language, livelihood, and lands. But current efforts by First Nations, in particular Mi'kmaw people through the *Mi'kmawey Kina'matnewey*, are working to change the undesirable outcomes of a previous era. They represent a new era of politics in Canada that is seeking the dismantling or devolution of Indian Affairs and new political and legislative action to ensure that First Nations can enter into their own agreements to implement their own choices. These new relations are significant in Canada, and have yet to unfold fully, just as the vision and educational strategy for Mi'kmaw education are still unfolding. Nonetheless, it is a process of great magnitude and importance.

It is important to understand the doubts and some peoples' discounting of local capabilities in this process because we were all contaminated with a colonial European education that is built on racist assumptions that targeted Aboriginal people as inferior. This was the contagion of our education, which created doubt. But we must be reminded that all provinces and their leadership had the same beginnings at some point in their development of an education system. They clearly must have had the same doubts, yet they laid out their vision and their responsibilities and changed all along the way to the current, not-so-perfect model, with its ever-changing knowledge base and divergent needs of their society. No education system is perfect, yet all produce remarkable results in some students and terrible results in others. This random achievement in schools, however, is not directly related to success in life or in parenting or in caring for others.

First Nations have demonstrated their preparedness to act and assume what we consider the most important part of our future, despite the systemic discrimination that has created a theory of unreadiness among First Nations. Perpetuated by government bureaucrats constantly asking if First Nations are ready to assume educational jurisdiction, or any other, we are assuredly on a path toward determining our selves and our future. This is itself self-determination at its core. It is historic, informative for other nations, and most enabling for us who have long been denied this opportunity. It is troublesome, untidy, and at different times frustrating, but it is a right and an opportunity all other Canadians enjoy and have enjoyed. This is our right and our chance to consider our children's rights and future under the Aboriginal and treaty rights in the *Constitutional Act, 1982* that the courts have affirmed. Our journey has been to think boldly, be brave, assert the foundation and base we want our children to inherit, and choose among all available options for structures and governance. We should not have to resort to provincial systems or standards, but we must be ready to make our own ever better because they were developed based on our needs, hopes, and aspirations. They inspire us to create our own curricula and hold them up to scrutiny periodically if they do not seem to meet our needs.

Every First Nations student recognizes the dilemmas and fragmentations in his or her educational experience. We talk freely and openly about them. A major obstacle to educational achievement has been finding the courage to live what we believe. This quest for wholeness, authenticity, and spirituality is embedded in the educational reforms urged by Indigenous knowledge. Indigenous knowledge presents several goals for educational reform: acknowledging the sacredness of life and experiences; generating the spirit of hope based on experience as a connection with others in creating a new and equitable future; generating the meaning of work as a vocation and as a mission in life; and developing the capacity to do everything to open a new cognitive space in which a community can discover itself and affirm its heritage and knowledge in order to flourish for everyone. In the dynamics of Indigenous knowledge, purposeful, meaningful lives are dignified and spiritual. This is what we strive for, and hope that educational reform will help us achieve.

Each nation-state is offered an opportunity to rededicate itself to protecting humanity, redressing the damage and losses of Indigenous peoples, and enabling Indigenous communities to sustain their knowledge for their future and the future of humanity.

We are the carriers of the knowledge linking us back to our responsibility to the earth, and we are the signposts pointing the direction to the health and healing of the planet. If this knowledge becomes lost to humankind, then it is entirely possible that our time will run out. (Clarkson, Morrisette, and Regallet, 1992, p. 43)

We each must understand our complicity, and take an active role in repairing the damage already perpetrated on the planet. We must take responsibility for ourselves, our understandings of our history, and the history contained in our knowledge, discourses, and institutions. We must be able to distinguish when the discourses are for Aboriginal people. The seed that lies beneath the snow lingers on among Indigenous peoples, and we will emerge in the spring with the seed nourishing the nation, the languages, the cultures, and our communities with the water of love and care, commitment and self-determination. We do not lose hope. Likewise, we have hope in others who can learn from the experience of the marginalized, from their understanding of mutual respect and partnership, and from their quest to create their own education and future. As Sandy Grande has aptly noted,

it is not only imperative for Indian educators to insist on the incorporation of Indigenous knowledge and praxis in schools but also *to transform the institutional structures of schools themselves*. In other words, in addition to the development of Native curricula, Indigenous educators need to develop systems of analysis that help theorize the ways in which power and domination inform the processes and procedures of schooling. *They need pedagogies that work to disrupt the structures of inequality*. (Grande, 2004. pp. 5-6. Emphasis added)

This is an important time for change, and everyone can benefit as we understand our roles and responsibilities to ourselves and to our creation and to our planet.

For educators, Aboriginal or not, it is not enough to rebel against injustices unless we also rebel against our lack of imagination and caring. To understand education, one must love it or care deeply about learning, and accept it as a legitimate process for growth and change. To accept education as it is, however, is to betray it. To accept education without betraying it, you must love it for those values that show what it might become. You have to have enough love of learning to have the courage to remake it, imagine it, and teach it. My friend Rita Bouvier often shared with me what her mother taught her in her Michif language. She said, "*Nitanis*, passing on what we know is an act of love" (Bouvier, 1994). Decolonizing education, then, is the act of love that generates my passion and my activism and my truths. It is, then, a call for action for all educators to take on as well.

Na tliaj. Wela'lioq

References

Aboriginal Language Task Force (ALTF) (2005). *Towards a new beginning: A foundational report for a strategy to revitalize First Nation, Inuit and Métis languages and cultures*. Report to the Minister of Canadian Heritage by The Task Force on Aboriginal Languages and Culture. Retrieved from http://www.afn.ca/uploads/files/education2/towardanew-beginning.pdf.

Administration of Indian Affairs (1843–1873, 1902–1916). *Department of Indian Affairs Annual Reports*. Ottawa.

Aikenhead, G. (1998). *Rekindling traditions: Cross-cultural science & technology units*. Retrieved from http://capes.usask.ca/ccstu.

Aikenhead, G. & Mitchell, H. (2011). *Bridging culture: Indigenous and scientific ways of knowing nature*. Don Mills, ON: Pearson Education.

Apple, M. (1982). *Cultural and economic reproduction in education: Essays on class, ideology and the state*. London: Routledge & Kegan Paul.

Apple, M. (1997). What postmodernists forget: Cultural capital and official knowledge. In A.H. Halsey, H. Lauder, P. Brown, & A. S. Wells (Eds.), *Education: Culture, economy, and society* (pp. 595–604). Oxford: Oxford University Press.

Apple, M. W. & Christian-Smith, L. K. (Eds.) (1991). *The politics of the textbook*. New York: Routledge.

Armstrong, J. (2006). Sharing one's skin. *Cultural Survival 30* (4),16-17. Retrieved from http://www.culturalsurvival.org/publications/cultural-survival-quarterly/canada/sharing-one-skin.

Assembly of First Nations. (1988). *The Aboriginal language policy study*. Ottawa, ON: Assembly of First Nations Education Secretariat.

Assembly of First Nations. Education Secretariat Aboriginal Languages Steering Committee (1990). *Towards linguistic justice for First Nations*. Ottawa, ON: Assembly of First Nations Language and Literacy Secretariat.

Atleo, E. R. (2004). *Tsawalk: A Nuu-chah-nulth worldview*. Vancouver: UBC Press.

Atleo, E. R. (Umeek). (2011). *Principles of Tsawalk: An Indigenous approach to global crisis*. Vancouver: UBC Press.

Auditor General of Canada. (2000). Indian and Northern Affairs Canada: Elementary and secondary education. *Report to the House of Commons*, chap. 4. Ottawa: Minister of Public Works and Government Services Canada.

Auditor General of Canada. (2004). Indian and Northern Affairs Canada: Elementary and secondary education. *Report to the House of Commons,* chap. 4. Ottawa: Minister of Public Works and Government Services Canada.

Auditor General of Canada. (2010). Indian and Northern Affairs Canada: Elementary and secondary education. *Report to the House of Commons,* chap. 4. Ottawa: Minister of Public Works and Government Services Canada.

Augustine, S. J. (2008). Oral histories and oral traditions. In R. Hulan & R. Eigenbrod (Eds.), *Aboriginal oral traditions: Theory, practice, ethics.* Halifax: Fernwood Publishing.

Avison, D. (2004). *A challenge worth meeting: Opportunities for improving Aboriginal education outcomes.* Prepared for the Council of Ministers in Education Canada.

Ball, J. (2004). As if Indigenous knowledge and communities mattered: Transformative education in First Nations communities in Canada. *American Indian Quarterly, 28,* (3/4), 454–480.

Barrett, J. (2009). *Researching with those who are not human: Animist research in the academy: Learning through spirit.* Unpublished paper with the Aboriginal Learning Knowledge Centre, University of Saskatchewan, Saskatoon.

Barsh, R. (1982). Her majesty's subjects. *Nations I* (1), 4–10.

Battiste, M. (1986). Micmac literacy and cognitive assimilation. In J. Barman, Y. Hébert, & D. McCaskill (Eds.), *Indian education in Canada Vol. I* (pp. 23–44). Vancouver: UBC Press.

Battiste, M. (1987). Mi'kmaq linguistic integrity: The Mi'kmawey School experience. In J. Barman, Y. Hébert, & D. McCaskill (Eds.), *Indian education in Canada: The challenge, Vol. II* (pp. 107–125). Vancouver: UBC Press.

Battiste, M. (1993, August). Annie Battiste: A Mi'kmaq family history. *Cape Breton Magazine,* 64, 23–42.

Battiste, M. (2000). *Reclaiming Indigenous voice and vision.* Vancouver: UBC Press.

Battiste, M., Bell, L., Findlay, I. M., Findlay, L., & Henderson, J. (2005). Thinking place: Animating the Indigenous humanities in education. *Australian Journal of Indigenous Education 34,* 7-19 [Special Edition].

Battiste, M., Bell, L., & Findlay, L. M. (2003). Decolonizing education in Canadian universities: An interdisciplinary, international, Indigenous research project. *Canadian Journal of Native Education 26* (2), 82–95.

Battiste, M., & Henderson, J. Y. S. (2000). *Protecting Indigenous knowledge and heritage: A global challenge.* Saskatoon, SK: Purich Publishing.

Battiste, M., Kovach, M., & Balzer, G. (Eds.) (2010). Celebrating the local, negotiating the school: Language and literacy in Aboriginal communities. *Canadian Journal of Native Education,* 32 (Supplement), 4–12.

Bear Nicholas, A. (2008). *Educational policy for First Nations in New Brunswick: Continu-ing linguistic genocide and educational failure or positive linguistic rights and educational success?* Retrieved from http://www.educatorsforimmersion.org/resources.html PDF/Genocide_in_Educational_Policy.pdf.

Belanger, J. M, (1817). *Grammaire de la langue Mikmaque.* Quebec: Le Francais.

Berry, T. (1988). *The dream of the earth.* San Francisco: Sierra Club.

Blaeser, K. (1996). *Gerald Vizenor: Writing in the oral tradition.* Norman: University of Oklahoma Press.

Bock, P. (1966). The Micmac Indians of Restigouche. National Museum of Canada, Bulletin No. 213. *Anthropological Series 77.* Ottawa.

Bouvier, R. (1994). Teaching our children what we know: An act of love – Unpublished paper prepared for Partners on Action: A Vision for the Future - A Forum on Indian and Métis Education, Saskatoon, Saskatchewan, March 24–26, 1994. ·

Brant Castellano, M. (2000). Updating Aboriginal traditions of knowledge. In G. Sefa Dei, B. L. Hall, & D. Goldin Rosenberg (Eds.), *Indigenous knowledges in global contexts: Mul-tiple readings of our world* (pp. 21–36). Toronto: University of Toronto Press Incorpor-ated.

Brant Castellano, M. (2004). Ethics of Aboriginal research. *Journal of Aboriginal Health,* 1(1), 98–114.

Brant Castellano, M., Davis, L., & Lahache, L. (Eds.) (2000). *Aboriginal education: Fulfilling the promise.* Vancouver: UBC Press.

Bromley, W. (1814). Second address on the deplorable state of Indians. Halifax, NS: Re-corder Office.

Cajete, G. (1986). *Science: A Native American perspective: A culturally based science edu-cation curriculum.* (Unpublished doctoral dissertation). International College, Los An-geles, CA.

Cajete, G. (2000) Indigenous knowledge: The Pueblo metaphor of Indigenous education. In M. Battiste (Ed.) *Reclaiming Indigenous voice and vision* (pp. 192–208). Vancouver: UBC Press.

Canada. (2010). Opening Statement to the Standing Senate Committee on Aboriginal Peoples Indian and Northern Affairs Canada—Education Program and Post-Secondary Student Support. May 12, 2010 Retrieved from http://www.oag-bvg.gc.ca/internet/Eng-lish/oss_20100512_e_33879.html.

Canada. Chrétien, House of Commons Debates, June 25, 1969, p. 10, 582.

Canada. Department of Indian Affairs. (1880-1936). Department of Indian Affairs Annual Reports. Ottawa.

Canada. Department of Indian Affairs. (1932). Sessional Papers, Report of the Department of Indian Affairs. Ottawa.

Canada. Department of Indian Affairs. (1971). *Subcommittee on Indian Education*. Ottawa.

Canada. Department of Indian Affairs and Northern Development. (1966). *Survey of the contemporary Indians of Canada. Vol. 1 & 2*. 1966.

Canada. Department of Indian Affairs and Northern Development. (1973). Chrétien, Honourable Jean, "Letter to Mr. George Manuel" February 2, 1973; Speech, Honourable Jean Chrétien, Minister of Indian and Northern Affairs, to the Council of Ministers of Learning, 23 June 1972.

Canada. Harper, S. (2008). Prime Minister Harper offers full apology on behalf of Canadians for the Indian Residential Schools system. 11 June 2008 Ottawa. Retrieved from http://www.pm.gc.ca/eng/media.asp?id=2149.

Canada. House of Commons. Standing Committee on Aboriginal Affairs. (1990). *You took my talk: Aboriginal literacy and empowerment: Fourth report of the Standing Committee on Aboriginal Affairs*. Published under authority of the House of Commons by the Queen's Printer for Canada.

Canada. Department of Justice. (n.d.). *Constitution Act, 1982*. Retrieved from http://laws.justice.gc.ca/en/const/annex_e.html.

Canada. Senate. (2011). *Report of the Standing Committee on Aboriginal Education. Reforming First Nations Education: From crisis to hope*. December 7, 2011. The Honourable Gerry St. Germain, Chair. December 2011. Retrieved from www.parl.gc.ca/content/sen/committee/411/appa/rep/rep03dec11-e.pdf.

Canada. (1969). Statement of the Government of Canada on Indian Policy (The White Paper). Retrieved from http://www.aadnc-aandc.gc.ca/eng/1100100010189/1100100010 191.

Canada. (1998). Statement of Reconciliation. Retrieved from http://www.aadnc-aandc. gc.ca/eng/1100100015725/1100100015726.

Canadian Association of Deans of Education (2010). *Accord on Indigenous Education*. Retrieved from http://educ.ubc.ca/sites/educ.ubc.ca/files/FoE%20document_ACDE_Accord_Indigenous_Education_01-12-10.pdf.

Canadian Council on Learning (2007). *Redefining how success is measured in First Nations, Inuit, and Métis learning*. Final draft. 1 Oct. 2007.

Carr Stewart, S. (2011). Post secondary education as a treaty right within the context of Treaty 6. *First Nations Perspectives: The Journal of the Manitoba First Nations Education Resource Centre Inc.* 4 (1), 84–109.

Chartrand, P. (1999). Aboriginal peoples in Canada: Aspirations for distributive justice as distinct peoples. In P. Havemann (Ed.), *Indigenous peoples rights in Australia, Canada, & New Zealand* (pp. 88–107). Auckland, NZ: Oxford University Press.

Clarkson, L., Morrissette, V., & Regallet, G. (1992). *Our responsibility to the seventh generation: Indigenous peoples and sustainable development*. Winnipeg: International Institute for Sustainable Development.

Cleary, L. M., & Peacock, T. D. (1998). *Collected wisdom: American Indian education.* Boston: Allyn and Bacon.

Conkling, R. (1974). Legitimacy and conversion in social change: the case of French missionaries and the northeastern Algonkian. *Ethnohistory 21*(1), 1–24.

Constitution Act, 1982, R.S.C. 1985, App. II. No 44 Schedule B to the *Canada Act 1982* (U.K.), 1982, c.11. S. 35. Retrieved from http://www.legislation.gov.uk/ukpga/1982/11/contents.

Cook, E. (1998). Aboriginal languages: History. In J. Edwards (Ed.), *Language in Canada* (pp. 125-143). Cambridge, UK: Cambridge University Press.

Council of Ministers of Education, Canada (CMEC). (2010). *Strengthening Aboriginal success. Summary report.* CMEC Summit on Aboriginal Education. Ottawa: CMEC.

Cummins, J. (1981). The role of primary language development in promoting educational success for language minority students. In *Schooling and language minority students* (pp. 3-49). Sacramento: California Department of Education.

Cummins, J. (1989). The sanitized curriculum: Educational disempowerment in a nation at risk. In D. Johnson & D. Roen (Eds.), *Richness in writing: Empowering ESL students* (pp. 19–38). New York: Longman.

Daes, E. I. (1999). Cultural challenges in the decade of Indigenous peoples. Unpublished paper presented at the UNESCO Conference on Education. Paris, France, 1999 July.

Delgado, R. (1990). When a story is just a story: Does voice really matter? *Virginia Law Review 76,* 95–111.

Denton, D., & Ashton, W. (Eds.) (2004). *Spirituality, action & pedagogy: Teaching from the heart.* New York: Peter Lang.

Descotes, R. (2013). Our home and unequal land. *Huffington Post Blog,* Posted: 03/21/2013 12:26 pm. Retrieved from http://www.huffingtonpost.ca/rachel-decoste/international-day-for-the-elimination-of-race-discrimination_b_2919650.html

Duran, E., & Duran, B. (1995). *Native American postcolonial psychology.* Albany, NY: State University of New York.

Durie, M. (2004). Exploring the interface between science and Indigenous knowledge. Paper presented at the 5th APEC Research and Development Leaders Forum, "Capturing Value from Science," Christchurch, NZ.

Ermine, W. (1995). Aboriginal epistemology. In M. Battiste & J. Barman (Eds.), *First Nations education in Canada: The circle unfolds.* Vancouver: UBC Press.

Ermine, W. (2002). The Cree First Nations sweat-lodge. In J. Downes & A. Ritchie (Eds.), *Sea Change: Orkney and Northern Europe in the later Iron Age 300 – 800.* Forfar, Scotland: Pinkfoot Press Balgavies.

Ermine, W. (2007). The ethical space of engagement. *Indigenous Law Journal, 6* (1), 193–204.

Ermine, W., Sinclair, R., & Jeffery, B. (2004). *Report of the Indigenous Peoples' Health Research Centre to the Interagency Advisory Panel on Research Ethics.* Indigenous Peoples' Health Research Centre, Saskatoon, Sask. Retrieved from http://www.iphrc.ca/.

Fanon, F. (1963). *The wretched of the earth*. New York: Grove Press.

Farmer, T. S. (2004). *Grade 12 Canadian history: A postcolonial analysis*. M.Ed. thesis, Department of Educational Foundations, University of Saskatchewan, Saskatoon, SK.

Findlay, I. (2003). Working for postcolonial legal studies: Working for the Indigenous humanities. *Law, Social Justice and Legal Development* (LGD) 1. Retrieved from http://elj.warwick.ac.uk/global/03-1/findlay.html.

Findlay, L. M. (2000). Always Indigenize! The radical humanities in the postcolonial Canadian universities. *ARIEL 31* (2000), 307–326.

Findlay, I. & Findlay, L. M. (2011). A new opportunity for co-operative education: Linking and learning with the Indigenous humanities. A paper presented to ICA Global Research Conference 2011, Mikkeli, Finland, August 24–27, 2011.

Four Arrows (2013). *<e-notes> First Nations File UN Racism Complaint Against Media/Government Demonization-8-an informative <e-notes>* for *24 February 2013*. Published by fourarrows@rogers.com (electronic copies available upon request).

Friere, P. (1973/1993*). Pedagogy of the oppressed*. New York: Seabury Press.

Giroux, H. (2000). Insurgent multiculturalism and the promise of pedagogy. In E. M. Duane & S. Smith (Eds.), *Foundational perspectives in multiculturalism*. New York: Longman Glasser.

Grant, A. (1996). *No end of grief: Indian residential schools in Canada*. Winnipeg: Pemmican Press.

Graveline, F. J. (1998). *Circle works: Transforming Eurocentric consciousness*. Blackpoint, NS: Fernwood Press.

Grande, S. (2004). *Red pedagogy*. New York: Rowman and Littlefield Publishers Inc.

Haida Nation v. *British Columbia (Minister of Forests)*. 3 S.C.R. 511 (2004).

Haig Brown, C. (2005). Toward a pedagogy of the land: Indigenous knowledge instructors' program. In L. Pease-Alvarez & S. Schecter (Eds.), *Learning, teaching and community* (pp. 89–108). Mahwah, NJ: Erlbaum.

Harmon, D. (2002). *In light of our differences: How diversity in nature and culture makes us human*. Washington, DC: Smithsonian Institution Press.

Harper, S. (2008). Prime Minister Stephen Harper's statement of apology to former students of Indian Residential Schools, on behalf of the Government of Canada. June 11, 2008. http://www.ainc-inac.gc.ca/ai/rqpi/apo/index-eng.asp.

Havemann, P. (Ed.) (1999). *Indigenous peoples rights in Australia, Canada, & New Zealand*. Auckland, NZ: Oxford University Press.

Hawken, P. (2007). *Blessed unrest: How the largest movement in the world came into being, and why no one saw it coming*. New York: Viking.

Hawthorn, H. B, et al. (1966/1967). *A survey of the contemporary Indians of Canada*. 2 Vols. Ottawa: Information Canada.

Heit, M. & Blair, H. (1993). Language needs and characteristics of Saskatchewan Indian and Métis students: Implications for educators. In S. Morris, K. Macleod, & M. Danesi (Eds.), *Aboriginal languages and education: The Canadian experience.* pp. 103–28. Oakville, ON: Mosaic Press.

Henderson, J. Y. (1997). *Mi'kmaq concordat.* Halifax, NS: Fernwood Press.

Henderson, J. Y. (2007). *Treaty rights in the Constitution of Canada.* Toronto: Carswell Press.

Henderson, J. Y. (2008). *Indigenous diplomacy and the rights of peoples: Achieving UN recognition.* Saskatoon: Purich Publishing.

Henderson, J. Y. & Marshall, J. B. (1980, 1986 updated). *Secular lnapskuk.* Sydney: Union of Nova Scotia Indians.

Hinton, L. (2001). Teaching methods. In L. Hinton & K. Hale (Eds.), *The green book of language revitalization in practice.* New York: Academic Press.

hooks, b. (1994). *Teaching to transgress.* New York: Routledge.

hooks, b. (2003). *Teaching community: Pedagogy of hope.* New York: Routledge.

Indian and Northern Affairs Canada. (1998). *Gathering strength — Canada's Aboriginal Action Plan.* Notes for the address by the Minister, Jan. 7, 1998. Ottawa, Ontario.

Indian and Northern Affairs Canada. (2002). Literature reviews commissioned by the Minister's National Working Group on Education in support of their work. Retrieved from http://www.ainc-inac.gc.ca/pr/pub/krw/wal_e.html.

Indian and Northern Affairs Canada. (2004). Demographics. Retrieved from www.ainc-inac.gc.ca/gs/dem_e.html.

Indian and Northern Affairs Canada. (2004). Elementary and secondary education. *Report to the House of Commons,* chap. 4. Ottawa: Minister of Public Works and Government Services Canada.

International Labour Organization. (1989) International Labour Organization Convention (No. 169) *Concerning Indigenous and tribal peoples in independent country* 27 June 1989.

Ireland, B. (2009). *Moving from the head to the heart, addressing 'The Indian's Canada problem' in reclaiming the learning Spirit – Aboriginal learners in education.* Aboriginal Education Research Centre, Saskatoon, Sask. and First Nations and Adult Higher Education Consortium, Calgary, Alta. Retrieved from http://www.ccl-cca.ca/pdfs/ablkc/AboriginalLearnersEdu_en.pdf.

Johansen, B. E. (2004). Back from the (nearly) dead: Reviving Indigenous languages across North America. *American Indian Quarterly, 28* (3/4), 566-582.

Johnston, A. A. (1960). *A history of the Catholic Church in eastern Nova Scotia. vol. II.* Antigonish: Francis Xavier University Press.

Johnston, B. (1988). *Indian school days.* Toronto: Key Porter Books.

Joint Committee of the Senate and House of Commons on Indian Affairs. (1959). *Minutes of proceedings.* Ottawa: Queen's Printer.

Kanu, Y. (2005). Decolonizing Indigenous education: Beyond culturalism: Toward post-cultural strategies. *Canadian and International Education, 34* (2), 1-20.

Kennedy, J. H. (1950). *Jesuit and savage in New France*. New Haven, CT: Yale University Press.

Klug, B. J. & Whitfield, P. T. (2003). *Widening the circle: Culturally responsive pedagogy for American Indian children*. New York: Routledge Falmer Press.

Knight, D. (2001). *The seven fires: Teachings of the bear clan as recounted by Dr. Danny Musqua*. Saskatoon, SK: Many Worlds Publishing.

Knockwood, I. (1992). *Out of the depths: The experiences of Mi'kmaw children at the Indian residential school at Shubenacadie, Nova Scotia*. Lockport, NS: Roseway Publishing.

La Duke, W. (2005). *Recovering the sacred: The power of naming and claiming*. Cambridge, MA: South End Press.

Lavallée, L. F. (2009). Practical application of an indigenous research framework and two qualitative indigenous research methods: Sharing circles and Anishnaabe symbol-based reflection. *International Journal of Qualitative Methods, 8*(1), 21–40.

Leavitt, R. (1995). Language and cultural content in Native education. In M. Battiste & J. Barman (Eds.), *First Nations education in Canada: The circle unfolds* (pp. 124-138). Vancouver: UBC Press.

Le Clerq, C. (1691). *New relation of Gaspesia*. W. Ganong (Trans. & Ed., 1910). Toronto: The Champlain Society.

Little Bear, L. (2000). Jagged wordviews colliding. In M. Battiste (Ed.) *Reclaiming Indigenous voice and vision* (pp. 77-85). Vancouver: UBC Press.

Longboat, T. L. (2005). *More than words: Cayuga immersion programming in Six Nations*. (Unpublished master's thesis). Canadian Heritage and Developmental Studies, Trent University, Peterborough, ON.

Lunney Borden, L. (2010). Transforming mathematics education for Mi'kmaw students through mawikinutimatimk. (Unpublished doctoral dissertation). University of New Brunswick (Canada), ProQuest, UMI Dissertations Publishing, 2010. NR82763.

Macedo, D. (1999). Preface. In L. M. Semali & J. L. Kincheloe (Eds.), *What is Indigenous knowledge? Voices from the academy*. New York & London: Falmer Press.

Maillard, M. L'Abbe. (1759). *Ideograms with translation in Micmac written in Roman alphabet. Eucologe*. Archives de l'Archdiocese de Quebec.

Maillard, M. L'Abbe. (1863). Lettre de M. l'Abbe Maillard sur les Missions de l'Acadie et Particulierement sur les Missions Micmaques. *Soirees Canadiennes III*: 291–426.

Martin, P. Promising practices in Aboriginal education. *Monthly Outreach*. Retrieved from http://www.maei-ppw.ca/.

Mather, A. & Wong, R. (2011). Employing equity in post-secondary art institutes. In D. Coleman & S. Kamboureli (Eds.), *Retooling the humanities: The culture of research in Canadian universities*. Edmonton: University of Alberta Press.

McConaghy, C. (2000). *Rethinking Indigenous education: Culturalism, colonialism, and the politics of knowing.* Flaxton, Qld: Post Pressed.

McGregor, C. (2013). *Aboriginal Inquiry: Lifting all learners: An impact assessment of the Aboriginal Enhancement Schools Network (AESN).* Dr. Catherine McGregor, Principal Investigator. The Office of the Federal Interlocutor, Aboriginal and External Relations Branch, Aboriginal Affairs and Northern Development Canada. Retrieved from http://inquiry.noii.ca.

McLean, M. & Wason-Ellan, L. (2006). *When Aboriginal and Métis teachers use storytelling as an instructional practice.* A grant report to the Aboriginal Education Research Network, Saskatchewan Learning. Retrieved from http://www.education.gov.sk.ca/storytelling.

Memmi, A. (1969). *Dominated man: Notes toward a portrait.* Boston: Beacon Press, 1969.

Micmac News (1974–75). The Micmac language. Dec.-June. 1978. The Shubenacadie Residential School. Aug., Sept., and Nov.

Mi'kmaq Education Act (S. C. 1998, c. 24). Retrieved from http//laws-lois.justice.gc.ca

Mulhall, A. (1996). Cultural discourse and the myth of stress in nursing and medicine. *International Journal of Nursing Studies, 33:* 455–468.

Nakata, M. (2007). The cultural interface. *Australian Journal of Indigenous Education 36* (Supplement), 7–14.

National Indian Brotherhood (NIB) (1972). *Indian control of Indian education.* Policy Paper presented to the Minister of Indian Affairs and Northern Development. Ottawa: National Indian Brotherhood.

Noddings, N. (1992). *The challenge to care in our schools.* New York: Teachers College Press.

Noddings, N. (1984). *Caring: A feminine approach to ethics and moral education.* Berkeley: University of California Press.

Norris, M. J. (2008). The role of First Nations women in language continuity and transition. In G. Guthrie Valaskakis, M. Dion Stout, & É. Guimond (Eds.), *Restoring the balance: First Nations women, community, and culture* (pp. 313–379). Winnipeg, MB: University of Manitoba Press.

Nova Scotia. (1820). Statutes of Nova Scotia. *An act to prevent the sale of spirituous liquors to Indians, and to provide for their instruction.* Halifax.

Nova Scotia. (1829). Statutes of Nova Scotia. *An act to prevent the sale of spirituous liquors to Indians, and to provide for their instruction.* Halifax.

Nova Scotia. (1842). Statutes of Nova Scotia. *An act to provide for the instruction and permanent settlement of the Indians.* Halifax.

Nova Scotia. Administration of Indian Affairs. (1843–1873). *Department of Indian Affairs Annual Reports.* Ottawa.

Nova Scotia. *Department of Indian Affairs* (1880-1936). *Department of Indian Affairs Annual Reports.* Ottawa.

Orr, J., Paul, J. J., & Paul, S. (2002). Decolonizing Mi'kmaw education through cultural practical knowledge. *McGill Journal of Education, 27* (3), 331-354.

Organization of American States. (OAS). (2001). Third Indigenous Summit of the Americas, Declaration of Quebec City, 20–22 April 2001.

Ottmann, J., & Pritchard, L. (2009). *Aboriginal perspectives and the social studies curriculum: A Review of literature.* Prepared for the Calgary Regional Consortium. Retrieved from *www.crcpd.ab.ca/uploads/userfiles/edd217485154.pdf.*

Owen, H. (1987). *Spirit: Transformation and development in organizations.* Potomac, MD: Abbott Publishing.

Pacifique, Rev. R. P. (1939). *Leçon grammaticales theoriques et practicque de la langue Micmaque.* St.-Anne-de-Ristigouche, PQ: Micmac Messenger.

Palmer, P. (1980). *The promise of paradox.* San Francisco: Jossey-Bass.

Palmer, P. (1993). *To know as we are known: Education as a spiritual journey.* San Francisco: Harper Collins.

Paul-Gould, S. (2012). *Student achievement, fluency, and identity: An in-depth study of the Mi'kmaq Immersion Program in one community.* (Unpublished master's thesis). St. Francis Xavier University, Antigonish, NS.

Paul-Gould, S., Sock, S., Murray-Orr, A., & Tompkins, J. (2013). An inquiry into an established Indigenous language immersion program: A case study of a Mi'kmaw immersion program. In D. Newhouse & J. Orr (Eds.), *Aboriginal Knowledge for Economic Development Volume I.* Compiled by the Atlantic Aboriginal Economic Development Integrated Research Program. Halifax, NS: Fernwood Press.

Peat, F. D. (1994). *Lighting the seventh fire: The spiritual ways, healing and science of the Native American.* New York: Carol Publishing.

Peters, N. (2012). *Tales told in school: Representations of the Mi'kmaq in Nova Scotia school curriculum.* Paper presented at Canadian Association for the Study of Indigenous Education, Congress of the Humanities and Research Council, Fredericton, NB.

Poole, R. (1972). *Towards deep subjectivity.* London: Allen Lane, Penguin Press.

Porsanger, J. (2004). An essay about indigenous methodology. *Nordlit, 15,* 105–120.

R. v. Côté, 3 S.C.R. 139 (1996).

R. v. Sundown, 1 S.C.R 393 (1999).

R. v. Van der Peet, 2 S.C.R. 507 (1996).

Rand, S. T. (1850). *Micmac tribe of Indians.* Halifax: James Bowes & Son.

Rigney, L-I. (1999). Internationalization of an indigenous anticolonial cultural critique of research methodologies. *Wicazo Sa Review, 14* (2), 109–121.

Royal Commission on Aboriginal Peoples. (1996). *Report of the Royal Commission on Aboriginal Peoples, 5 Vols.* Ottawa: Canada Communication Group.

Sargent, D. (1936). *Catherine Tekakwitha.* New York: Longmans, Green and Company.

St. Denis, V. (2007). Aboriginal education and anti-racist education: Building alliances across cultural and racial identity. *Canadian Journal of Education 30* (4), 1068–1092.

St. Denis, V., Bouvier, R., & Battiste, M. (1998). *Kiskinahmahkewak: Aboriginal teachers in publicly funded schools.* Regina: Saskatchewan Education.

St. Denis, V. & Hampton, E. (2002). *Literature review on racism and the effects on Aboriginal education.* Indian and Northern Affairs Canada, Literature reviews of the National Working Group on Education. Ottawa.

Saskatchewan Education. (1984). A five-year action plan for native curriculum development: Report of the Native Curriculum Review Committee. Regina: Saskatchewan Education.

Saskatchewan Human Rights Commission (2003–2004). Annual Report. Retrieved from saskatchewanhumanrights.ca/+.../SKHR_AnnualReport_2003-2004.pdf.

Saskatchewan. Joint Task Force on Improving Education and Employment Outcomes for First Nations and Métis People. (2013). *Voice, vision and leadership: A place for all. Final Report.* Gary Merasty Chair. Retrieved from http://www.ae.gov.sk.ca/joint-task-force.

Saskatchewan Instructional Development and Research Unit (SIDRU) (Fall 2004). *Mi'kmaq education evaluation project.* M. Tymchak, Project Advisor, Faculty of Education, University of Regina.

Schissel, B. & Wotherspoon, T. (2003). *The legacy of school for Aboriginal people.* New York: Oxford University Press.

Semali, L. M., & Kincheloe, J. L. (Eds.) (1999). *What is Indigenous knowledge? Voices from the Academy.* New York: Falmer Press.

Sherwood, J. (2010). *Do no harm: Decolonizing Aboriginal health research.* (Unpublished doctoral dissertation). School of Social Work, The University of New South Wales, Australia.

Sinclair, R., (2003). *PAR and Aboriginal epistemology: A really good fit.* Retrieved from http://www. aboriginalsocialwork.ca/special_topics/par/epistemology.htm.

Skutnabb-Kangas, T. (2000). *Linguistic genocide in education or worldwide diversity and human rights?* Mahwah, NJ: Lawrence Erlbaum Associates.

Smith, L. T. (1999/2012). *Decolonizing methodologies: Research and Indigenous peoples.* London: Zed Books.

Smith, L. T. (2000). Kaupapa Maori research. In M. Battiste (Ed.), *Reclaiming Indigenous voice and vision* (pp. 225–247). Vancouver: UBC Press.

Smith, L. T., Battiste, M., Bell, L., & Findlay, L. M. (2003). An interview with Linda Smith. *Canadian Journal of Native Education, 26* (2), 169–186.

Sock, S. (2012). *An inquiry into the Mi'kmaq immersion program in one community: Student identity, fluency and achievement.* (Unpublished master's thesis). St. Francis Xavier University, Antigonish. N.S.

Statistics Canada. (2008). *2006 Census: Educational Portrait of Canada, 2006 Census: Aboriginal population: The proportion of Aboriginal people with a university degree has grown*. Ottawa: Statistics Canada.

Statistics Canada. (2010). *Aboriginal Peoples in Canada. Aboriginal language indicators for Inuit, Métis, and off-reserve First Nations children in Canada*. Retrieved from http://www.statcan.gc.ca/pub/89-645-x/2010001/c-g/c-g008-eng.htm.

Suzuki, D. (1997). *The sacred balance: Rediscovering our place in nature*. Vancouver: Greystone.

Thwaites, R. G. (Ed). (1856-1896). *The Jesuit relations and allied documents. 73 Vols*. Cleveland: Burrows.

Tisdell, E. J. (2003). *Exploring spirituality and culture in adult and higher education*. San Francisco: Jossey-Bass.

Truth and Reconciliation Commission of Canada. (2012). *Interim Report*. Ottawa. Retrieved from http://www.attendancemarketing.com/~attmk/TRC_jd/Interim%20report%20English%20electronic%20copy.pdf.

Tymchak, M. (2001). *School plus: A vision for children and youth*. Final Report of the Minister of Education, Government of Saskatchewan, Task Force and Public Dialogue on the Role of the School. Saskatchewan Instructional Development and Research Unit, Regina. Retrieved from *www.srsd119.ca/continuousimprovementfiles/SchoolPLUSOverview.pdf*.

UNESCO. (1996). *Declaration of the principles of international cultural co-operation*. Retrieved July 2008 from: http://www.unhchr.ch/html/menu3/b/n_decl.htm.

UNESCO. (1999). *Declaration on Science and the Use of Scientific Knowledge, Science for the Twenty-First Century*. Budapest, Hungary, June 26–July 1, 1999. Retrieved from http://www.unesco.org/science/wcs/eng/declaration_e.htm.

UNESCO. (1999). World Conference on Science for the twenty-first century: A new commitment. Retrieved from: http://unesdoc.unesco.org/images/0012/001207/120706e.pdf. Union of Nova Scotia Indians. (UNSI) (1979). *Survey of Indian education 1971-79*. Dalhousie University, Halifax: School of Public Affairs.

United Kingdom. *British North America Act*, 30–31 Vict., c. 3 (1867).

United Nations. CERD (1965). UN *Convention on the Elimination of All Forms of Racial Discrimination*, Resolution 2106 (xx) 21 December 1965.

United Nations. *Charter of Human Rights* (1948). Adopted by General Assembly resolution 217 A (III) December 10, 1948. Retrieved from http://www.ohchr.org/EN/UDHR/Pages/Language.aspx?LangID=eng.

United Nations. Secretary General. (2012). Report on the status of the convention on the rights of child (A/67/225).

United Nations. HRC (1967). 197 UN *International Covenant on Civil and Political Rights*, [ICCPR] G. A. Res. 2200 (XXI), 21 UN GAOR, Supp. (No. 16), UN Doc. A/6316 (1967) came into force on 3 January 1976.

United Nations. (1967). *International Covenant on Economic, Social, and Cultural Rights* (1967), G.A. Res. 2200 (XXI), 21UN GAOR, Supp. (No. 16) at 49, UN Doc. A/6316 (1966); Can. T.S. (1976, No. 46). Adopted by the UN General Assembly on 16 Dec. 1966 and entered into force on 3 Jan. 1976. Canada acceded to this covenant on 19 Aug. 1976.

United Nations. (1989). *Report of the United Nations seminar on the effects of racism and racial discrimination on the social and economic relations between Indigenous peoples and states.* UN Commission on Human Rights, 45th Sess., UN Doc. E/CN.4/1989/22, 1989.

United Nations. (2009). *Report of the Expert Mechanism on the Rights of Indigenous Peoples. Study on lessons learned and challenges to achieve the implementation of the right of Indigenous peoples to education.* Retrieved from http://daccess-dds-ny.un.org/doc/UN-DOC/GEN/G09/151/81/PDF/G0915181.pdf?OpenElement.

United Nations. *Convention on the Rights of the Child.* (1989). GA res. 44/25, 20 November 1989.

United Nations. *Convention on Biodiversity.* (1992). CBD I.L.M.818, 1992. Retrieved from http://www.cbd.int/convention/.

United Nations. (2007). *Declaration on the Rights of Indigenous Peoples.* UN Doc. A/61/L. 67.

United Nations. Expert Mechanism on the Rights of Indigenous Peoples. (2009). *Study on Lessons Learned and Challenges to Achieve the Implementation of the Rights of Indigenous Peoples to Education: Report of the Expert Mechanism on the Rights of Indigenous Peoples to the Human Rights Council.* UN Doc. A/HRC/EMRIP/2009/2.

United States (US). (1991) *Aroostook Band of Micmacs Settlement Act* 25 USC 1721 (1991 Amendment).

Upton, L. (1979). *Micmacs and the colonists: Indian-white relations in the Maritimes, 1713-1867.* Vancouver: UBC Press.

Vetromile, Rev. E. (1866). *The Abnakis and their history.* New York: James B. Kirker.

Warnock, J. (2004). *Saskatchewan: The roots of discontent and protest.* Montreal/NewYork/London: Black Rose Books.

Wiessner, S. & Battiste, M. (2000). The 2000 revision of the United Nations draft principles and guidelines on the protection of the heritage of Indigenous peoples. *St. Thomas Law Review, 13* (1), 383–414.

Willett, V. (2001). *Islands of culture: The experiences of post secondary Cree language teachers.* M.Ed. thesis, Department of Educational Foundations, University of Saskatchewan, Saskatoon, SK.

Williams, R. B. (2006). *36 tools for building spirit in learning communities.* Thousand Oaks, CA: Corwin Press.

Wilson, A. & Battiste, M. (2011). *Environmental scan of educational models supporting Aboriginal postsecondary education.* Report prepared for the Commonwealth of Australia as represented by the Department of Education, Employment and Workplace Relations to the Review of Higher Education Access and Outcomes for Aboriginal and Torres Strait Islander People, Canberra, AU.

Wilson, S. (2008). *Research is ceremony: Indigenous research methods*. Halifax: Fernwood.

Wilson, S. (2013). Using Indigenist research to shape our future. In M. Gray, J. Coates, M. Yellow Bird, & T. Hetherington (Eds.), *Decolonizing social work*. Farnham, Surrey UK: Ashgate Publishing Ltd.

Index

C

Courtin, Martin 42

cultural inclusion 27–28, 72, 101, 103, 105–07, 163–64

culture 30–32, 181–83
    transmission of 32
    superiority of 97–98

Cummins, Jim 91, 143–44

D

Daes, Erica Irene 185–86

Declaration on Science and the Uses of Scientific Knowledge 117–18

decolonizing science 75, 84–85, 117–24

decolonizing the humanities 108–17, 121, 124, 161

Delgado, Richard 136

Denny, Alex 17–18, 139

Department of Canadian Heritage 130

Department of Indian Affairs 48, 55, 58, 88, 90

Department of Indian Affairs and Northern Development (DIAND) 60

Department of Indian and Northern Affairs 59

discrimination 97, 186
    definition 97
    in education 107; *see also* Eurocentric education
    right to protection from 30, 83–84, 140, 173
    in science 26, 75, 84–85, 95–97, 117–24
    See also racism; whiteness

disenfranchisement 57

Durie, Mason 95

duty to consult 169–70

E

education 21–22, 29–33, 104, 175
    as propaganda 29–31, 56, 159
    possibilities for transformation 175–91
    post-secondary 185–87
    See also Aboriginal education; Eurocentric education

Ermine, Willie 98, 105, 160, 182

H

I

J

K

L

language. *See* Aboriginal language

Lazore, Dorothy 34, 91

learning spirit 18–19, 25–25, 71, 176, 178
    recognizing and affirming 180–85

Le Clerq, Christian 36–37, 108

Little Bear, Leroy 108–09

Longboat, Tricia 156

M

Mackey, Jeremiah 56

Maillard, Antoine Pierre 42–46, 50

Malagawatch (Grand Council of Mi'kmaq meeting place) 41–42

Marshall, Murdena 17

Martin, Paul 101–02

Membertou 40–41 methodologies 69, 72,
    in education 32, 66, 103–04, 107, 111, 142
    Eurocentric 102, 103–04, 119–20, 186
    Indigenous 73, 74–77

Memmi, Albert 132–33

methodologies 69, 72,
    in education 32, 66, 103–04, 107, 111, 142
    Eurocentric 102, 103–04, 119–20, 186
    Indigenous 73, 74–77

Mi'kmaq
    education: reform 87–94, 188; *see also* Aboriginal education
    initial relationships with Europeans 36–38, 47
    introduction of Catholicism 37–46
    literacy 43–46, 50, 53
    relations with the French 38–46
    relations with the English 38, 44–46, 48–49

Mi'kmaq Education Act 79, 90

Mi'kmaw kina'matnewey 66, 90–91, 168, 188

Mi'kmawey school; bilingual education 87–90
    Mi'kmaw immersion 91–94

Michell, Herman 119

U

W

Marie Battiste, Professor of Educational Foundations, founder and first Academic Director, Aboriginal Education Research Centre, University of Saskatchewan, is a Mi'kmaw scholar, knowledge keeper, and educator from Potlotek First Nation, Nova Scotia. Marie earned degrees from the University of Maine (B.S.), Harvard (Ed.M.), and Stanford (Ed.D.). She has also received honorary degrees from the University of Maine at Farmington, St. Mary's University, and Thompson Rivers University. A Fellow in the Royal Society of Canada, she has also received the Distinguished Academic Award from the Canadian Association of University Teachers, the National Aboriginal Achievement Foundation Award in Education, the Saskatchewan Centennial Medal, the 125th Year Queen's Award for Service to the Community, the Distinguished Researcher Award from the University of Saskatchewan, and Eagle Feathers from the Mi'kmaq Grand Council and Eskasoni community. She has edited two highly influential books from UBC Press, texts that continue to be taught nationally and internationally: *First Nations Education: The Circle Unfolds* (1995) and *Reclaiming Indigenous Voice and Vision* (2000). She has co-authored, with J. Youngblood Henderson, *Protecting Indigenous Knowledge: A Global Challenge* (Purich 2000), identifying threats to Indigenous knowledge from global patenting and intellectual property regimes while affirming the linguistic and land-based grounds of resistance to paternalism and predation. A prolific writer and speaker, she has developed an international profile for advancing the decolonization of education, the development of Indigenous voice and vision, antiracist education as violence prevention, and the institutionalization of the Indigenous humanities, science, and knowledge.

Notes

Notes

Notes

Notes

Notes

Notes